The Wolf-Man

THE
WOLF-MAN

CONVERSATIONS
WITH FREUD'S PATIENT—
SIXTY YEARS LATER

Karin Obholzer

Translated by Michael Shaw

CONTINUUM · NEW YORK

1982

The Continuum Publishing Company
575 Lexington Avenue, New York, NY 10022

Originally published under the title of
Gespraeche mit dem Wolfsmann

Copyright © 1980 by Rowohlt Verlag GmbH,
Reinbek bei Hamburg

English translation copyright © 1982 by
The Continuum Publishing Company

Printed in the United States of America

Library of Congress Cataloging in Publication Data

Obholzer, Karin.
  The Wolf-Man.

  Translation of: Gespraeche mit dem Wolfsmann.
  Includes bibliographical references.
  1. Mental illness—Case studies. 2. Psychoanalysis—
Case studies. 3. Neuroses—Case studies. 4. Wolf-Man,
1887–   . I. Wolf-Man, 1887–   . II. Title.
RC465.02413   616.89′14′0924 [B]   82-5041
ISBN 0-8264-0190-2   AACR2

Contents

· I ·
THE
WOLF-MAN

An Art Nouveau
Personality

"Are you planning to learn Russian from him?" The pensioner, supporting himself on crutches, was pointing at his neighbor's door, which had no nameplate on it. The inquisitiveness in his eyes behind the round glasses was undisguised and a suggestive smile hovered around his lips. Once again, I had wasted my time climbing to the fifth floor of this old apartment building in Vienna's inner city but could at least be sure now that I had come to the right place. For weeks, I had been trying to find the address of the Wolf-Man, whose real name I had only known as Sergej P. until a short time ago. Although I had tried repeatedly to find him at home, I had never had any luck.

But because his neighbor now began informing me in great detail about the Wolf-Man's schedule, things worked out better during my next visit. The Wolf-Man is rarely at home, I was told. He sleeps late. More than once, people have rung his bell around ten-thirty, and he came to the door still half asleep and asked reproachfully: "Why are you here this early? I am still sleeping." Sunday is the only day he gets up around nine, leaves, and doesn't get back until evening. Tuesday and Thursday mornings, the maid straightens out his apartment, so he leaves earlier than usual for his noon meal. "He is Russian and a widower, you know," the pensioner said meaningfully, as if to excuse a way of life he seemed to consider odd.

"I write under the pseudonym 'Wolf-Man.' How do you happen to know my address?" The slight old gentleman, his full white hair combed back, his expression an odd mixture of reproach, rejection, and friendliness, opened the door around eleven o'clock on a Wednesday when I had returned to see him. I liked him immediately. "I don't give interviews," he said. "Come in."

He asked me to wait in a windowless foyer and disappeared briefly. When he returned, a loosely fitting jacket, its top button carefully closed, covered his shirt. He led the way into a cabinet with dark, flowery wallpaper that obviously served as his study. He pointed to an old-fashioned sofa and sat down behind the desk standing next to it. "My book is interesting only for experts," he said, surprised that I should think of writing about him. "In Vienna, hardly anyone is interested in psychoanalysis."

Then he told me that, because of an appointment at the dentist's, he would have no time for me on that day. "But I will call you and I will also show you a few paintings," he promised.

My next visit began with telepathy. Having waited for two weeks for the Wolf-Man's call and having heard nothing, I decided to go to his apartment to remind him of his promise. As I was getting dressed, the telephone rang. "This is the Wolf-Man," said a voice with a slight Russian accent.

"I was on my way over," I answered as astonished as he. "But that's telepathy," he decided, delighted. "That's something you will have to mention. But don't write how you found me because then there'll be no end of people coming here and bothering me."

"I am pleased that you are interested in my paintings," he said by way of greeting and immediately began showing me around in his unheated apartment. There was a conventionally furnished bedroom, the largest room in the apartment, which he had presumably shared with his dead wife Therese. There was a smaller room next to the kitchen, and the study which I had seen before. Still lifes with flowers and landscapes, both impressionistic in character, were hanging on the walls. He called my attention to two oil paintings above the sofa that had not been painted by him. They were of his father and sister. An acquaintance had sent them from Russia in the early twenties, that liberal period when Lenin was publicizing the New Economic Policy in an effort to get the economy going.

"I find this landscape especially successful but this one less so," he said, looking at his own work like an impartial critic, and adding that he valued Velásquez and the impressionists especially highly and that his preference among modern painters was van Gogh.

"I hardly paint any more these days," he sighed. "You know, when you are as old as I am, washing the brushes, that sort of thing, becomes very burdensome. . . . Acquaintances have been urging me to move into an old peoples' home. But I don't feel like that at all. I am used to living alone."

We went back into the study with its inadequate electric heater, he sat down and, lost in thought, began running his fingers over a letter from a funeral institute that lay, clearly visible, on his desk. The formalities regarding his burial had already been attended to. It was his wish to be laid to rest in the same cemetery in the Wienerwald where his wife Therese and his mother had been buried before him. "One would be glad to die earlier," he said, and pushed the ashtray toward me. That was the beginning of our acquaintance. At the time, in early 1973, the Wolf-Man had turned eighty-six.

A few weeks earlier, the memoirs of the Wolf-Man, originally published in the United States,[1] had been brought out in German translation. The book had come to my attention by chance; I had read it through in one night, and decided to find this man. After several unsuccessful attempts—I only knew the first letter of his last name—a simple logical reflection led me to the Wolf-Man's address.

I couldn't really have said why I found this book so fascinating or why I felt attracted to this man. For me, there was something romantic about his life, the story of a wealthy Russian aristocrat who had lost his fortune and had had to spend the rest of his life as an émigré. When I came to know him, he struck me as a character invented by Schnitzler, an Art Nouveau personality. Sometimes, when I thought of him, I felt he was the kind of man to whom one gave orchids.

I had looked for the Wolf-Man because I wanted to write about him for the daily that employed me at the time. I was at the beginning of my journalistic career, and an interview with this surviving monument of Russian history and of the history of psycho-

1. Muriel Gardiner, ed., *The Wolf-Man: With the Case of the Wolf-Man by Sigmund Freud* (New York: Basic Books, 1971).

analysis would be a scoop, of course. My story was published and attracted some attention and praise, but I had expected more. The following years showed me how such stories continue.

In the psychoanalytic texts that form part of his memoirs, the Wolf-Man's illness is referred to as an obsessional neurosis. This did not mean very much to me and I wanted to investigate further. I also would have liked to discover why Freud had treated him for four years, for what I had read had not made that clear to me. But I was to busy at the time and could not concern myself with the Wolf-Man further.

One and a half years later, in the summer of 1974, Editions Stock approached me. The Paris publisher had obtained my address from a fellow journalist at the Austrian Broadcasting Company because I had been the only journalist to have succeeded in tracking down the Wolf-Man. It was my feeling that Stock wanted a romantic story: turn-of-the-century Vienna, the monarchy, the Lipizzaner horses, Freud, etc. Although I had no way of knowing whether the Wolf-Man would be able to add anything to his memoirs, I decided to go ahead. And by the sustained interest he took in my work, the publisher helped me get through the next few years during which my story grew.

I visited the Wolf-Man and suggested a series of conversations that would later be turned into a book. The old man seemed pleased. "But I must seek advice, I must inquire," he said. This startled me a little; it was the first time I became aware of the compulsive character of my future conversational partner, a character that was going to give me a good deal of trouble as time went on.

The Wolf-Man explained at length whose counsel would have to be obtained before he would feel up to making a decision: he wanted to write to Muriel Gardiner, the editor of his memoirs, who lived in the United States; and to Dr. E., an Austrian analyst who had emigrated to the United States and was working at the Freud archive in New York, and ask both for permission. Every summer, E. spent several weeks in Vienna and still analyzed the Wolf-Man during those visits. The matter was also to be discussed with Dr. S., a professor and the director of the Vienna Psychiatric Hospital at the time, with whom the Wolf-Man had a session once a week. I had got to know S. through a piece I had done for the paper and formed an idea of the other two analysts on the basis of that knowledge. I believed they would object to the interviews and tried, unsuccessfully, to talk the Wolf-Man out of his plan.

"I am sorry but I can't do it," he told me sadly over the phone some two weeks later. Muriel Gardiner had sent a telegram urging him not to give any sort of interview, and the Wolf-Man did not seem to have the courage to go against that ban. But I am not a person that gives up easily, once she has become involved in something. I visited the Wolf-Man from time to time, started asking him questions, and tried to establish a personal relationship with him.

Every time I came, the Wolf-Man was very pleased, told me a great deal, and went into much detail. One day he had me sit at his desk while he settled down on the sofa. Had he stretched out, we would have found ourselves in the classic position of analyst and patient. On another occasion, he wanted me to look through two volumes of reproductions of Russian paintings. Time and again, he called my attention to a painting with the title *What Is Truth?* He explained that Russian has two words for *truth*, *pravda*, which means truth in the everyday sense, and *iistina*, for the truth that lies behind appearances. What is truth? We kept asking ourselves that question, and it is in the search for both kinds of truth that our conversations were conducted.

"It seems that I want you to write something after all," the Wolf-Man said one day. "But it must not be published until after my death. You must understand, I cannot do otherwise." We decided to meet in my apartment from then on, for the Wolf-Man preferred that arrangement to my visiting him. My original plan had been to take two or three weeks leave, to spend several hours each day with the Wolf-Man, to work on the material and to ask supplementary questions. My partner was dead set against this procedure. He did not want to meet more often than once every two weeks. What could I do? Although this was difficult for me, I had to adapt to the slowness of an old man and live in perpetual fear that he might die, considering that his eighty-eighth birthday was approaching.

From September 1974 to January 1976, we met every two to three weeks and talked for several hours on each occasion. After this, the Wolf-Man came less often because he became more and more tired, realized that he had already told me the important things, and was becoming even more repetitious than before. When I had not heard from him for some time, I went to see how he was getting on. Although he became weaker by the day, he could not be persuaded to go into an old peoples' home. In July 1977, he suffered a circulatory collapse in the foyer of his apartment building. Dr. S. had him moved to the psychiatric hospital, where he remained until his death on May 7, 1979.

Our first conversations and those held during my visits in the psychiatric hospital were recorded from memory. I made tapes of the rest. Forty hours of tape constitute the basis of this text.

The difficulties that had to be overcome in the writing of this book were many—work on it dragged on for more than five years— and it seems almost superfluous to emphasize that it was only the sympathy the Wolf-Man and I felt for each other that made it possible to complete it at all. This sympathy may also explain the confidence I felt. I was firmly convinced that I would finish this frequently threatened project, although over long periods there was really no justification for such confidence.

At the very outset, it was the problem of identification that preoccupied me. I wondered which of the persons who surface in his memoirs would be most like me and decided to try to adopt the role of his older sister, Anna. However odd this may appear when one considers that he was more than half a century older, it was a plausible role for me because it was the one I had played in my own family. The Wolf-Man, in any event, seems to have enjoyed my occasionally treating him somewhat condescendingly, or teasing him when I felt he was becoming too involved in his suffering. Once, I visited him in a skirt that fell all the way to the floor because I wanted him to think back to the turn-of-the-century atmosphere and rekindle his memory of Anna, who had been two and half years older and had committed suicide. For years afterward, he would rave about the elegance of my dress on that occasion. . . . And yet it took me by surprise when he told me one day that he identified me with his sister.

I did everything in my power to create a more personal, friendlier atmosphere than is customary between analyst and patient. In spite of this, the Wolf-Man saw me as a new kind of analyst, one more on top of all those he had come into contact with in the course of his life. I am no psychoanalyst; yet the transfer situation mentioned above made possible something like a final analysis of this famous patient in which the effect of his analyses became the object of investigation. My financial and emotional independence permitted me a distance a psychoanalyst could not have achieved so readily.

It was only natural for a person my age to assume that one becomes more rational and serene as one gets older. But the Wolf-Man made me see the full tragedy that lies behind Jean Cocteau's phrase, "The awful thing about old age is that one remains young." He still had the problems of his youth, problems involving women and money. And the way he felt about his teeth had remained the same, so that ever-recurring complaints about his dentures accompanied our conversations.

While relations with his tailor had become more even, he continued to attribute an importance to clothes that seemed inordinate in a man his age. He always came immaculately dressed, wearing an elegant pinstripe, a dark suit, or sports clothes. The importance clothing had in his life became apparent when I suggested that we use the self-timer to take a picture of the two of us. On his next visit, he presented himself in a dark suit. Because my camera had suddenly begun malfunctioning, we had to postpone the picture taking. During that afternoon, he repeatedly came back to the subject of clothes. "I think I look too solemn today," he said. "It is better if I wear something sportier." I agreed. "So I'll wear sports clothes next time. But you, you must dress elegantly. Let's do it that way: I'll be in sports clothes, and you'll be elegant."

The contract became a painful hurdle for us. I had not known that where material of some scope is concerned, a contract becomes a necessity. When Editions Stock pointed this out to me and I told the Wolf-Man, he looked on this as a complete breach of faith. "First you make me believe that this is an arrangement between friends, and now you come with a lawyer," the learned jurist expostulated.

I had to visit Dr. S. at his office and explain everything to him. Dr. S., thin, and playing the role of the cool and unapproachable analyst, said to me, "The patient has the right to express himself critically about his treatment." But he insisted that the matter be discussed with Dr. E., who would arrive in August, as he did every year. It was already June, but once again I felt the fear that the Wolf-Man might die before a contract could be drawn up and signed. Dr. S. stated that he would be willing to testify that our conversations had in fact taken place, should that become necessary.

When Dr. E. finally arrived, it was difficult to persuade him to talk to me. The Wolf-Man, who was at least as excited about the contract as I, informed me that I should first write a letter requesting an interview. The letter having been mailed, E. called me and we agreed to meet in an apartment in the Schwarzspanierstrasse where he lived during his stay in Vienna.

E., dark haired and also thin, conducted himself with considerable arrogance. He, who had encouraged the Wolf-Man in his letters of the year before to meet with me, now wanted to persuade him to tell me that he could not agree to the publication of the interviews. . . . E. suggested to me that I would not only have to wait for the Wolf-Man's death, but also for the death of a person close to him about whom he had told me a great deal. E. also gave me to understand that he did not care for books written by laymen, and that only psychoanalysts had the necessary qualifications in these matters.

The Wolf-Man would not go along with his analyst. Both of us considered him unfair. E. attempted to convince his patient that this was not so, but had no success. Finally, we discussed the matter with a lawyer E. had suggested. I had declared my willingness to buy the rights of the Wolf-Man. The purchase price and the lawyer's fee were to be paid immediately, and the rights would pass to me after the Wolf-Man's death. When everything had been settled, the Wolf-Man suddenly pulled back: "I will have to think about this some more," he said. My nerves were beginning to give way, and the Wolf-Man's lawyer was also losing patience. Yet toward the end of September 1975, both of us finally signed the agreement after the matter had dragged on for nearly half a year. In retrospect, the Wolf-Man viewed the contract as a personal accomplishment, as a sort of final success in a life that had not been successful.

But the greatest hurdle was the writing of the text. It is almost impossible to convey what it means to be writing a book that one wants to see in print, yet to know that one must wait for someone's death before that can happen. It would lead too far, I believe, were I to start describing the psychological conflicts, the writing blocks, and the despair that this situation produced.

The forty hours of tape with the unending repetitions of an almost-ninety-year-old man often became a labyrinth I could no longer find my way out of. Occasionally, I must have lost my way in the neuroses of my partner, in his obsessional doubting and brooding over the selfsame matters, the meaninglessness of his life in which he had never had anything but bad luck, where almost everything had been failure, where he had made nothing but mistakes.

Over extended periods, I was incapable of work on the manuscript. The moment I sat down at my desk to deal with the material, I was overcome by an infinite weariness, nothing came to mind, I felt depressed. Absurd trivia overwhelmed me: whether and how I should write footnotes, whether I should use abbreviations and, if so, which names to abbreviate. There were weeks and months when I could not make a decision about these inconsequential matters. Obsessional doubts and brooding kept me from my work. But one thing is certain: today, I know what an obsessional neurosis is.

It goes without saying that the taped material had to be edited, for in their raw state, taped protocols do not yield a readable book. But it was my goal to stick as closely as possible to the spoken word because I wanted to retain that curious style with its repetitions and discontinuities that psychoanalysis, age, and perhaps an obsessional neurosis produce.

The older he became, the more the Wolf-Man became fixated on certain stereotypes of which he could free himself less and less. I must have heard certain phrases a few hundred times. I believe no one will blame me for saying frankly that there were occasions when my conversational partner got on my nerves. And nothing much remained of that Art Nouveau romanticism I had seen in him at the beginning of our acquaintance. In spite of all this, our mutual sympathy remained the strongest sentiment. And I owe this man a debt of gratitude.

In the Mirror
of Psychoanalysis

"Our records from so many sources, thorough, detailed, profound, make it possible for the lay person as well as the scientist to judge the extent to which psychoanalysis can help the seriously disturbed person,"[1] writes editor Muriel Gardiner in her book *The Wolf-Man*. Like Anna Freud in her preface, she tries to draw a positive picture of the therapeutic effect of analysis. The Wolf-Man appears as a harmless, satisfied, almost happy pensioner. Important parts from the life of this famous patient as he tells them in the following interviews have been omitted. Over stretches, the book conveys too harmonious a portrait of the Wolf-Man.

Freud published six extensive case histories but only analyzed four patients himself. The Wolf-Man is thus one of those famous cases on which all of psychoanalytic literature rests. Because this patient could be observed for such a long time, it would therefore have been all the more important to draw the most accurate picture possible of the conditions under which he lived. It is only natural that Anna Freud, the daughter of a famous father, and Muriel Gardiner, a psychoanalyst and follower of Freud's teachings for decades, should both be less than objective.

After the treatment had ended, Anna O.'s attitude toward analysis is hostile. As an adult, little Hans flees from the importunities of analysts. Only the Wolf-Man is "able and willing to cooperate ac-

1. Muriel Gardiner, ed., *The Wolf-Man: With the Case of the Wolf-Man by Sigmund Freud* (New York: Basic Books, 1971), p. vii.

tively in the reconstruction and follow-up of his own case,"[2] as Anna Freud writes in the preface. She expressly speaks of "our Wolf-Man"[3] and presents him as if he were a model student of psychoanalysis.

It is true that the Wolf-Man owed a debt of gratitude to his analysts, and the financial dependence in which he found himself during the last years of his life did not permit him to express his opinion in public. It could only be published after his death.

The book *The Wolf-Man* contains not only the memoirs of the patient and Freud's case history, but also a postscript by Ruth Mack Brunswick and a short account of his life in old age which was written by the editor, Muriel Gardiner.

I will begin by giving a summary of his life and of the most important texts on the Wolf-Man: Sergius P. was born on January 6, 1887, the son of wealthy aristocratic landowners, on an estate in southern Russia. When he is five years old, his parents move to Odessa. The family spends its time between Odessa and a castlelike manor house in the country. Sergej and his sister Anna, who is two and one-half years older, are brought up by nannies, governesses, and tutors. The hypochondriacal mother is kept busy by her illnesses while the father, a well-known liberal, spends his time in politics and occasional bouts of depression. A grandmother is believed to have committed suicide. In a situation that parallels *The Brothers Karamazov*, the grandfather vies with his son for the affection of the latter's bride. An uncle had suffered from paranoia and died in total isolation on a remote estate.

It cannot be surprising that with such a family background, a person should make a career of being a patient. Yet initially, Sergej developed normally. He attends the gymnasium, and it is not until he contracts gonorrhea at age eighteen that he suffers severe depressions. He recovers but has a serious relapse when, a year later, his sister surprises everyone by committing suicide.

To divert himself, he attends Petersburg University but finds himself unable to follow the lectures. He becomes a patient of the well-known neurologist Bechterev, who uses hypnosis. He then visits a number of sanatoria in Germany where he is treated by

2. Ibid., p. xi.
3. Not in English original.—TRANS.

outstanding specialists such as Kraepelin and Ziehen. His father had seen Kraepelin earlier because of melancholia.

In the sanatorium of Neuwittelsbach near Munich, he falls in love with a nurse. Therese is a few years older, divorced, and the mother of a girl. A curious back and forth begins. At times, Therese seems to yield to his advances, at others she wants to put an end to the relationship. The previously timid and reserved young Russian reacts so confusedly that Kraepelin diagnoses him as he had his father, i.e., manic-depressive. Doctors, family, and acquaintances are all opposed to any relation between the aristocrat and the nurse.

Sergej finally leaves Therese and returns to Russia. The father has died recently and laid down in his testament that the son will not receive his inheritance until age twenty-eight. Disputes arise between him and his mother over the inheritance, but a short time later, an uncle leaves him a considerable fortune, so that he now has money at his disposal. He seems cured of his passion for Therese.

Although he does not feel ill, he decides to return to Germany to consult Professor Kraepelin on the subject of his earlier depressions. He is unable to stay away from Therese; the journey reveals itself as a pretext for seeing her again. The meeting precipitates a profound depression and he returns home in an extremely poor psychological state.

He now goes to a sanatorium near Frankfurt am Main but finds it impossible to stay for long. He consults Professor Ziehen in Berlin, who recommends a stay in the sanatorium of Schlachtensee. Mother and aunt have come to Berlin and are staying in a pension nearby. Occasionally, he visits Therese in Munich. Both physician and mother hope that the relationship will gradually cool and refer to Therese as a woman "with whom no man could get along."[4] Sergej comes to share this view and wants to return to Russia. He meets Therese a final time. A quarrel with her prompts him to write a farewell letter. He returns home in a state of profound depression.

In Odessa, he is now being treated by Dr. Drosnes, a young physician who has read Freud and who dabbles in psychoanalytic treatment. Sufficiently insightful to admit that his knowledge is inadequate, he proposes that Freud be consulted. Sergej sets out

4. Gardiner, *Wolf-Man*, p. 75.

with the physician and a medical student whose task it is to give him injections for his digestive difficulties and to be the third in their card games.

That is the "breakthrough to the woman"[5] says Freud when he hears about Therese, and he also agrees that Sergej may see her again, although not until the patient has a few months of analysis behind him. Freud's method and personality make such an impression on Sergej that he continues in treatment. Since the analysis takes only an hour a day, the three young Russians have time to amuse themselves in Vienna, the capital of the former Austro-Hungarian monarchy.

Only a year later—Drosnes and the medical student have already returned to Odessa—does Freud allow Sergej to see Therese again. She is now the proprietress of a small pension in Munich and grief over the separation has affected her so deeply that she looks terribly run down. He suddenly decides to marry her but must bow to the rule of psychoanalysis according to which he can take such a step only after treatment has come to an end. Some time later, Therese joins him in Vienna.

Four years later, a few days before the outbreak of the First World War, the analysis ends. Sergej returns to Odessa while Therese remains in Bavaria with her small daughter Else. She is to follow him a short time later. Suddenly, war erupts between Germany and Russia and it is difficult to obtain a Russian visa. Yet Therese does finally get to Odessa and the long-planned wedding takes place.

Therese cannot get along with her mother-in-law or the other relatives. The young couple therefore spends the winter months in Moscow, where the Wolf-Man, who has returned to his studies, is preparing for his examinations. In the spring, he passes the state law examination in Odessa. New disputes with the mother develop. It is learned that Therese's daughter Else, whom she had left in the care of her brother in Munich, has fallen ill.

Therese is given permission to leave the country; the Wolf-Man stays in Odessa. But Else's condition deteriorates and it is impossible to send money to Germany. He decides to follow his wife. In Bucharest, where he is detained by the French, he learns that the

5. Ibid., p. 56.

Red troops marched into Odessa a few days after his departure (1918).

He travels via Vienna, where he also visits Freud, who recommends a reanalysis because there is a small, nonanalyzed residue. A few months later, during which time Else dies, he returns to Vienna with Therese. The treatment drags on for half a year.

It has become impossible for the Wolf-Man to return to Bolshevist Russia. By a lucky coincidence, he finds employment at an insurance company where he will work until he is pensioned in 1950.

The wealthy aristocrat has become an impoverished émigré. This change in circumstances again triggers severe depressions and decides him to seek treatment from Freud. But Freud is already too ill and recommends his student Ruth Mack Brunswick.

The Wolf-Man leads the life of an ordinary citizen, works as a minor employee in an insurance company, goes out into the country with his wife on Sundays, and paints landscapes as a hobby. Therese, who had married a wealthy man, must adapt to new conditions. She seems to be losing her joie de vivre, neglects her appearance, and turns to saving money as her principal interest in life. A few days after Hitler's march into Austria in March 1938, the Wolf-Man, coming home from work, finds his wife dead. She had killed herself.

Muriel Gardiner, an American who was studying medicine in Vienna at the time, was close to the Psychoanalytic Circle. The Wolf-Man became acquainted with her while he was being analyzed by Ruth Mack Brunswick. She took Russian lessons from him; later, when she stopped, he visited her once when her insurance policy was renewed. After Therese's suicide, he runs into her on the street; she is so moved by his despair that she helps him obtain an exit visa to travel to Paris and London, where he is to meet Ruth Mack Brunswick, who helps him deal with this fresh blow.

In his case history, "From the History of an Infantile Neurosis,"[6] Freud describes the patient as "entirely incapacitated and completely dependent upon other people."[7] "The patient . . . remained for a long time unassailably entrenched behind an attitude of obliging apathy. His unimpeachable intelligence was, as it were, cut off

6. Ibid., pp. 153–262.
7. Ibid., p. 154.

from the instinctual forces. . . . It required a long education to induce him to take an independent share in the work. . . . His shrinking from a self-sufficient existence was so great so to outweigh all the vexations of his illness."[8]

Freud calls the patient's illness "a condition following on an obsessional neurosis which has come to an end spontaneously, but has left a defect behind it after recovery."[9] In his text, he deals primarily with the rise and effect of this neurosis in early childhood.

"I dreamt that it was night and that I was lying in my bed. My bed stood with its foot towards the window; in front of the window there was a row of old walnut trees. I know it was winter when I had the dream, and nighttime. Suddenly, the window opened of its own accord, and I was terrified to see that some white wolves were sitting on the big walnut tree in front of the window. There were six or seven of them. The wolves were quite white, and looked more like foxes or sheepdogs, for they had big tails like foxes and they had their ears pricked like dogs when they pay attention to something. In great terror, evidently of being eaten up by the wolves, I screamed and woke up. . . ."[10]

From this dream which the patient had at the age of four and for which he was given his psychoanalytic pseudonym, Freud derives the cause of the neurosis. Fairy-tale material (like "Red Riding Hood," "The Wolf and the Seven Kids"), a story about a tailor—in his later life, tailors play a preeminent role—and a tailless wolf his grandfather had told him about have been reworked in the dream. But behind the dream, according to Freud, there lies an experience from early childhood that provided the basis for his castration fears: at the age of one and a half, he had fallen ill with malaria and slept in his parents' room instead of in his nanny's, as was customary. During an afternoon, "he witnessed a coitus a tergo, three times repeated," where he could see "his mother's genitals as well as his father's organ."[11] In this primal scene, the white wolves stand for the parents' white underwear. Freud attributes the number three to a spontaneous idea of his patient.

8. Ibid., p. 157.
9. Ibid., p. 154.
10. Ibid., p. 173.
11. Ibid., p. 182.

To answer possible doubts about this interpretation of the dream by his readers, the author writes, "There are more things in heaven and earth than are dreamed of in our philosophy."[12]

In addition to this primal scene, there are seduction attempts by the older sister and threats of castration by the nanny at a later time. When, during a journey by the parents, disputes arise between a newly hired English governess who proves difficult and possibly an alcoholic, and the nanny, there takes place a change of character in the boy and the symptoms of obsessional neurosis surface. From this time on, he is excitable, suddenly becomes afraid of animals, yet torments bugs and caterpillars and begins to suffer from the odd compulsion to blaspheme after his mother teaches him biblical history in an attempt to divert him.

The primal scene results in a deterioration of relations to the father. The Wolf-Man identifies with the mother, the woman, whose castrated state he observed at the time. But he represses his homosexual inclination. This complex condition manifests itself in a malfunctioning of the anal zone: "The organ by which his identification with women, his passive homosexual attitude to men, was able to express itself was the anal zone. The disorders in the function of this zone had acquired the significance of feminine impulses of tenderness, and they retained it during the later illness as well."[13] Intestinal difficulties were still present during analysis: "Spontaneous evacuations did not occur for months at a time, unless a sudden excitement from some particular direction intervened. . . . His principal subject of complaint was that for him the world was hidden in a veil, or that he was cut off from the world by a veil. This veil was torn only at one moment—when, after an enema, the contents of the bowel left the intestinal canal; and he then felt well and normal again."[14]

It is in connection with the intestinal difficulties that Freud sees the problems his patient had with money: "In our patient, at the time of his later illness, these relations (to money) were disturbed to a particularly severe degree and this fact was not the least considerable element in his lack of independence and his incapacity for

12. Ibid., p. 158.
13. Ibid., p. 220.
14. Ibid., p. 217.

dealing with life. He had become very rich through legacies from his father and uncle; it was obvious that he attached great importance to being taken for rich, and he was liable to feel very much hurt if he was undervalued in this respect. But he had no idea how much he possessed, what his expenditure was, or what balance was left over."[15]

Freud sees the Wolf-Man's disturbed relation to women as the second problem that must be addressed. The Wolf-Man feels drawn to servants and falls in love obsessionally when he sees a woman in a certain position. It is this position that is also taken by the nanny Gruscha, who makes her appearance very late in the analysis; it is a very distant childhood memory: "The posture which, according to our construction of the primal scene, he had seen the woman assume, was of no less significance; though in this case the significance was limited to the sexual sphere. The most striking phenomenon of his erotic life after maturity was his liability to compulsive attacks of falling physically in love which came on and disappeared again in the most puzzling succession. These attacks released a tremendous energy in him even at times when he was otherwise inhibited, and they were quite beyond his control." These compulsive loves were "subject to a definite condition, which was concealed from his consciousness and was discovered only during the treatment. It was necessary that the woman assume a posture which we have ascribed to his mother in the primal scene. From his puberty he had felt large and conspicuous buttocks as the most powerful attraction in a woman, to copulate except from behind gave him scarcely any enjoyment."[16]

For social reasons, Freud refuses to report anything more detailed about his patient's difficulties. But analysis, the becoming conscious of those childhood experiences that have caused the neurotic disturbances, is to make it possible to cure the patient.

After four years of analysis and a reanalysis of half a year, the Wolf-Man is discharged by Freud as cured, yet again feels in need of analysis in October 1926. Ruth Mack Brunswick initially treats him for five months and, after about two years, irregularly for a number of years. While Freud had advised reanalysis to deal with an unre-

15. Ibid., p. 215.
16. Ibid., p. 185.

solved transference remnant, such remnants have once again made their appearance.

According to Ruth Mack Brunswick, the Wolf-Man has meanwhile undergone a significant change in character. Whereas Freud had described him as compulsively honest and conscientious, his new analyst comes to know another side of the man. He has become guilty of all sorts of minor dishonesties, concealing from Freud, for example, that he has the family jewels in his possession, a secretiveness that becomes all the more peculiar when one considers that Freud had often helped him out financially. His present symptom is the *ideé fixe* that his nose has been conspicuously and incurably deformed by blackheads. Occasionally, complaints about his teeth take the place of those about his nose. Just as, at an earlier time, he had gone from tailor to tailor, eternally dissatisfied, he now goes from one dermatologist to the next, or from dentist to dentist.

Ruth Mack Brunswick diagnoses this illness as hypochondriacal paranoia. She is of the opinion that in Freud's analysis, the transference was not sufficiently "lived through" and that the more recent illness has thus become possible. Toward the end of the analysis, when treatment would stagnate for long periods, Freud had set a time limit, which is the strongest weapon the analyst can use to combat the patient's resistance. But then the treatment had terminated satisfactorily after all. Mack Brunswick comments: "This time limit resulted in the patient's bringing sufficient material to produce a cure, but it also enabled him to keep just that nucleus which later resulted in his psychosis."[17] Is there such a thing as being cured on the one hand, yet retaining the nucleus of a psychosis which is, after all, something rather substantial? And as to the reason the patient who formerly suffered from an obsessional neurosis should suddenly have become paranoid, she writes: "Why the patient developed paranoia instead of reverting to his original neurosis is hard to say. It may be that the first analysis robbed him of the usual neurotic modes of solution. One asks oneself if the patient was perhaps always latently paranoid."[18]

17. Ibid., p. 304.
18. Ibid., p. 305.

In her contribution, "The Wolf-Man in Later Life,"[19] Muriel Gardiner tells how, after the war, she meets the now famous patient again. She recounts short meetings at intervals of several years, speaks of his paintings that she sells for him in the United States, and quotes from his letters. Occasionally, there is talk about affairs that trouble the Wolf-Man, about the time of his retirement, the last years of his mother, who had moved in with him after Therese's death, and of the illness of his housekeeper Tiny, here called Gaby.

There is one experience that made a special impression on the Wolf-Man and that takes up a correspondingly large number of pages: during the occupation, he wanders unthinkingly into the Russian sector and paints what appears to be an empty factory. As he is about to return home, he is prevented by Russian soldiers, who take him inside the building, which turns out to be a military post. He is suspected of espionage and detained for several days. Only after he has been questioned for some time can he convince the Russians of the harmlessness of his painting.

The reader discovers that even now, the Wolf-Man consults psychiatrists and psychologists when he finds himself in difficult situations. In the fall of 1955, he establishes contact with one psychoanalyst; later, he gets regular help from another.

In her final chapter, "Diagnostic Impressions," Muriel Gardiner describes the Wolf-Man in these terms: "The chief feature is the prominence of his obsessional doubting, brooding, questioning, his being completely engrossed in his own problems and unable to relate to others. . . . What the Wolf-Man experiences as depression is sometimes a reaction to a real loss and sometimes the despair caused by his obsessional doubts, guilt, self-reproaches and feeling of failure."[20]

Muriel Gardiner quotes other analysts who also describe the Wolf-Man as a compulsive personality. It seems that the defect that remained with the patient from his obsessional neurosis could not be removed completely either by Freud or by Ruth Mack Brunswick. "Some manifestations of this defect will remain after the Wolf-

19. Ibid., pp. 311–67.
20. Ibid., p. 361.

Man's analysis: periods of depression, of doubting and vacillation, ambivalence, feelings of guilt and strong narcissistic needs. They were modified and reduced by analysis but not destroyed. However, the positive results of the Wolf-Man's analysis are impressive indeed."[21]

How impressive, the reader will be able to judge for himself, once he has read the conversations that follow.

21. Ibid., p. 365.

·II·
CONVERSATIONS
WITH
THE WOLF-MAN

Freud the Father

WOLF-MAN: You know, I feel so bad, I have been having such terrible depressions lately . . . (looks at me mistrustfully). Now you probably think that psychoanalysis didn't do me any good.
OBHOLZER: Not at all, why should I? People sometimes feel bad, don't they? Do your depressions have a specific cause?
W: I'd rather not discuss that. So, you are interested in psychoanalysis? It does seem that interest in it keeps coming back. In physics, you can discover something, but one cannot look inside the human brain. That's why people are interested. It used to be different.

Some twenty years ago, I wrote a few articles on psychoanalysis and inquired at some journals about getting them published. Nobody wanted them at the time. One editor said to me, "Einstein's theory of relativity is something you can understand, but what do you do with psychoanalysis?" That annoyed me a great deal at the time. Freud was a genius, there's no denying it! All those ideas that he combined in a system. . . . Even though much isn't true, it was a splendid achievement.
O: I've been here a few times to see how you were. But you were never in. The last time, I wrote you a note. . . .
W: It's a good thing, by the way, that you used such a large piece of paper, otherwise I might have overlooked it. It'll be best if you send me a postcard before you come. There've been a number of times when I wasn't at home. Dr. E. of the Freud archive in New York spent four weeks in Vienna. Usually, he only stays three. This time, he stayed four. He observes me because he is interested in what becomes of Freud's patients. He always asked me to come very early

in the morning, sometimes also at night. That was an effort for me—
I had to get up earlier. Normally, I prefer sleeping later. And on
Tuesday afternoon, I see Dr. S., although it's useless.

O: Then why go?

W: I have no idea. E. said once I should go, so I went, and then I just
kept going. You know him, don't you?

O: S.? Yes, I interviewed him once.

W: A year ago, I reserved a place in an old peoples' home because E.
and S. insisted. I was told it would be about a year until they could
take me. I should inquire about now, but I don't feel like it. They
only give you one room, whereas here I have two, the bathroom and
the kitchen. But everything is becoming very difficult for me, like
climbing up to the fifth floor; there's no lift (*he moans*). My God,
everybody wants to get old and no one knows what it means. I no
longer have the courage to go on vacation; just packing is too much.
I used to go to the Semmering Pass or into Styria. All of Austria is
beautiful. I had the idea of moving to New York, but that was
probably just a fantasy. I don't even speak English.

O: Freud writes that your illness erupted because you got the clap.

W: The what?

O: Gonorrhea.

W: I beg your pardon?

O: Go—norr—hea.

W: That we have to talk about these unpleasant things!

O: What's so terrible? It can happen to anyone. Perhaps it will
console you when I tell you that I had the clap myself.

W: I am amazed you should tell me. You really seem to trust me!
Here's what happened: In the gymnasium, I had a friend, and this
friend had an older friend who arranged it. There was a café with
three girls in it. And this friend knew that these girls were in that
café and that they could also be put to a different use. . . .

O: What sort of girls?

W: Waitresses. And they also had a room. . . .

O: Did the people that owned the café know about that?

W: Yes, they must have known, tolerated or even arranged it;
perhaps they made a little money off it.

O: How old were you at the time?

W: Seventeen.

O: Was that your first sexual experience?

W: Yes. In any event, we went and I asked the friend—you'll have to excuse my telling you these terrible things—whether one should use a prophylactic or not. And he answered, "The whore will laugh at you." So we didn't take any along. And then, by way of a joke, he said that there's a superstition that the name of the first woman with whom one has sexual intercourse will also be the name of the woman one marries. And that was true in our case. Her name was Maria, I remember, and my wife's name was actually Maria Therese. So it was true.

And in the case of this friend . . . I should mention that he was an acquaintance of my violin teacher's whom he once brought to the estate because it had struck my father that I had no companions. He took me to the café. And the girl whom he knew there was called Nadja. And that was also the name of the violin teacher's daughter. At first, the father didn't want her to marry him because he wasn't a good match. But then he did, and they did get married. You see, by chance, the superstition turned out true. In any event, that was all there was to it.

O: The gonorrhea came later?

W: Yes, later. I got it from a peasant girl. That was a year later. I felt confident; I thought, that can't happen in the country. People always said that it was risky to go to prostitutes. And out in the country it is less dangerous. The opposite turned out to be true. She was even married, but I think her husband was doing his military service. In any event, I didn't think it would happen here, I thought it might happen in the other situation.

O: And you gave the peasant girl money, or were you in love?

W: No, no, you always gave something, that was a matter of good manners. At least I think so, it's so long ago. In any case, I got it from that peasant girl. A fellow student told me at the time that he had chronic gonorrhea. That really frightened me terribly. I imagined I had the same thing. The word *chronic*, you understand, was terrible. A physician used a catheter; it took a long time and was painful. What do they do today?

O: You get penicillin injections.

W: It wasn't that simple in my time. In any event, I was dissatisfied with the physician. Then I found a professor who treated me. After some time, he told me: "You can get married tomorrow. For a while, there will be a drop on your member, but that's of no consequence and will pass." Although he had told me that, I worried. I knew there was no reason. Nonetheless, it was an obsessive idea. No one knew anything about gonorrhea. I was feeling terrible. My sister asked me: "What's wrong with you? Are you in love?" I told her to guess. She didn't find the right answer. Don't you think she should have been able to guess?

O: How could she have?

W: The only one to notice something was a certain Viktor. I'll tell you about him some other time. He was a student who used to come to the house. I met him, and he understood immediately that I was ill, psychologically. "What is troubling you?" he asked. "You look completely changed." I: "No, it's nothing." He: "Oh yes, you look completely changed." He'd noticed something.

Then I traveled to Berlin with my mother and sister. They went to a sanatorium there. We took a student along, a certain Hasselblad— his grandfather or great-grandfather had come from Sweden. Odd, isn't it? One always took strangers along. And this Hasselblad had an uncle, a certain Professor Anton, who was a psychiatrist in Vienna. He happened to be in Berlin at the time and this Hasselblad asked me if I wanted to speak with his uncle. I went to see him and he diagnosed the whole thing as puberty neurosis. "It will pass," he said, and suggested that we take a trip. We went to Italy. That was a diversion, and all those ideas went away. Hasselblad was a good traveling companion for me because he was a calm person and had had gonorrhea himself. He had had it repeatedly in the past, and then he got it again in Rome. That's when I saw that it isn't so terrible. That was really the most important success.

O: That was very reasonable.

W: The advice had been correct. I just thought of something! Let's call the thing by its name. Even before the gonorrhea, I had had bad luck with my penis, my member. You know those insects they call ticks. On the estate, we ran around in the bushes, lay in the grass, climbed trees. In any event, something was suddenly itching. I rubbed and scratched. Finally I noticed that it was taking on enormous dimensions. The member had swollen; it was big and red. I told my father. And he called one of our servants who had done medical work in the army. He was not a real doctor, only half a one, but he knew something about these things. And he removed the tick in some way, and it passed. I think I spent two weeks in bed and was given ice bags.

O: How old were you?

W: Around eight. That may have contributed to the fact that the gonorrhea made such an impression on me. But I had . . . I don't know whether I told my friend about it. Then there was something else. When I was about fifteen, that spot itched me once. But that was during the winter, in Odessa. I scratched and saw that something was wrong, that it was swollen and red. I told my father. There happened to be a physician in the house at the moment, a neurologist. He looked at me and said, "That's gonorrhea." I had never had intercourse with a woman, so that was impossible. And my father—there you see what sexual education was in those days— my father started in on me: "You've been to women! Do you want to die of syphilis? Do you want to rot?" I kept saying, "I am not aware of it. Perhaps it's an infection that the wind blew in my direction." That was meant as a joke—it's a cold, you know. He said, "Don't talk nonsense." He had a specialist come to the house, of course, who discovered that it wasn't gonorrhea at all. Something below the skin had become infected. perhaps I hadn't kept my member clean enough. He gave me some kind of medicine and it went away. You see, that's the threat from the father. That may also have contributed to the fact that the gonorrhea made such a terrible impression on me. I don't know, of course.

O: So the gonorrhea got better. Then your sister killed herself. But why you then went to Freud is something I still don't understand. What did you tell Freud you were suffering from?

W: Well, depressions.

O: So it's because of the depressions that you went?

W: Yes, actually it was because of Therese.

O: You mean you began psychoanalytic treatment because you had fallen in love? Isn't it perfectly normal to be a little confused in a situation like that?

W: Well, perhaps things would have taken care of themselves without Freud. But everyone was against Therese: the doctors, my mother, my relatives. They all said that she was a woman with whom one could not live. Had I decided to go see Therese, things might have been all right without Freud.

O: And Dr. Drosnes, you physician in Odessa, was he also against her?

W: Yes. Perhaps, if he had said. "Go to Therese," everything would have turned out well. But he didn't say it. So I didn't know what to do. I could not prevail, and so we went to Vienna. And if Freud had not said "That's the breakthrough to the woman," and that I could see Therese, I would not have stayed on. No one had any idea that it would take all that time. I had assumed it would go very fast, and that everything would be all right afterwards. That's how Drosnes had explained it to me in Odessa: "There is something called psychoanalysis, and there is a Professor Freud who has invented a new method that is splendid. What he has invented borders on the miraculous. For he believes that some childhood experience, a trauma, is the cause of an illness. And if one remembers this event, one gets one's health back. In five minutes." That pleased me, naturally, that everything could be explained by a trauma.

O: And did Freud tell you that it would take all that time?

W: No. At first, it looked as if it would take a few months. And then it dragged on and on. Freud was a genius even though not everything he said was true. If you had seen him—he was a fascinating personality. . . . He had very serious eyes that looked down to the very bottom of the soul. His whole appearance was very appealing. I felt sympathy for him. That was transference. He had a magnetism or, better, an aura that was very pleasant and positive. When I told him about my various states, he said: "We have the means to cure what you are suffering from. Up to now, you have been looking for the causes of your illness in the chamber pot." In those days people tried to get at psychic states by way of the physical. The psychological was completely ignored. And it was also a temptation. Everything was explained.

O: And what did he tell you to do?

W: At first, I stayed in a sanatorium. Freud said that he had other patients there, so he saved himself a trip. I stayed there for about six weeks. I found it fascinating that a doctor should tell me, "We have what it takes to cure your illness." That was faith.

O: And you lay down on the bed during the very first hour, and he sat at the head?

W: He also told me why. There was a girl who tried to seduce him as he was sitting at the other end.

O: Is that it?

W: Everything was so new and interesting for me, you understand. I was used to the old psychiatrists. . . . He said that one should say out loud whatever came into one's mind, just the way the thoughts came.

O: He said, "Treatment means that you have to say everything that occurs to you"?

W: Everything that occurs to you.

O: Did he explain why?

W: No, he did not go into details. He must have thought that the important things are in the subconscious and that they emerge through free association. When he had explained everything to me, I said to him, "All right then, I agree, but I am going to check whether it is correct." And he said: "Don't start that. Because the moment you try to view things critically, your treatment will get nowhere. I will help you, whether you now believe in it, or not." So I naturally gave up the idea of any further criticism.

O: Why?

W: Well, because he said that if I continued to criticize, I would make no progress, because I always want to prove something. He writes somewhere that I had the tendency to clear up contradictions. But that may be the very opposite of my character, because contradictions are constantly battling each other inside me. And precisely in those cases where I should be logical, I fail. In theoretical matters, I am logical. I would rather be logical where feelings are concerned. . . . But it is interesting that he should have said, "Don't criticize, don't reflect, don't look for contradictions, but accept what I tell you, and improvement will come by itself." That's how he succeeded in bringing about a total transference to himself. Is that a good thing, do you suppose? That's the question. Too strong a transference ends with your transferring to individuals who replace Freud, as it were, and with your believing them uncritically. And that happened to me, to a degree. So transference is a dangerous thing.

O: Probably.

W: If you look at everything critically, there isn't much in psychoanalysis that will stand up. Yet it helped me. He was a genius. Just imagine the work he did, remembering all those details, forgetting nothing, drawing those inferences. He may have had six, seven patients a day, and all the things he wrote. He was witty, a very intelligent man, there's no disputing that. And that he made mistakes . . . to err is human. And it's also clear that he overestimated his work.

O: I daresay everyone does.

W: If he hadn't overestimated it, he might not have done it.

O: When you speak of Freud, you make such a cool and rational impression. You keep saying stereotypically, "Freud was a genius." But your relationship to him was emotional.

W: With whom?

O: With Freud.

W: Well, actually, I worshiped him. That's because of Father. Father disappointed me because he preferred Sister. So the relationship to Father wasn't good. Homosexual or not, I was very attached to Father and would have liked him to spend time with me and to introduce me to management. And then my father died and I had no father at all and came to Freud. And Freud said, "You were lucky that your father died, otherwise you would never have become well." You see, I just remembered that he said that. . . .

He probably meant that this transference would not have occurred otherwise, from Father to him, to see Father in him. Perhaps it was good luck that I came to him just after my father had died. You see the importance he attributed to transference. One can obviously obtain improvement through transference. I had a conflict with my father, you see, internal, not overt. There was no overt conflict, only an inner one, and then my father died and Freud says to me, "You were lucky . . ." So he meant that if my father had not died, I would not have succeeded in making a transference to him.

O: Did you have difficulty expressing everything that occurred to you?

W: Well, sometimes things did occur to me that I really didn't want to mention. But I followed the rule and always mentioned everything. During my childhood, I had blasphemous thoughts, insulted

God, and so on. And with Freud, it was the same thing. I thought, Freud is a scoundrel—that's the sort of thing that came into my head. And I expressed that. He put up with it stoically.

O: Did you tell him things like that more than once?

W: Not often.

O: You just thought it?

W: The idea occurred to me.

O: Freud is a scoundrel! And what did he say?

W: He suffered it stoically. According to Freud, a psychoanalyst must be a kind of god.

O: Well . . .

W: But don't you believe that psychoanalysis harms a person when he has to make a decision on his own and relies on it?

O: Probably. Did he smoke during analysis? He smoked a great deal, didn't he?

W: Yes, yes.

O: And did you smoke too?

W: No, I didn't. I was lying down.

O: One can smoke lying down.

W: Then I would have had to ask for an ashtray, and that wasn't possible. I didn't smoke so much in those days.

O: But Freud did smoke?

W: Yes, almost all the time.

O: And then I have read that at the beginning, when he started an analysis, he would invite the patient to his house for dinner.

W: No, he didn't.

O: So that was no longer the case when you were seeing him. And they say he sometimes had refreshments served.

W: No, no.

O: Never? At what time during the day did you see him?

W: Sometimes in the morning, sometimes in the afternoon.

O: Many patients find it unbearable that the analyst is like a blank wall, that he acts so impersonally, that he says nothing about himself, and they develop enormous aggressions against him.

W: No, I never did. He did sometimes give his views.

O: But generally, he did not talk about himself.

W: Not much, but some. He discussed painting, for example, and that a son of his had wanted to become a painter, that he gave up that idea and became an architect. He did mention a few things but not much, not much at all.

O: And you saw him every day?

W: Yes, every day except Sundays.

O: Every day for one hour, an hour every day for four years.

W: Yes, there's something incredible about it.

O: And your mother didn't mind your spending four years in Vienna?

W: No. She could see that I was getting better, and had no objections.

O: And what did Freud charge per hour?

W: Forty crowns.

O: About how much is that in today's money?

W: That's difficult to say. I will give you a figure for purposes of comparison. In Germany, you paid ten marks per day in a first-rate sanatorium. Ten marks included everything, treatment, physician, your room. What's ten marks? It's ridiculous.

O: And ten marks was how many crowns?

W: The Russian ruble was about two and one-half francs. And these currencies were all equal: crown, Swiss frank, French franc. And the mark was worth a little more.

O: In other words, forty crowns per hour was about thirty-five marks or sixteen rubles, and a day in a sanatorium cost ten marks. That was certainly expensive.

W: It was. In Russia, minor employees had to live on one hundred rubles per month. So you can imagine how cheap everything was. Well, it's certainly a drawback of psychoanalysis that it is only for the wealthy. Hardly anyone can afford that kind of treatment. Nowadays, I couldn't afford it myself. And here's something else: for many, money is a problem that makes them ill. And that problem is totally ignored.

O: So Freud was certainly not poor if he had eight or ten consultations per day.

W: That's true, but he wasn't so very smart. He bought bonds from the Austrian government.

O: He did?

W: Yes, and he lost money.

O: Did you know the Freud family?

W: Only by sight. I later became acquainted with his son Martin. At the time I was being treated by Freud, I saw him walk up the stairs and then his sister, Anna Freud, who was a girl at the time, perhaps fifteen.

O: Did you know other patients?

W: Only by sight. I later saw two of them on the street, but I can't say that they looked healthy. One was a Jewish baron, that's what Freud told me. Remember that in Austria, Jews could become noblemen. He was very fat when I saw him during office hours, elegantly dressed, and normal looking. But then, after the war, he looked terrible and was in the company of an altogether impossible woman. One could tell that he had come down in the world, that somehow he had not become well. But I know no details, you understand. And the other one was also curiously dressed. I saw patients during office hours and asked Freud, who is that one, or that one.

O: And he told you?

W: Not their names.

O: When you read the "History of an Infantile Neurosis" for the first time, what did you think?

W: I didn't think much about it.

O: Did you believe at the time that everything Freud had written in that text was correct?

W: I didn't think about it. That was because of transference.

O: And today?

W: There is that dream business. I never thought much of dream interpretation, you know.

O: Why not?

W: In my story, what was explained by dreams? Nothing, as far as I can see. Freud traces everything back to the primal scene which he derives from the dream. But that scene does not occur in the dream. When he interprets the white wolves as nightshirts or something like that, for example, linen sheets or clothes, that's somehow far-fetched, I think. That scene in the dream where the windows open and so on and the wolves are sitting there, and his interpretation, I don't know, those things are miles apart. It's terribly farfetched.

O: But it is true that you did have that dream.

W: Yes, it is.

O: You must have told him other dreams.

W: Of course, but I no longer remember the dreams I told him.

O: And that didn't impress you when he interpreted dreams?

W: Well, he said it doesn't matter whether one takes note of that or not, consciously. The effect remains. I think that assertion would have to be proven. I prefer free association because there, something can occur to you. But that primal scene is no more than a construct.

O: You mean the interpretation Freud derives from the dream, that you observed the coitus of your parents, the three acts of coitus?

W: The whole thing is improbable because in Russia, children sleep in the nanny's bedroom, not in their parents'. It's possible, of course, that there was an exception, how do I know? But I have never been able to remember anything of that sort.

In logic, you learn not to go from consequences to cause, but in the opposite direction, from cause to consequences. When, where we have an *a*, we also have a *b*, I must find a *b* when *a* recurs. If one does it the other way around, and concludes from effects to cause, it's the same thing as circumstantial evidence in a trial. But that's a weak argument, isn't it? He maintains I saw it, but who will guarantee that it is so? That it is not a fantasy of his? That's one thing. We had best begin with the theory. And secondly, when one makes something conscious that was in the subconscious, it doesn't help at all. Freud once said, "I am a spiritual revolutionary." . . . Well, I also have to look at psychoanalysis critically, I cannot believe everything Freud said, after all. I have always thought that the memory would come. But it never did.

O: One might say that your resistance up to the present day is so strong that you don't want to remember.

W: Well, that would also be a supposition, wouldn't it? But it is no proof.

O: No, it's no proof. And that story about your sister . . .

W: Well, the story about the sister is something I remembered. I could not remember the other things. What he meant by the wolves. But I do know this: she was aggressive, and that is the reason the complex did not go away, somehow continued to have effects.

O: What do you mean?

W: Regarding my sister, there was this childhood seduction when she played with my member. That's something very important when it happens in childhood. I was very small when this seduction took place. It must have been before my fifth birthday because my father sold that estate when I was five. I can remember that we had sat down between the doors and she played with my penis. But must that necessarily have such consequences, or is it already a sign of sickness that something like that has consequences? Perhaps it also happened to other little boys and had no effect, I don't know.

O: Most children do have sexual experiences.

W: I have a female acquaintance who told me once that when her son was small, perhaps six years old, a cousin came for a visit. As she enters the room, she sees the girl playing with his member, and hears her say, "How prettily it hangs from his behind" (*laughs*). So you see, that sort of thing happens, it's no reason for someone to turn into a neurotic. It had no consequences. I'll admit that it wasn't as systematic as what my sister did. But you see, when we looked at those pictures of naked women, I pressed a little against her. . . . Freud describes that.

O: I can't recall just now.

W: We looked at a book with pictures of naked women, I don't know what sort of book. And I remember that I felt like expressing something sexual and moved closer to my sister. In any event, she got up and left.

O: How old were you at the time?

W: Difficult to say; ten perhaps, perhaps a little older. She rejected me, in any case. That may also have importance. But after all, it was normal. She couldn't have done anything else, otherwise it would really have been incest. It should not have such consequences. Very well, he came close to her, but after all, it was his sister, and that must not happen between brother and sister. She got up and left, and that should have put an end to the matter. Well, this sister complex is really the thing that ruined my entire life. For those women who resemble my sister, I mean as regards social position or education, well, that was a prohibition again, that was incest again. There may also be an inheritance of these psychological illnesses, but we won't discuss that.

In any event, here we have a recollection. It is not a fiction, not an inference, and not a construct. And it has been explained. And it was useless, for the choice of Therese, my wife—this was again a person who was to be below me socially. Or, let's be perfectly frank: either socially inferior, or for money.

O: So these women bear no resemblance to your sister.

W: They bear none. If they take money, they are not sisters. The others are the sisters. By the way, Freud told me that he used to use hypnosis.

O: Yes, in the beginning.

W: In the beginning, and then he stopped. I think that being hypnotized is dangerous because it is also a kind of transference. It's not the same, because under hypnosis, one isn't aware that one puts one's trust in someone. But when there is transference, you know when your trust is excessive. One can adopt a more critical attitude. . . . But basically the two things are similar, of course. When I do what transference shows me, it is really like being hypnotized by someone. That's the influence. I can remember Freud saying, "Hypnosis, what do you mean, hypnosis, everything we do is hypnosis too." Then why did he discontinue hypnosis? I cannot remember. You must have read something about it. Why did he confine his method to conversations with his patients, and stop using hypnosis?

O: As far as I know, he believed that hypnosis would be ineffective in the long run, that something more rational had to be found.

W: Certainly. The rational is the explanation by these constructs. I actually believed when I came to Freud that recollection must come at some time. And that's really how he described it. But no recollection came in my case.

O: And besides your analysis, what did you do in Vienna during those four years?

W: I took fencing lessons, for example.

O: Had you already learned fencing in Russia?

W: Yes. There was a relative who was an officer and he suggested that I take fencing lessons as a form of gymnastics. And here, in Vienna, there was a fencing master, a former Italian officer, who had a fencing club. Well, those were completely different times. People believed in progress and thought that the condition of mankind could only improve. That things couldn't get worse. About Russia, people believed that if democracy came, it would be paradise.

And Vienna was completely different, the capital of an empire, with lots of soldiers. That gave the city a certain splendor. There was something else: Jewish comedians were always best. And there was a theater, "Budapester Affairen" it was called, it was a Jewish theater. It was magnificent how interesting, how witty, how intelligent it was. There are no theaters like that nowadays.

O: And there are almost no Jews left.

W: And in the Prater, there was Venice in the Prater, all that is gone too.* Things were completely different. Nowadays, for example, they often put on French plays in the Josefstädter Theater. I used to like French plays in France. What esprit, what intellectual content! But what you see these days. . . . And then, my hearing has become poor.

Well, you asked what I had done in Vienna. Dr. Drosnes was here, and we also had a student along. I suffered from intestinal difficulties and a student from the elder Drosnes's sanatorium gave me enemas. And that student who gave me those enemas we took along to Vienna. That was the student's task. But the real motive was different. Drosnes was a passionate card player. And he played a Russian game that is similar to bridge, where you need three players. And that's why the student was taken along, and so we often played cards until three o'clock in the morning. But actually that student was not needed. And when I was being treated by Freud and told him about it, he said—you know how psychoanalysts play around with subconscious homosexuality—well, that promotes subconscious homosexuality, and he could no longer give me enemas. When Freud treated me, I was fine. I felt very good. We went out, to cafés, to the Prater, it was a pleasant life.

O: But then Freud set a final date and said that treatment must be over by then.

W: But he wrote that things moved along after that.

O: Yes, but what happened before? Why did it come to that in the first place?

W: Well, because it lasted such a long time. Four years, that's a long time.

O: But the analysis is supposed to have stagnated.

* Formerly a place of amusement in the Prater that used stage sets to convey the atmosphere of Venice.

W: Allegedly.

O: But you didn't notice anything?

W: I wasn't really aware of it.

O: Nothing struck you as odd?

W: No, nothing did. I was simply glad that it was ending. Those four years were beginning to feel a little long.

O: He hints that you took refuge in resistance.

W: But he wrote that things moved along afterwards. He set that date and then it went all right, allegedly.

O: But setting a date is the ultimate weapon, when there is no other way of dealing with a patient. Treatment must have stagnated for a long time before that.

W: To judge by his comments, of course. I cannot give you any detailed information about that. I was not aware of that.

O: You mean you always talked about something.

W: I always talked about something. But he didn't find what he was after, whatever it was. But you see, all those constructs must be questioned. Do you believe in all those constructs of the psychoanalysts?

O: No. But in this case, what do you mean by construct?

W: Well, that scene with the white wolves: those are the parents and the coitus, and that's how it is all supposed to have started. Do you believe that?

O: No, I don't really. But my question is this: What made Freud say that treatment was stagnating?

W: One would have to bring Freud back to life and ask him, wouldn't one? I don't know what went on in his brain.

O: Didn't that story about Grusha, the servant girl who was on the estate in your early childhood, come to light after that?

W: That's very hazy. I no longer know precisely. I cannot remember. I cannot even remember this Grusha. She was a maid, I believe. But I cannot remember details.

O: Freud writes that after he set a final date, more material came to light.

W: It's so long ago. I have no idea.

O: And he also writes that you had very little social interest: "For this reason, the patient was without all those social interests which give a content to life."[1] And during the analysis, he said he could observe how things got better.

W: Yes, I remember that sentence. But I don't think there's much in it.

O: You mean it isn't correct . . .

W: I don't believe so.

O: . . . that you attitude has changed.

W: No, what change would there be? That I took my exam? I was never much interested in politics. Those are social interests.

O: No, why? It can also be an interest in other people.

W: I did have acquaintances.

O: While you were in analysis?

W: Later, there was Therese. And as regards the date he set, he said that there was no conclusion. And then I was glad that it was over because being there for four years wasn't all that pleasant.

O: It wasn't pleasant?

W: Well, I wanted to get back to Russia, don't you see. . . . You asked what I did. Well, what did I do precisely? To begin with, I sent for the books for my studies. I chose the law because there are no experiments as there are in the natural sciences. What jurists read in their books is precisely what they hear in their lectures. You don't have to attend the university, you can simply take the exams. The Jews did that. There was a quota. They studied abroad, but that wasn't recognized. So I prepared for the exams—that took some of my time—I saw Freud, and went to the theater or the cinema with Therese.

Something occurs to me: One day, the Russian consul asked me to the consulate. Somehow, he had found out that I was Russian. I went, and he asked what I was doing, that sort of thing. I told him that I was ill and being treated by Freud. And he said, "Why aren't you a member of the Russian colony?" But how could I have introduced Therese there? I wasn't married yet. I did not marry her until later, in Russia. So that wasn't possible. That she didn't speak Russian would have been the least of it. But that she didn't speak French was much more serious. In Russia, a girl had to know

1. Muriel Gardiner, ed., *The Wolf-Man: With the Case of the Wolf-Man by Sigmund Freud* (New York: Basic Books, 1971), p. 214.

French. But there was no persuading Therese. . . . So I made up some excuses. That took care of the matter. The consul probably thought, there's a wealthy Russian. . . . You know how that is, they want donations and all sorts of things. Later, they worked against the Bolsheviks. I once had to testify about that. But I didn't know anything.

O: You couldn't have gone by yourself?

W: I couldn't have left Therese all alone. What do you think? She would have gotten jealous.

O: Was she that jealous?

W: She certainly was.

O: And you, you weren't jealous?

W: For a while, I was. She sent me a picture in which she was decked out like an actress. I was jealous then. But that went away.

O: And when the treatment was over you gave Freud a present?

W: Freud said that a present would be suitable so that the feeling of gratitude wouldn't become too strong. It was he who suggested that I give him something.

O: So he took it for granted that you would be grateful?

W: Yes.

O: And what did you give him?

W: A princess, Egyptian statuary, rather tall.

O: Was it ancient Egyptian?

W: Yes.

O: That must have cost a fortune.

W: I can't remember. Probably. Considering my situation at the time, it was of no consequence. It was a fine piece, an antique. A recently made one would have been without value, after all. He had all kinds of old things. But the way, he said once that this is the way it was among the Egyptians: when they adopted new gods, they did not drop the old ones. They did not replace the old ones with new ones. They kept the old ones and added the new ones. And he felt that my psyche is, or at least was, more or less like that. I am open to new insights but do not relinquish old ties. . . .

O: He also mentions that in your case history.

W: That complicates things, of course, because the old and the new struggle with each other. You know the expression "object cathexis." When I cathect a new object, I do not drop the old one. And that must lead to confusion.

O: Actually, it's a fine quality.

W: But it complicates things.

O: Was Freud referring to something specific?

W: No. He gave that as a purely theoretical view. But why I picked on something Egyptian, I don't know. If I were an Arab . . .

O: And after four years, at the end of the treatment, Freud discharged you as cured, as it were.

W: Freud said that when one has gone through psychoanalysis, one can become well. But one must also want to become well. It's like a ticket one buys. The ticket gives one the possibility to travel. But I am not obliged to travel. It depends on me, on my decision.

That point of view meant that he recognized free will, doesn't it? But on the other hand, they have that sarcastic question in psychoanalytic books: Where is this free will supposed to come from? Everything is determined. According to Freud, one really would have to say that once everything has been cleared up, the person should have to become well. And not that he is free to decide for health or not. But that idea with the ticket invalidates that. Actually, no one worries about these questions any more, about free will. The concept of "will" has altogether disappeared.

O: Probably because it doesn't get one anywhere. But Freud tended to believe in determinism.

W: Then he should have said that once all those childhood matters have been cleared up, if they are the causes of inhibitions and symptoms, then it must disappear. If it is true that everything originates in childhood and that, when everything is remembered, the illness disappears, it must disappear. And one cannot say that the patient is then free to choose. There's a certain contradiction here. Well, psychoanalysis has come to a halt. Schopenhauer said that the principle of reason[2] is not applicable to man. If it cannot be applied, if logic cannot be applied to man, science cannot develop either. Then all of psychology is a pseudoscience.

---

2. In German, *"der Satz vom Grunde."* Reference is presumably to Schopenhauer's *"Über die vierfache Wurzel des Satzes vom zureichenden Grunde"* [On the Fourfold Root of the Principle of Sufficient Reason]—TRANS.

O: There are people who would say that, of course.

W: Well, according to Freud, it was a science. But through this qualification that one must have the will, he really overthrows the entire structure.

O: In what connection did he use that comparison with the ticket?

W: I asked him whether one becomes well when everything has been cleared up and he answered no, that's not the way it is, and used the comparison with the ticket.

O: But he did help you?

W: Well, he enabled me to marry Therese. That was a decision that wasn't easily made, but I did manage. I finished my studies, and then spent thirty years at the insurance company. I conducted myself more or less normally. My depressions had got better. But it's a question, of course. I don't know, perhaps we are touching on too difficult a topic. He helped me, provided there are no conflicts. Not everything depends just on whether I was helped or not. Everything also depends on chance, on the people I come in contact with, what situations I find myself in.

How hot it is today! Actually, I should be used to it—in Odessa it was also very hot all the time. I cannot remember ever having suffered as much from the heat as this year. Last year, it was also very hot. But I didn't feel it as much. But in summer, I always feel worse than in winter.

O: I think I'll go, it's getting late.

W: It's nice that you come (*looks into the ashtray*). We smoked a lot.

O: How much do you smoke a day?

W: Thirty cigarettes.

O: Me too, more or less.

W: Why do you smoke? You have things to do, you have a profession. I didn't smoke for a long time, it's only recently that I have been smoking this much.

O: Do you think people smoke this much when they are dissatisfied?

W: Probably you haven't found the right man.

O: But that's no problem, really. . . .

W: But you clearly haven't found the right man.

O: What about your obsessional neurosis now?

W: I believe you are born with something like that, there's nothing one can do about it.

O: Do you mean to say that you still suffer from obsessive ideas?
W: I don't discuss the present. You see, it isn't normal, blaming oneself all the time for the mistakes one has made.
O: What would be normal?
W: There are people who simply forget, or who blame others. . . .
O: Are those people normal, I wonder?

Residues of Transference

WOLF-MAN: As I told you, Gardiner wrote that she objects to any kind of interview. You have to understand, I can't do it. . . . A Russian émigrée wrote her, by the way. And she sent along a letter to me, in Russian. Gardiner sent everything back. She really had the obligation to show me what that woman had written in Russian. But she didn't—very well, it probably wouldn't have led anywhere.

OBHOLZER: You mean she could have been a friend to you?

W: Something like that.

O: You are obviously to be protected from everything and everyone. No one must come near you.

W: You can see for yourself. On the other hand, I have an obligation because she took some trouble with my book. She negotiated with the publishing house and so on. That was quite a lot of work.

O: But it also benefited her.

W: Well, you know, that transference. I also transferred to her, and transference is dangerous. I relied too much on others; then you are really lost in the end.

O: So when the First World War broke out, you went to Russia. Therese joined you there. You got married. Then Therese's daughter became ill, and she went to Germany. You followed her a little later and visited Freud on the way. And he said that there were some unanalyzed residues, and you returned to him for treatment. What were those residues, actually?

W: That's another story, those residues. That's a good question. You think logically (*laughs*).

O: Well, what were those residues?

W: It's unappetizing. But I'll have to tell you about that as well since you already know so much about me. It is embarrassing. Should I? Or better not? This is the way it was: I once had diarrhea, and Dr. Drosnes came to the estate. I tell him I have diarrhea. He takes a little bottle wrapped in paper from his pocket and says, "This is calomel." He pours some into a cup and says, "Take it." The result was that it got worse.

O: The diarrhea?

W: The diarrhea. The next time, I tell him that it didn't help, it got worse. And he says, "I didn't give you enough."

O: What was that medicine called?

W: Calomel.

O: Never heard of it.

W: Later, a general practitioner told me that it is only given to horses, not humans. I am telling you that what happened was that I couldn't eat anything all winter long. I lived on tea, milk, things like that. Just a little tea, and I had to run to the toilet. It was terrible. All the mucous membranes were torn. And what happened as a consequence? The consequence was that these attacks of diarrhea stopped. But a new situation developed.

O: Constipation, I imagine.

W: Yes, a constipation that nothing could be done about. When I took medicine, I got diarrhea again. I helped myself with those enemas that Freud then forbade. I have already told you about that. I used another medicine he prescribed. And that has stayed with me to the present day: my intestines don't work by themselves. I have to take something twice a week. At times, I take it only once a week, but then I have pains. It's terrible what this man did.

O: You had no intestinal difficulties before that?

W: Before that, everything functioned perfectly.

O: And the diarrhea . . .

W: That only happened once, when he gave me this calomel. You see, that's also something very unpleasant. One has to take something, one doesn't know whether it will work, one gets pains. . . . That intestinal thing was really the reason I stayed with Freud at that time. He said, "That's something we still have to deal with."

O: The second time around.

W: Yes. At that time, the English were in Odessa, and I could have gone. It was stupid of me that I listened to Freud and stayed in Vienna. And it dragged on all winter long.

O: Because of the intestinal disorders.

W: Because of the intestinal disorders. I could have been smart and told him, "Look, professor, that's impossible." I got to know a relative of his once, or perhaps it was an in-law, a certain Schütz. He was Austrian but had studied in Russia. I told him that I had asked Freud whether I should stay in Russia if the Bolsheviks came to power there, or whether I should go abroad. And Freud said, "It's better to stay in the country one was born in." I told Schütz that and he said, "You know, Freud knows human intelligence very well, but he doesn't seem to know the Bolshevist intelligence."

He thought everything was so simple—a few things change, everything else remains the same. I don't know. . . . You see, someone as intelligent as Freud. When I came back from Russia and asked, "What's your opinion about the World War?" all he could say was, "Our attitude toward death is wrong." That's no position, as far as I am concerned. I went through analysis and he was a very smart man, of course. But even he was only human, you see, and to err is human.

O: And what became of your intestinal disorders?

W: I somehow got it to come by itself, a few times. And he wrote, "We've been successful!" No such thing! I don't know, of course. Perhaps, had I gone there and speculated, and the communists had come, perhaps I would not be sitting here with you, talking. I don't know. But reason told me: "Go there right now, and settle your affairs." And I said to him, "I would like to go because of my financial affairs." And he answered, "No, stay here. There is this and that still to be resolved." And so I stayed. And that's why it became too late. When I went to the English later, they said "There are no visas, the Red Army is already in Odessa." And just imagine, in 1938, after the death of my wife, when I went to the English for a visa, they still had the documents relating to my case.

O: So it was because of transference that you stayed?

W: Transference is a positive relationship, and I believe that psychoanalysis takes you back to childhood, and that you then react more or less like a child.

O: I sometimes get the impression that you bore Freud ill will for not continuing to play the role of father until the end of his life.

W: I am not blaming him. I blame him for not having allowed me to travel to Russia. You see, that intestinal business came through psychoanalysis. I lost my fortune. Those are the negative aspects of psychoanalysis, and there's no reason not to discuss them.

O: Of course not. So you blame him for what happened with your fortune.

W: He should not have kept me back. But one can interpret that anyway one pleases. One could also say that he may have saved me from a danger. That could also be. I don't know.

There was a family in Odessa, very wealthy people, their name was Anakran. And a son of theirs attended the same gymnasium I did. We also ate our noon meal there, and where the food was handed out, one stood in line with a plate in one's hand. I always observed this Anakran, the way he was standing there, with the plate in his hand. He looked like a Roman patrician, a very good-looking individual. He married a *chansonnette* later. And he was the first in Odessa to own an automobile. Yes, and then he had an accident and was killed on the spot.

Then there was a cousin of this Anakran who was very ugly. He was a student at the time and someone brought him to the estate once. I don't know whether we knew him, or what. In any event, he was the most harmless person imaginable. And what did my mother tell me later? He served with the Bolsheviks and was shot to death. So you see, among Russians it's a matter of luck whom you run up against. One person will shoot you, another lets you go.

There's no way of knowing. I might have tried to save my fortune, people would have found out, and perhaps they would have shot me too. It can turn out either way. But reason told me, "Go home and settle your affairs, and don't stay because of your intestine." That was pointless! I have to tell you that. Those are facts. One can't overlook them. That doesn't mean that I am attacking Freud. But he was no god, either.

Well now, transference is a double-edged sword. On the one hand it helps, on the other, there's something wrong with it. For if I look on Freud as father and believe everything he says, I can make mistakes. He said, for example, that I should not go and settle my affairs, although that was precisely the right moment. But because there was transference, I stayed. Transference is already a certain falsification of reality because the person involved is not my father. But I act as if he were. You see that there are certain dangers. And I paid for having stayed. Suddenly, it was too late. Had it been my father, he would have understood politics better than Freud. . . .

O: Your father?

W: Of course, because he knew the political conditions in Russia about which Freud knew absolutely nothing. He did not concern himself with politics at all. He was unfamiliar with it because psychoanalysis deals with the individual. And in politics, it's more or less a matter of mass psychology, or whatever. Just consider his opinion when I asked him what he thought about the First World War. "We have the wrong attitude toward death." That's no standpoint. Well, it's a very difficult task we have set for ourselves. We are supposed to take a position on psychoanalysis. At least that's the way I understand it.

O: Yes, it isn't simple. And have you never been back to Odessa since that time?

W: No. I still have the ticket I used. Perhaps I should leave it to you in my will. . . . Some time ago a female acquaintance tried her best to talk me into taking a trip to Russia. She inquired around; they would give me a visa. But what's the point?

O: And how long did your mother remain in Russia?

W: She left in 1923. She first went to Italy, to an Italian uncle, and then she stayed with my cousin in Prague because my mother and my wife did not get along. Unfortunately. She would occasionally come to Vienna for a month, and I went to Prague once. My mother came with a Soviet passport. She was given permission to leave the country. Once, when I was questioned by the Russian occupation authorities after the Second World War, I said that my mother had come legally. And the official who was interrogating me said, "That probably cost a great deal of money."

O: Your mother had enough money left to pay for that?

W: Yes, apparently. She still had jewelry.

O: Then she left before Stalin took over. Lenin died in 1924.

W: During Lenin's rule, it was quite liberal for a time. There was a famine and Lenin was making propaganda for the New Economic Policy. At that time, my cousin could send me things. The pictures of my father and sister, I've already shown them to you. I just happen to remember something: some reviewers of my book write that I was unable to get dressed by myself while I was being treated by Freud. That's nonsense, of course. One of these fellows copies from the other.

O: There's something about dependent . . .

W: Well, a psychological dependence, but not that I couldn't put on my own clothes. I remained in Vienna by myself, so who would have dressed me? And I also worked . . .

O: No, I remember, it was Mack who wrote about getting dressed. "The man who had come with his own physician and orderly, who had been unable even to dress himself, was now working hard at any task obtainable and supporting to the best of his ability a sick and disappointed wife."[1] The psychoanalysts started that, not the journalists.

W: You are sticking up for your profession. That Mack could commit such a stupidity! How could she have written that? It's nonsense. She was a very determined person, by the way. I did not see her again later. She was found dead in her bathtub.

O: Did she kill herself?

W: No, I think it was heart failure. In any event, Mack writes that I had paranoia. Perhaps I got well so quickly because I wanted to prove that she was wrong.

O: You didn't care to have paranoia?

W: I didn't care to have paranoia. Besides, Gardiner wrote that too, and it was confirmed by everyone, that there is no such thing as a paranoia that comes and goes. It doesn't exist. If someone really suffers from paranoia, it doesn't go away.

O: You were feeling bad and wanted to return to Freud for treatment. And he sent you to Mack. Why?

W: Freud already had cancer, cancer of the palate. And he no longer accepted students, or only very few. . . . He had little time. I remember that I was going somewhere in a taxi with him and that I talked to him. He already had difficulty speaking. He said that he

1. Muriel Gardiner, ed., *The Wolf-Man: With the Case of the Wolf-Man by Sigmund Freud* (New York: Basic Books, 1971), p. 267.

could not treat me but that there was an American woman, a student of his, who would. He gave me her address. When Hitler came, she went to America. . . . I believe the whole thing is not clearly described in the book.

O: Well, the reader is surprised that suddenly, after having been with Freud for so many years, you lose your psychological equilibrium again.

W: I suppose you're right. Had I been cured, something like that should not have happened.

O: And with such severity.

W: And how severe it was. It was worse than everything else, worse than that gonorrhea business.

O: You had a blackhead on your nose and that completely unsettled you. How was something like that possible?

W: How was it possible? Well, you see, with the gonorrhea, there was the idea that I had something that was terrible and that mustn't be. Even though I knew that there was no permanent harm. There was only this drop—it didn't really matter, yet I suffered. Well, how did Freud explain it? You know better than I.

O: Better than you? No, no.

W: It's paradoxical but that's the way it is.

O: No, that isn't so.

W: Well, in any case, it went on for a time until I overcame that, and I thought it didn't matter. And then it passed and came back. With the nose, it's similar. Well now, how did it start? You are asking me this question, and I can't even answer. You must have suffered from depressions.

O: Yes.

W: Did you have *idées fixes,* or did you get along without *idées fixes*?

O: *Idées fixes,* I don't know if that's the right term. When I have depressions, I imagine that no one likes me.

W: Well, that's something similar.

O: I don't know if that's a fixed idea.

W: It's something very similar. When one is disfigured, you know, people don't like one either. So you see, it really comes to the same thing. But how it came about. . . . This is the way it was: my sebaceous glands had become enlarged, and those very delicate veins on the nose swelled somewhat and became red. And I remember that I thought once, You have lost everything, but you could also have been disfigured.

O: Now I see.

W: I remember now. It was an idea that came to me, an odd idea, really. There are worse things than losing money. If one is disfigured, that is worse. That's actually a normal thought. But that precisely this thought occurred to me showed, I think, that I was reacting to something external—that one must not be disfigured, let's say. Well, then I got the blackhead on my nose and went to the insurance doctor and told him, "Look, I have a blackhead here." He gave me an ointment and said: "Come back in three weeks. If it doesn't go away, it's no blackhead but a gland that has become inflamed."

I smeared ointment on it, but it didn't help, and I went back to him. He had a look and said, "There's nothing to be done." I: "Am I to spend the rest of my life with a pimple on my nose?" "Well, yes, there's nothing to be done," the doctor says. You see, that was the first thing that impressed me. I asked Freud whether he could recommend a dermatologist. He recommended Ermann, and I went to see him. He was a Jew, an old man. And he said, "It is a swollen gland that can be removed." And he pressed it and removed it. As a result, the nose became inflamed, of course.

Besides, I had trouble with the sebaceous glands. I already had that in Odessa, where I also complained that those glands were swollen. At the time, a physician said, quite correctly, "When you are old and your skin is like parchment, you won't have that anymore because there will be no more fat on your skin." Very well. This Ermann removed the gland. Because of it, probably because of the pressure, the veins became dilated. The nose looked lopsided and was reddish. I went back to Ermann and he said, "You could have an electrolysis treatment." Electrolysis means that the nerve end is killed. He did that, and what developed was the kind of thing pockmarked people have.

O: Holes.

W: Holes, small holes were created, and they began irritating me, you understand. I kept looking in the mirror to see whether they were going away. But they didn't. I told myself, I am going to consult another physician. They recommended a famous dermatologist to me; Kren was his name. He has since died—both died a long time ago. So I went to see this Kren. And he looks at my nose and asks, Who did that? I answered, "Well, I'd rather not give you his name." He said: "But that's terrible. How can anyone do a thing like that? Electrolysis leaves scars. That's not at all what should be done. Diathermy is the only thing."

When I came back after the electrolysis treatment, my wife clapped her hands together and said, "You look terrible, there is blood, blood, blood all over your face." It looked awful; then it healed, but small indentations remained. That embarrassed me. And so I went to this fellow Kren, and when I told him "electrolysis," he clapped his hands together and made a fuss—why would anyone do a thing like that? And then he said, "Scars never disappear," and at the very moment he said that, I thought, I am disfigured. Because he said that they never disappear. There you have another instance of transference.

O: To this doctor, this Kren?

W: Yes, to this doctor. I was dissatisfied with the other one.

O: Transference here means that you believed what he told you.

W: I believed what he said. He claimed that it was badly done. No one had told me that before. It embarrassed me at first. But then it became awful. I was horrified. All I could think of was how horrible it was.

O: Those were the states Mack referred to as paranoia.

W: Yes, yes, and then I cured myself. Now I'll tell you something else. At some time or other, it went away. A few years passed; it was no longer visible. I thought, I'll have some fun, I'll go to Kren and see if he can find the scars. Because he had said that scars never disappear.

O: What did he say?

W: He didn't remember, of course, that I had been his patient. Years had passed. I said to him, "Look, I have these small red veins on my nose." He looks at them and says, "They can be removed. I answer: "They can be removed? By diathermy?" And he exclaims, "For heaven's sake, that will leave scars!" But he didn't find the scars. You see, I had only wanted to see what he would say. Because he had said that scars never disappear.

O: And he had recommended diathermy before.

W: Yes, and then he said something entirely different. I remember very well with what horror he pulled back and called out, "For heaven's sake, that will leave scars." But then he didn't see them. And that settled the matter.

O: And when Mack called your states paranoia, that was the last straw?

W: Well, Mack interpreted my states by saying that not everything had been psychoanalytically interpreted by Freud. That's her explanation. But my explanation is different. Because I know that I attributed very little importance to what she said to me. The treatment did nothing for me until she made that remark about paranoia. Only then did I begin to concern myself with it. Paranoia was nothing new to me.

I had an uncle who lived like King Ludwig II of Bavaria. An extreme case of misanthropy. That was one case, and then I had a cousin on my mother's side. He was the son of my mother's older sister. He had paranoia in a less serious form. In the end, he landed in an insane asylum in Prague. But for decades, he was not in an institution and no one knew that he had paranoia. My mother lived in Prague for a time and she told me about him. Things like this: Suddenly, on the street, it strikes him that he is being followed. He jumps on a streetcar, rides around, quickly jumps off again and on another, in order to mislead the fellow. . . .

O: And there was nothing there?

W: Nothing.

O: He only believed he was being followed?

W: Once, he visited us with his father. I thought, if he stays for two weeks, I'll go mad. He kept changing his mind all the time. It was awful. So I know what paranoia is. And then he would take nothing but milk because he believed that everything else was poisoned. And that woman suddenly tells me I have paranoia. I didn't care for that, of course. And I suddenly had the will not to be considered paranoid.

I was very proud that Freud had written about me "his impeccable intelligence," and so on. He was an enemy of religion, and I had told him that as a child, I had already had doubts because of the contradiction that people talk about the loving God on the one hand, and the great amount of evil in the world on the other. There's something wrong, I thought to myself. And so I was proud of course, because he said that only a child could think with such logic, and praised me as a thinker of the first rank, etc. And now I was suddenly to be labeled a paranoid.

So, I gathered all my strength, stopped looking in the mirror, and somehow overcame these ideas. It took a few days. In a few days, it was gone.

O: It went that fast?

W: Yes, it was gone after a few days. That is my greatest accomplishment. Even today, I cannot understand how I succeeded. With such rapidity, you see, and so simply, actually. So you can see that an incorrect diagnosis can sometimes bring it about that the patient gathers all his healthy forces to overcome a certain condition. I believe I had most success while I saw Mack because I took a stand against the psychoanalysts, made a decision on my own. Stop constantly thinking about your nose! That's why it was so salutary. It was a much greater success than with Freud because I rejected transference.

O: And what Mack called unresolved transference residues, how do you explain that?

W: I have no idea how she explained it. I paid so little attention to what she said to me. Identification with the woman—something like that, I think. She didn't say anything new, in any case. She said the same thing Freud had already written. And I actually did not react to her, and did not pay attention. I still remember: "Sometime, talk with a decent woman about indecent things, because you have done that so rarely in your life."

O: Mack said that to you?

W: That's what she said to me.

O: What is it supposed to mean?

W: You know, in psychoanalysis, everything revolves around the sexual.

O: And she considered herself a decent woman?

W: She considered herself a decent woman. One doesn't discuss indecent things with a decent woman. That's the generally recognized principle. But her interpretation of dreams, that sort of thing, I took no note of. I had to write down dreams. . . . Only the moment she said "paranoia," that made an impression on me. And then things really happened with fantastic speed.

O: And yet I don't quite understand how all that could have happened. You were not in a particularly grave situation at the time, and then there was that relapse that was worse than anything that went before.

W: Well yes, it was a very serious relapse. It was a crisis which Mack helped overcome. One could also believe that a person is not completely cured if he undergoes such a crisis. Actually, there was no reason. It was a genuine illness. And if I had become completely well through Freud's treatment, it should have been impossible for me to slip into such a state.

O: Perhaps you had problems with your wife.

W: Certainly not. I did have problems with her, especially in Russia, because of the quarrels with my mother.

O: But—you'll excuse me for being so indiscreet—Mack writes something like that. She claims that you had other women at the time.

W: You can't call it having other women. For that matter, what man is always faithful to his wife?

O: So you wouldn't consider it something out of the ordinary?

W: No, it was temporary, you know. Well, there you raise a question one would have to go into at greater length. That wasn't right, of course, that I was unfaithful occasionally. . . . But it is . . . Very well, I'll stop discussing it for now. Well, that's all there is to tell. I saw that he was not finding those scars. But the question is, how could such an *idée fixe* arise after I had been treated by Freud for such a long time? Mack thought that there was a little grain, as it were, that had remained undissolved, and that grain was paranoia. But Gardiner did not make that diagnosis, and Dr. E. did not make it; no one diagnosed it as paranoia. She is the only one to have made that finding. And paranoia doesn't go away when people really have it. And with such speed, in a few days—there's no such thing. She was mistaken, and because of that error, I gathered all my strength and overcame it. Now, what were you saying? You said something about those other women?

O: I said that you had some sort of difficulties, perhaps sexual difficulties, with your wife. And you answered that that wasn't so because a man is sometimes unfaithful.

W: What she writes is something else. That's another problem. Somehow, Mack was against my wife.

O: Really?

W: Yes, I think there was also some jealousy because Freud had found her very beautiful.

O: Your wife?

W: Yes, and she was very beautiful, and he found her very likable, etc. And Mack . . .

O: She wasn't beautiful?

W: No, she wasn't. She was a Jewish type. Well, she wasn't ugly either, a pronounced Jewish type. Perhaps that bothered her a little. She wasn't actually ugly. She was very vigorous. I remember that I once complained about my financial situation and she answered: "You are better off than I am. It's true, my income is greater, but so are my expenses. And you don't have so many expenses." She twisted things so that the wealthy person is actually the poor one because he has such large expenses. That's typically American. Yes, it's a curious thing how that could come about. Who knows the answer?

O: Yes, and why . . .

W: And what did she write about the women? That had no connection with the matter. But she put it in.

O: She writes: "He resorted to his former habit of following women in the street. . . . He now frequently accompanied prostitutes to their lodging. . . ."[2]

W: Well, I sometimes did talk to a woman and then go with her. But that was only temporary.

O: But your wife didn't know?

W: Of course not. Other men do the same thing.

O: That's true. So Mack knew your wife?

W: Yes, I don't recall why, but she said once I should come with Therese. And then she said, "She isn't beautiful at all." She had something against my wife. I think it was jealousy because Freud had praised her. You know how women are, even when they are psychoanalysts.

O: But she didn't say that to your wife?

W: No, not to my wife, but to me. "She doesn't suit you," she said. She actually incited me against my wife. Well, those are difficult matters.

2. Ibid., p. 272.

O: But that isn't right.

W: Of course it wasn't right. And then she wrote something—it's nonsense what she wrote. That I sometimes went with a woman had nothing at all to do with my nose. Well, she was an orthodox psychoanalyst. She believed everything Freud said, of course. Do you believe in psychoanalysis?

O: I am skeptical.

W: You are skeptical.

O: Some of the things Freud discovered are probably true. I find his system impressive. But I doubt that it is practicable as a method of treatment. But then, I hope that's something I will find out from you.

W: Well, there are these two extremes. When there is no transference, it doesn't help. But when there is transference, there's the danger that you will then transfer to others and no longer make your own decisions. I think that was my situation. Because the tie to Freud was too strong, I then transferred to other figures who could somehow stand for the father. I've already told you about the money, that I didn't undertake anything. That was an absolute mistake.

And before I left Russia, I should have asked my acquaintances, how do I save my money? We knew a wealthy shipbuilding family, they were decent people, they could have helped me. But no, I walk into the bank and talk to the bank director. And he said to me, "If you are going to Germany and Austria, you had best take crowns and marks." That's what I did. He said that, of course, because he wanted to get rid of those undesirable currencies. But the transference continued to work. After all, that's a bank director. . . . It's only an example. So transference is a dangerous thing. When one looks at everything critically, not much of psychoanalysis stands up. But it helped me. You see, Mack made an incorrect diagnosis, and through this incorrect diagnosis she cured me.

O: How long have you been living in this apartment?

W: Since 1927. In Russia, we became acquainted with Austrian officers who subsequently went to Sankt Georgen on Atter Lake and set up a small soap factory. They suggested that we should move to Sankt Georgen for good, and that I would be given a position there. My wife spent an entire winter in Sankt Georgen. And I lived here in Vienna, in Floridsdorf. There was a terrible housing shortage after the war; one had to get out of bed at six in the morning and run around all over to find a room. It took a long time until I found one. Later, I even found two.

And this apartment here, my wife simply didn't want this apartment. I liked it because there is light for painting. Then, quite unexpectedly, she called me at the insurance company, she had taken the apartment. Later she always said that she hated this apartment. "Then we'll move," I said. But she didn't want that either. She was always in favor of saving. Later, when we had saved money, we invested in mortgage bonds. I really wanted to buy a house, but she didn't. She wanted to save. She was German. And when the Nazis came and eliminated the gold clause in the mortgage bonds, she may have had the feeling that she had said something false. . . .

O: And you worked for an insurance company.

W: Yes, it really wasn't pleasant. One had to bring in customers. Really nothing out of the ordinary. I would rather have worked at a bank. But who can say whether that would have been better. Actually, I would have preferred being self-employed, but my wife wanted something stable, dependable.

O: What would you have liked to do, had you been on your own?

W: I would have liked to be a businessman, for example.

O: And before you found the job, did Freud help you financially?

W: Someone wrote somewhere that I and my wife lived at Freud's expense. That's not true. He just helped occasionally. He said, "I took money from you, now you take some from me." He had foreign patients and students and therefore had foreign currencies, dollars and pounds, and so he occasionally gave me some.

O: But he collected money for you once a year.

W: No, no, I know nothing about that.

O: But Mack writes, "Freud collected a sum of money for this former patient . . . and repeated this collection every spring for six years."[3]

W: But no, that isn't true.

O: That isn't true? But . . .

W: No, what happened was that I sometimes went to him and he gave me a few pounds. But no large sums. He helped a little until I had that job. Then that stopped.

3. Ibid., p. 266.

O: And you didn't receive that gift every year?

W: But I already had that position in 1922.

O: Why does Mack write that you did?

W: She's imagining things.

O: And what about the jewelry?

W: An acquaintance brought that jewelry with him from Russia.

O: Yes, and she writes . . . But did you never read the book?

W: Oh yes! What does she write?

O: She writes: "He therefore told no one that the jewels were in his possession. In his fear of losing Freud's help . . . ."[4]

W: No, that isn't true either. That's nonsense. The jewelry, that was a necklace we received. And I believe that we received eight thousand schillings for that necklace, and we used that money to buy the apartment. Why make a secret of that?

O: Why does Mack say you did?

W: No, it may have been something else. I think Freud continued giving me money for a time after I already had the job, and Mack objected to this and said, "You have that job now, you need nothing more from Freud.

O: But Freud knew that you had the job.

W: Of course, of course.

O: Or did you conceal it from him?

W: No, I told him. In any event, those were mere gifts, nothing regular. And then I had the job. I recall that I went to him once. . . . He had two adjoining rooms and entered the second and asked me to wait in the first. That's where he got the money he was going to give me, and I followed him. He cried out, "Don't come in here!" Did he think, "My God, what is this man doing, perhaps he is going to kill me?" I turned right around, of course.

O: But he should have known you better than that.

W: Well, in any event, he shouted. And then, when my wife killed herself, he did not receive me. The Nazis were there and the maid said, "He is ill, he cannot receive you." So I actually didn't see him again after the death of my wife.

When I was in London, I could really have visited him. He knew that I was there. But he didn't feel like it. Mack considered the

4. Ibid., p. 267.

whole thing dangerous because of the Nazis. That the Nazis would perhaps find out that I had connections with psychoanalysis. And Gardiner also wrote that there was a risk. But things turned out all right.

O: Freud knew that you were in London?

W: Of course he knew.

O: You mean he should have written you that he would like to see you?

W: Don't you think? I realize he had cancer, and then there were the Nazis, and he was quite old by then.

O: He died soon afterwards.

W: He died soon. He was very ill.

O: I sort of agree that he should have invited you.

W: I had expected it. Mack said that it would be dangerous for me. I don't know, I didn't feel that it would be dangerous. . . .

Gardiner sent me one hundred dollars at the time. But we had put some money aside and I did not need it, so I sent it back to her. Immediately thereafter, the Gestapo called me in: "You deprived Germany of foreign currency." I had to go three or four times and they kept coming back to the subject. I said: "I didn't need it. It didn't occur to me." Once I was there, someone started talking Russian to me. He knew Russian. And then he said, "The matter has been settled."

O: And it is through Mack that you became acquainted with Gardiner?

W: First, I gave Russian lessons to an Englishwoman. Her name was Strachey. Then I was treated by Mack, and Gardiner was also there—she was also being psychoanalyzed by her. I saw Gardiner in Mack's waiting room, but I didn't know that this woman would play a role in my life. Mack also wanted to take Russian lessons, but then she didn't have the time. And she said, "Gardiner wants to take Russian lessons," so I made her acquaintance. That relation is very old, but we never got close. We exchanged nothing but letters. Mack, well . . . I always had the impression that Mack didn't like me somehow. And Gardiner wrote me after the war that Mack had always spoken enthusiastically of me, of my intuition and logic— that surprised me a little at the time.

On the other hand, I thought, then she must like me. Because she once said to me, "You remind me of an American artist who has suffered a great deal." His name was Brunswick. But she married him. And if I resembled the man she married, she must have found me likable in some way. At the time, I also got to know Stechel, who is a Freud disciple. He had a dog with a Russian name, and would ask him, "Who is the first psychoanalyst in the alphabet?" And the dog answered, "A—bra—ham." It's a fact, I saw it myself. He asked the dog, "Who is the first psychoanalyst," and the dog, "A—bra—ham."

O: That's amusing.

W: And then E. said to me, "The princess always spoke of you in the highest terms. . . . This is the way it was with the princess: she was a great admirer of Edgar Allan Poe, you know. And somehow she put me in the same category, not for my achievements, of course, but on the basis of character. I read once that a French critic called that *bas romanticisme,* low romanticism, where there is talk about death and masochism and sadism, and it all ends in madness. I am not the same type as Edgar Allen Poe. . . .

O: That was Marie Bonaparte?

W: Yes. I read her book, I think she wasn't quite normal either. She was a big hulk of a woman. When I was in Paris, she invited me to dinner, but I refused. I was in such a state after the death of my wife. . . . (*long pause*)

O: There is one thing I don't quite understand: you say you don't want to discuss the present. Why not? Perhaps I am being naive, but it would seem to me that someone who has so many years of analysis behind him, that such a person could talk about anything, or almost anything.

W: Now that you bring it up, I must tell you something quite terrible. . . . I have a lady friend.

O: So what.

W: She might show up here and surprise us.

O: Would that be so terrible?

W: She would probably be very jealous. She is a very impulsive woman. There might be a scene. This morning, quite by chance, I ran into this woman at the tobacco store. That's the reason I am so restless today. . . . It's not likely that she will come today, of all days. But I am always nervous when you are here. She comes very infrequently, you realize. . . .

O: I am sorry, but I couldn't know.

W: I thought I might say that you are taking Russian lessons from me.

O: Why don't you?

W: Because she knows that I no longer give lessons. I thought, if worse comes to worst, I'll say that you are a former student . . .

O: . . . who happens to have dropped by for a visit.

W: If worse comes to worst, if worse comes to worst. I must tell you this. I kept wondering, should we meet in a café? But then chance might have it that she comes to that very same café. I've had too much bad luck in my life, so many stupid accidents have happened to me. . . .

O: Then it would probably be best if you came to my apartment.

W: To your apartment?

O: Yes.

W: Well yes, I'd prefer coming there. I'd rather travel the distance than have something unpleasant happen. . . . I'm glad we found a solution. My God, all that is terribly disagreeable. This woman doesn't understand me at all. And she also thinks nothing of psychoanalysis.

O: Do you plan to get married?

W: I cannot marry her because she absolutely does not understand me. And that is why there are constant quarrels. She insists on getting married.

O: How old is she?

W: Sixty. We had broken off once; that's when I should have said, "No more." Today, I can no longer end it; she is ill.

O: How long have you known her?

W: About twenty-five years.

O: And when did you stop seeing her?

W: Twenty years ago. Only for a few weeks. Then we ran into each other on the street. And she said, let's make up. I shouldn't have done that.

O: It seems you had a good deal of success with women.

W: Almost too much, I myself don't understand why.

O: I do. When I compare you to the average Viennese, who thinks of nothing but eating and drinking. . . . If you no longer want this woman, why not simply stop.

W: No, I can no longer do that.

O: Then keep her and look for a second one with whom you get along better.

W: It's too late for that.

O: And your friend knows nothing of your existence as the Wolf-Man?

W: She knows that I was treated by Freud, but she knows nothing about the book.

O: You haven't told her?

W: She would assume that writing a book makes one a millionaire.

O: And that article I wrote about you. She hasn't read that either?

W: Fortunately she hasn't.

O: Does she work for a living?

W: She worked as a domestic once. But then she was ill and lived off her mother, and now she lives off me.

O: Your interest in commonplace women is really something that hasn't changed.

W: You have read my book? Then you know, the intellectual woman was my sister.

O: One would have expected that sometime after the analysis was over, this fixation on commonplace women would have come to an end and that you would have looked for a woman on your intellectual level.

W: I had female colleagues, but they weren't really intellectual women. My wife Therese wasn't very intelligent either, but at least she had an understanding for psychoanalysis. In any case, there are very few intellectual women. And it would have been difficult for a woman to measure up to my sister. My sister was really very intelligent—there weren't many that could have come up to her. Actually, you are an exceptional woman also.

O: Me? You think so?

Further Childhood Material

WOLF-MAN: You know, there are times when I feel very weak. Well, you mustn't forget, I'll be eighty-eight this coming January. That's an age where one can't expect much. What's your opinion of what Gardiner wrote about me?

OBHOLZER: What she writes is friendly enough.

W: There isn't much in the book about the period after the Second World War. You know, my teeth keep causing me such trouble these days. I have two sets of dentures. One makes me ill, the other hurts. And without teeth I look awful. Eating is a terrible chore. The oldest set is the best. What was I going to . . . I wanted to tell you about this Viktor.

This mademoiselle, our governess, had been among Poles before she came to us, not just among the wealthy and aristocratic but also in the houses of ordinary mortals. She had been with a family—I believe the father was an army doctor, and the son's name was Viktor. We heard a great deal about this Viktor. She always started telling us something, she went on, and finally she forgot why she had begun . . . in any event, she told us about this Viktor. And then, by chance, I don't remember the circumstances, I got to know Viktor.

Russians tend to be slow. At least there's a Russian proverb—perhaps it applied only to the older Russians and is no longer valid today: thinking with the brain at the back of one's head. That means that the Russian is intelligent, but that it takes him much too long to find the answer to something. He knows things only when it is too late; it takes him too long to come up with the right answer. People in the Mediterranean countries are quicker than the Germans or Russians, one might say. And this Viktor gave the impression of having no Russian characteristics, as if he were like the Italians or Spanish. He was lively, he was very small, we became friends.

Naturally, I never concerned myself with politics. And my father published a liberal journal. And because no one knew what name to give it, my mother suggested *Quo Vadis* would be best.

O: And is that what it was called?

W: No, no, it was called something like *Southern News*, it cannot be translated literally, something like *Süddeutsche Zeitung, South-Russian News*, you understand? It was a monthly. Well, I became friends with this Viktor, whom I found very likable, and one day he came wearing a little ribbon in his buttonhole with the Austrian colors, yellow and black. I ask, "What have you got there in your buttonhole?" And he said that he had founded a league. You know that the Russian students were all revolutionaries. But he had founded the very opposite, a monarchist league. And that was the insignia.

It was the time of the Russo-Japanese War, and some people were great patriots because it really troubled them that Russia, this colossal country, had lost. It was a terrible disgrace, little Japan defeating this big country. In that year, 1904, Viktor was also patriotic. It didn't bother me, I thought, what do I care? My father's paper was decidedly liberal. While the liberals were not outlawed, it was an opposition party from the point of view of the government. And with few exceptions, the journalists who came to his house did not make a special impression on me. I remember one, a Jew, for there were many Jews in Odessa, especially journalists. He came to my attention, and much later I read in the paper that there was an extreme nationalist party in Israel and that he was the leader of it. He apparently went to Israel and became a famous man. I took pictures at the time, he was in them, but when Hitler came, I tore them up.

My father would give large parties in those days and invite the journalists. There was a certain period when there was much dancing. Sometimes students were also invited. It was always a political affair. And my mother, who took no interest in politics, once had the idea—she probably did not realize that these two things don't go together—of inviting both the journalists and the students to the same dance. Viktor also came.

In any case, I don't know if it was chance or intent, this party took place on December 14. December 14 was the day of the Decembrist uprising. On December 14, 1825, after the death of Czar Alexander, there had been the Decembrist uprising against the czar. I don't know whether my father settled on that date to celebrate the event or whether it was just chance. In any case, those students who were less interested in politics came, Viktor with his badge among them, and then the newspapermen. And one of them recognized that that was a monarchist enterprise and was horrified (*laughs*). And he said to my father, "Don't you know that a monarchist comes to your house?" The next day, my father reproached me for that and decided that it was inadmissible for me to be friends with a monarchist, that one of his colleagues had criticized him for it, etc. It was embarrassing for me, of course, to simply break off relations. . . .

O: Is that what you did?

W: Yes, I did, I did not invite him again. But I had to meet him one more time. We had already agreed to go to a resort by the sea. At that time, cars didn't exist yet—perhaps there was one automobile in all of Odessa. There were horse carriages. He rented such a carriage and I went with him to that vacation place. And as we are moving along, I suddenly see my father coming toward us. He had forbidden me to continue seeing this student. You can imagine that that was unpleasant. I didn't quite know what to do. He looked at me and at this Viktor. I simply did not greet him, and gave no sign of life. I don't know whether he recognized us or not, that was never cleared up.

O: You never discussed it?

W: No, we never did. He could have reproached me but he never said anything, and I didn't either, of course. I just understood that I had to stop seeing Viktor in all earnest, and I never did see him again. In any event, this episode must have made a deep impression on me. Later, when I read Merezhkovski's *Fourteenth December*, I found these Decembrists especially interesting, perhaps because of this incident. In school, no one ever told us anything about the Decembrist uprising, of course. You know, it's interesting, the Russian princes traced their origin to the Varangians, the Normans, and believed it had been an uprising of the Normans against the Germans because the czar was German. All this made such an impression on me that I later wrote a filmscript about this Decembrist uprising.

O: What became of it?

W: I tore it up, here, in Vienna, I don't remember when. I had no connections to literary circles.

O: Do you still remember the 1905 Revolution?

W: Yes, there was unrest, we barricaded ourselves, my father bought a Browning for defense. There was no death penalty, but at that time there were many executions. Then it was all over. People thought that everything had calmed down again. Around 1908, no one thought about it anymore.

O: Wasn't there a kind of revolutionary mood so that people had the feeling that things would not continue indefinitely as they were at the time?

W: Not really. After the 1905 Revolution, we went abroad. In 1906, the newspapers were full of talk about inflation. And I said to my mother, for my father had not come with us, "Shouldn't we send some of our money out of the country?" Just imagine, I had that idea! Me! I had no money myself, of course. But then, later, when I did have some, I didn't do it either.

O: What did your mother answer?

W: Nothing, she ignored it. One time, my mother traveled to Italy with my sister and they saw an empty villa on the shore of Lake Como. My mother asked my sister if she should buy it for her. My sister didn't want it, and that was that. My mother certainly would not have bought the villa for herself. Well, it's only because of the war that things turned out as they did. Otherwise, everything would probably have turned out differently, one can't say how, but I believe Russia would have become a parliamentary democracy. My father belonged to the Constitutional Democrats' Party.

O: What were they for?

W: I think they didn't know yet what they wanted, a republic or . . . A limited monarchy with a parliament, in any case. When the revolution broke out, they wanted something after the English model, not the American, because the president in America is too powerful. If a monarchy, then a constitutional one, but I believe they wanted a republic.

O: Did the Constitutional Democrats advocate the independence of the Ukraine?

W: Well, they weren't part of the Ukrainian movement, but the liberals were in favor of giving greater autonomy to those regions, and the paper said the same thing. You know, when I was a child, the word *Ukraine* did not exist. There were Little Russians and Great Russians, and the Ukrainians were called Little Russians.

O: Don't the Ukrainians have their own language?

W: Yes, the language is a little different.

O: Is it a dialect or a real language?

W: It is really a different language. Now there is the Ukrainian Republic, and I believe the language is even Ukrainian, much more so, in any event, than before. It used to be that only the peasants spoke Ukrainian.

O: Did you speak Ukrainian?

W: No, I spoke correctly.

O: Do you understand it?

W: Yes, it is close enough to understand. It is certainly the language that is closest to Russian, yet it is a language in its own right. I don't know whether I already told you that there was a student in my class who was Ukrainian. Otherwise, there's nothing of importance to tell about him. His name was Nikowsky. And there was a Ukrainian government from 1917 to 1919. It didn't last long; the Bolsheviks quickly put an end to it. He was in my class at school, but I had no contact with him. And then I read in the paper that he had come to Vienna as the foreign minister of this Ukrainian government and that he was staying at the Hotel Hapsburg.

I thought to myself, this fellow a minister? I'll visit him. First, a secretary came—yes, the minister will see you. He seemed to me to be two heads taller than he had been in school, was elegantly dressed, with pomade in his hair, an important man all of a sudden. I didn't talk with him for long. He mentioned, I remember, that my father's paper had sided with the Ukrainian movement. Later, I heard that he was the chairman of a party in America that fought for Ukrainian independence.

Well, today, let's stay with politics. I never took an interest in politics, but politics took an interest in me.

O: Politics never interested you especially?

W: I cared about painting and literature. Politics is really an eternal struggle, and then there are fanatics, and I have always found fanaticism unappealing. Women are especially fanatical in politics.

O: Whom are you thinking of?

W: But it's a well-known fact.

O: That's news to me.

W: Well, perhaps they don't make a display of it in public, but when you ask them their opinion in private, it's usually extreme. In my experience, at least.

O: That isn't really my experience.

W: Really? (*long pause*) Something else occurs to me that has to do with politics. The father of this Dr. Drosnes who had me see Freud, you remember, he had a psychiatric institute. And when I started getting those depressions, my mother consulted the father. And he said I should move about more, become a carpenter, plane, etc. I think that's the way it is done in some sanatoria—they have the patients work. In any event, we did that. We had a carpenter come to the house. Normally, we only spent summers on the estate; nothing went on there during the winter. I had the idea of staying there for some time and had this carpenter's bench brought to the estate. I can't remember that I actually used it. . . .

O: Did you enjoy planing?

W: Not much. In those days, psychoanalysis was still unknown, you see, so they tried things like that. In the sanatorium, the patients had to glue bags. In any case, the fact is that this carpenter's bench arrived at the estate. And in Russia, there was a political police, always somewhere nearby. There were two kinds of gendarmes. One had light blue uniforms—they were the rural police; one didn't see much of them. The others wore dark blue uniforms. They were—I don't know what to call them—nowadays people always say "secret police. . . ." Well, that was the political police. Suddenly, they called me in, although I had never gone in for politics. I went. A policeman greeted me, pointed to an armchair: "Sit down, please." Then an officer comes in and says, "We have been informed that a print . . ." How do you say, print machine?

O: Printing press.

W: ". . . a printing press has been transported to the estate and that proclamations against the government of the czar are being printed there." I say, "That's an error," and explained the facts. He was very polite. Apparently the story about the printing press was merely a pretext. Or did he really believe it? Suddenly, he started in on something else: "Tell me, why is your father so much against us?"

O: Against whom?

W: Against the czarist government. "Can't you get your father to work with us? If he worked with us, he could have a bigger career than you can imagine." Well, my father had organizational talent, that's what he was alluding to. I said, "Well, you see, I have no influence over my father, that's his affair." "And do you share his views?" I said, "Yes, I do." "Will you put that in writing?" I say, "Of course, if you wish. . . ."

O: The views of your father?

W: Of my father, yes, yes. I don't know how I formulated it, that I shared those liberal opinions. That was all. So you see, I even had a run-in with the czarist police. Yes, and the second time, I had no dealings with the police, but something happened that could have had unpleasant consequences for me. There was a law in Russia at the time that if a family had only one son, he need not go into the army. And if one had graduated from the Gymnasium, one could volunteer for a year.

I didn't concern myself with that, of course, because I knew I did not have to serve. Suddenly, I received a notice to present myself for a physical examination. I thought, this must be an error. I went and said: "Why did you send me this notice? I am an only son and exempt from military duty." The officer said, "We sent your father a questionaire and he didn't fill it out. Perhaps"—my father was already dead—"perhaps your father wanted you to serve. But because he was busy with his paper, he may have overlooked it. In any event, he hasn't filled out the questionnaire."

So I say: "What should I do? Why should I?" Well, the man took pity on me and said: "Don't go to the examination. Once you have been examined, there's nothing you can do. Then you'll have to serve as a common soldier and cannot volunteer." I left and turned the whole thing over to my mother, and she took care of it. What an episode that was. . . .

O: You didn't want to go into the army under any conditions?

W: No, no.

O: But as a child, you enjoyed playing with soldiers.

W: Yes, when I was a child, I liked the military, but that passed. When I was about ten, I used to read books about cadets and things like that. I was enthusiastic about it. At a certain age, one is enthusiastic. But you see, I would have had to serve as a common soldier. As a volunteer, it would have been for a year, otherwise it was for three or four. So it was serious business. And it was careless of my father not to have answered.

O: You think he forgot?

W: Of course. He has, that is . . . Perhaps your father wanted that? Why should he have? He overlooked it, he didn't answer. . . . I should mention that my mother had made up her mind to learn to speak impeccable English. She studied English throughout her life. She made translations from English into Russian. After her death, I found a few notebooks. I was amazed how well she wrote it. . . . When I was a mere child, my mother already recognized that English is more important than French. But that governess ruined everything for me.

O: What governess?

W: You read my book?

O: Yes, yes, of course.

W: Well, then you know that we had an English governess. My mother had been quite right, wanting us to learn English. But because of that person, it didn't work out—she was crazy or drank, whatever. In any event, I somehow didn't care for her, so I never learned English. French and German went better. If you have read my book, you know that we had a French governess and an Austrian tutor. But that was later. When I was small, we had a nanny.

O: Was the nanny there just for you or also for your sister?

W: Just for me.

O: And your sister had her own?

W: My sister no longer had a nanny. Well, in part, she was there for her, we slept in her room. But the English governess was really for my sister.

O: How old were you when you got that nanny?

W: I must have been quite small still.

O: So it wasn't from birth on?

W: Practically.

O: And who breast-fed you when you were a baby?

O: There was a wet nurse who didn't live far from the estate on which I was born. The son of the wet nurse was called "foster brother." Once, we went to see this brother, I remember. But I really have no memory of this wet nurse. I only remember this Nanja, the nanny. It must still have been at the age when consciousness has not yet fully awakened. When my father sold this estate on which I was born, I was five years old. So as regards all memories of that estate, I know that I was younger. I was very unhappy at the time that the estate was being sold. Nanja consoled me and said, "It's only places"—she always said "places"—"that are being sold, but the estate hasn't been sold."

O: What is that supposed to mean, "places"?

W: I didn't understand it either. In any case, I didn't believe her.

O: And up to what age did you sleep in Nanja's room?

W: Well, I don't know, up to seven or eight, something like that.

O: Just you, or your sister as well?

W: I have a vague memory that we were together at first, and then I was alone because my sister was already older.

O: And what sort of woman was Nanja?

W: Well, she was a simple person. . . . She had a son who died, and it seems she transferred her feelings to me. She liked me a lot. She continued living with us later, but at that time, in her old age, she was a little mad. She was very tender toward me and I had the feeling she loved me.

O: More than your mother?

W: My mother was cool by temperament. She did not have the capacity for being demonstrative. It isn't that she didn't love us children. . . . She couldn't express it. I remember the mother of one of my cousins—Schura was his name—she took him on her knee and kissed him . . . there was nothing like that in our family.

O: There wasn't?

W: In the morning, we gave her a kiss, and before going to bed at night, we again gave her a kiss, but otherwise there was no tenderness. Only when we were ill, then she spent a good deal of time with us. There was always the fear of catching colds. She was hypochondriacal.

O: Your mother?

W: Yes, she imagined she had all sorts of illnesses, and in the end she lived to be eighty-nine and died of old age. But I did miss that, tenderness from my mother. And my father wasn't the type either to express any sort of affection. The only thing he did was, he played with us. He taught me the Russian alphabet, but that was really all.

O: You are the scion of land-owning aristocrats. Did you have a title?

W: No, we had no title. Aristocrat, that was the class, the class was entered in the passport. *Dvorjanin.* And *grazhdanin* is ordinary citizen. Russia was a class society. My grandfather was no nobleman.

O: What class did he belong to?

W: The merchant class. He was a businessman, engaged in some sort of business, he became the owner of an estate and bought the land. That's how he became so wealthy. It was black earth, and prices rose enormously. It was good soil for grain. Black soil is the most fertile. It was that way all over the South, but often there wasn't enough rain. There were areas in Russia, in White Russia, for example, where you had sand or loam. In our part of the country, the peasants were very well off. There was never a famine, everyone always had enough to eat. It was different in White Russia, the people there were much poorer, one could tell that immediately. Just one detail: our peasants wore boots, in White Russia they wore shoes made of rags.

O: So your father was the first to be ennobled?

W: Yes, he was a lay judge, an honorary judge, and so he was raised to noble rank.

O: And your mother?

W: They were aristocrats. They also had an estate, but it wasn't as big.

O: So your mother came from a better family than your father?

W: If you want to put it that way.

O: Did people consider your parent's marriage a *mésalliance*?

W: No, no. My mother was really a talented person. Once, she spent an entire winter in Nice and then she returned with drawings, and everyone was amazed at how well she drew, especially hands and feet, which are the most difficult. Then she hired a painter from the school in Odessa. He came and looked at her paintings and said: "Well, that's all very well and good, but you have to work. You have to work nine hours a day." When she heard that, she never picked up a pencil again. She also had a literary gift. But it was just a talent. You see, the painter said one has to work. And that put an end to her interest.

O: So you inherited your artistic talent from your mother.

W: Well, painting is just a hobby. My father went in for music. He even wanted to attend the conservatory, that's how well he played the piano. My mother also had a humorous vein.

O: Your father didn't?

W: No, not really. But my mother did have one bad quality: she was jealous.

O: And then, after your fifth birthday, you lived in Odessa?

W: Yes, after my parents had sold that estate near Kherson, they bought a house in Odessa and an estate nearby. The manor was larger than the house in town. Should you ever find yourself in Odessa, you must visit our estate. It's an hour by railroad, the second or third stop. It was called Vasilyevka, from Basil, you see.

O: Was your father's name Basil?

W: No, Konstantin. My name is really Sergius Konstantinovich, and my sister's was Anna Konstantinovna. The railroad station near the estate was Vigoda. It was a village with a population of two hundred at the time.

O: Do you still have relatives in Russia?

W: I have lost all contact. My cousin, this Schura, wrote to me until 1945. After that, I know nothing; he suddenly stopped. I thought, either he is dead or it is not advisable to write. It was clear from his letters—Odessa was occupied by Rumanian troops at the time—that the Rumanians had given him a job in the city administration. That's the reason I believe he didn't fare well when the Russians came.

This Schura also sent me the two pictures I showed you. The estate was expropriated. They turned it into kolkhozes or something like that, and the house in Odessa also. Shura wrote me that after Hitler had made a present of Odessa to the Rumanians, the praetor [sic] established himself in the big house in the country. He had the roof repaired; probably it had been damaged. That's the last news I had of our estate. It was very stupid of me to ask that the pictures of my father and sister be sent to me. We owned two Kandinskys, you understand, which my father had bought in Munich. It would have been better had I asked him to send those. But I didn't know. . . . It's only later that I read that Kandinsky had originated abstract painting. Nothing really happened to my mother in Russia. That's because we had always treated the peasants well. No one complained about us. My mother even visited the peasants.

O: As regards your education, didn't your parents once make the remark that your fortune wouldn't always be there, that the time might come when you would have to work?

W: Unfortunately they didn't. I remember, someone once mentioned a Polish estate owner who had lost everything. I was about seventeen at the time, and I said, "I hope nothing like that ever happens to us." Just imagine, that thought occurred to me!

O: So you lived off the income from your estates?

W: No, not so much. We had loans, mortgage loans. When my father died, our fortune came to two million rubles. Yes, those were really interesting times, at least for people with money. For the workers, it's better now, of course, from the social point of view. But every civilization is based on there being people who have time for higher things. I am really quite dissatisfied with my education. The trouble was, everything was theory; one read books, one had a literary education, but no value was put on practical things.

In America, it is customary for the son of a manufacturer to take some unimportant job in his father's business so that he gets to know how the whole thing works. As the son of a landowner, I should have been taught farming. When I was twenty or twenty-two, my mother wrote that my father was planning to teach me the rudiments of farming. It's a little late, when you are twenty-two. And then my father died. He never got around to it. All these things would have interested me, but my father didn't bother with any of them. He thought, there's enough money and there always will be. No need to concern oneself with practical matters, with the running of the estate.

O: Did he know something about farming?

W: Not much, I believe, but a little. And then there was this mademoiselle with the romantic stories she told us. . . . I don't mean that everything in my education was bad, you understand. I find it right, for example, that I learned to ride a horse. My father sent me to riding school when I was ten. Then he had a painter come, which was a good thing since otherwise I probably would never have taken up painting. Violin lessons were a mistake. My father insisted that I learn to play the violin. And the violin teacher was afraid of losing the lessons and said, "It would be a pity to stop now."

But my father was intelligent enough to see that it would not be a pity since I had no interest whatever in the violin. My hand hurt; I couldn't stand all that scratching. One has to have a very fine ear and I didn't. The teacher said, "You will never be able to tune your violin yourself." So why bother taking lessons? It was completely unnecessary. If I had learned to play the piano, that would have been something. But the violin. . . . This is the way it was: my sister was learning to play the piano and I had to learn the violin. . . . What were we actually talking about.

O: Your education.

W: Education . . . horseback riding, that was a good idea.

O: Why?

W: Well, it's a beautiful sport. In the country, you have lots of opportunity for horseback riding. It was one of the chief occupations, riding and hunting.

O: So you also went hunting?

W: Of course.

O: Were you good at it?

W: Well, I was fair. I wasn't a really passionate hunter. When I was ten, I believe, I was given a Monte Christo for Christmas. Monte Christo was the name of a small rifle. I know I was still quite young. Actually, it's cruel, firing a Monte Christo at sparrows.

O: You did that?

W: Yes, yes. The most important thing when you hunted were woodcocks. They actually lived up North. In White Russia, there are swamps, rivers, and ponds. In southern Russia, there is a great deal of steppe. There were almost no trees, a few acacias, and the rest was fields, fields, fields. The park near our estate was about two kilometers long, but that was rare. In the fall, in September, October, the woodcocks migrate south. Everywhere where there were trees and bushes, they gathered, and then they flew zigzag. . . .

Well, in the fall, the most important time for hunting, they rested before setting out on their flight across the Black Sea. Yes, those woodcocks tasted very good. I have never really had woodcock here, you see, it's even the German word, *Waldschnepf.*

O: It's the same word in Russian?

W: *Waldschnepf,* yes, yes.

O: Did your sister hunt too?

W: No, she didn't. There were women who did hunt, but not my sister. My father said he was not worried about me, that I had healthy tastes because I went hunting, horseback riding, etc. But it didn't do any good either. I wound up as a patient of Freud's.

O: So your sister didn't have healthy tastes?

W: No, all she ever really did was sit around with a book. She had no interest whatever in clothes. She really should have been a man. It is a mystery to me why my sister killed herself. She was so talented. I cannot remember my sister except reading. She always said that she was no classical beauty. But then, who is? She certainly wasn't ugly. Do you remember her picture? She was fairly pretty. She did nothing for her appearance, nothing. And then that horrible death, mercury. If it comes to that, gas is better, the way Therese did it.

O: Didn't your sister have a friend?

W: Not as far as I know.

O: Perhaps she suffered because no one took an interest in her.

W: There would have been people to take an interest, but she didn't care for them, and then she always thought they they wanted her for her money. I just happen to remember, I had also written about it in my memoirs, but Gardiner took it out. It's a childhood recollection which, it seems to me, would be very important psychoanalytically, and I want to tell you about it. The estate was near a market town, some seven or eight kilometers away. We spent summers on the estate—it was a summer residence, you might say. And something happened there. My parents were abroad, and we had been entrusted to the care of my mother's younger brother. He later emigrated to Italy.

We had a gardener who was in charge of the rest of the servants, so to speak. You have to realize that this estate was rather far away, on the Dnieper. There weren't many children around. . . . And suddenly the daughter of this chief gardener and my sister Anna—

she was perhaps six at the time—disappeared. There was great excitement. I still remember my uncle running around, excited, wiping the perspiration from his face because it was his responsibility. These two girls, the chief gardener's daughter and Anna, were gone. We looked everywhere, of course, in the park and outside. Finally, they were found, they had hidden in a ditch.

Later, they were asked what they had had in mind, and they told who had had the idea. Whether it was my sister or the gardener's daughter, I don't know. They wanted to flee to this market town to hire themselves out as maids. How does an estate owner's daughter get the idea of wanting to learn to be a domestic? Identification may also have something to do with it. . . . And thinking of being a maid, that didn't leave my sister. There was something not quite right there. She was a sort of scholar, she did chemistry. And she said a few times, "When the mistress is ugly and the servant beautiful, that must be terrible for the mistress."

O: Your sister said that?

W: Yes, my sister, when she was already an adult. And once, when we were in that sanatorium in Germany, she said to me: "Being a maid is really the best profession. You do your work and the rest of the time is your own." And odd idea for a girl one always thought would turn into a second Curie or who knows what, who spent all that time reading, and then she says, "Being a maid is the best profession." There's something wrong there somewhere. But she said things like that. Perhaps that affected me somehow, I don't know. But Gardiner took it out.

O: Why?

W: I didn't find that passage. Something occurs to me, but it has nothing to do with this. My sister imagined she had a red nose, although she never did. And we agreed that we would ask "esonder"—that's "red nose" spelled backward—and then she would ask, "Esonder?" Then I looked at her and said, "No, no, you don't have one, everything is all right."

O: Oh yes?

W: I am telling you this because it seems I regard you a little as my sister.

O: I beg your pardon?

W: I believe I regard you a little as my sister.

O: Me?

W: Yes (*laughs*).

O: But why? Do I resemble her?

W: No, it isn't that. But it's so easy to talk to you.

O: I see. And it was also easy to talk to your sister. But it is not a matter of looks?

W: No, it isn't. Now you tell me, why did my sister kill herself? What a strange thing. She had no reason.

O: It really is incomprehensible.

W: No reason at all, she wasn't ill or anything.

O: Yes, and especially that no one noticed anything before she did it.

W: Who would have thought! She seemed normal.

O: She had no depressions?

W: Well, it wasn't called depressions. But she didn't complain, she didn't say, "I have such severe depressions." And why didn't Therese say anything? There was no reason there, either. If we had quarreled . . .

O: Don't your analysts have any theories about that?

W: Not really, I don't recall. My sister was young, after all, she was wealthy, and Father preferred her. She was his darling. Father disappointed me because he preferred Sister. I wasn't jealous of Sister because she really didn't accept that preference. And when she killed herself, I saw that Father somehow reproached her. He said, "Well, she was only a woman, after all, and needed a man." Yes, he said that. It was a disappointment to him because he wanted to give her money, had she wished to live abroad. . . . Her every wish would have been fulfilled. And she kills herself! With mercury! It was a horrible torture, her teeth fell out. Why does someone do a thing like that?

I remember, because you asked whether no one was interested in her. We knew a family who felt they were aristocrats on the one hand, yet there was also a revolutionary tradition. They had no money and money was the most important thing to that family. When we were in Berlin, a son of that family showed up, the oldest, a dashing fellow, but he already had gray hair. We laughed a lot when he told how, during the Russo-Japanese War, a ship keeled over and stayed like that, and that his gray hair dated from that moment. His sister attended the Kunstakademic in Berlin; she wanted to become a painter. And she told us that her brother suffered from depressions every time he had no money. Well, he suddenly showed up, very elegantly dressed, looking like an English lord, and proposed marriage to my sister Anna. And he said that if she turned him down, he would kill himself. But having heard that he had depressions, she didn't take that seriously. And he didn't kill himself.

O: What was your position in school?

W: I don't quite understand. You mean, did I learn well or poorly?

O: There are leaders in every class. . . .

W: But there were no politics in our gymnasium.

O: I don't mean that. Especially in boys' schools, there are always some who are the leaders, and the rest get beaten up.

W: No, that didn't exist in my school. I entered the second year of the gymnasium. At that age, one is already something of an adult. Here, you have elementary school. All children must attend. In Russia, elementary school was not compulsory. Only the children of the poorer people went. Then efforts were made to have those children also attend the gymnasium. That may explain why the students were so radical. In any event, elementary school was not compulsory. Here, it is. Did you also attend elementary school?

O: Of course.

W: How many years?

O: Four.

W: Well, you see, it's altogether different. At the gymnasium, I started in the second year. In the villages, there was nothing else, of course. The children of the peasants went to elementary school, the others were taught at home.

O: The nose plays an important role in the history of your illness, and Mack writes that your nose already made you suffer in school because it earned you the nickname Mops [pug].

W: Yes, well . . . but everybody had a nickname of some sort, you see, they just gave me that one.

O: And you found that unpleasant?

W: Yes, I did, I didn't care for it at all. But that was only in the lower grades, in the fourth, fifth, then it stopped. Those were awful boys, you know. The population of Odessa—it was that way in all port cities—did not have a good reputation. It was a very mixed population, Greeks, Georgians, Armenians, and so on. In a word, there was a good deal of rabble.

My father always said, "That's not a Russian city" because so many foreigners lived there. People from the southern countries, especially. There were also many Jews. Jews weren't allowed in Saint Petersburg, they were not allowed to live in the North, only in the West, in Russian Poland and in the South, in the Ukraine, that's where they could live. When one of them traveled to Saint Petersburg or Moscow, he had to have a kind of passport. Only those who had had a higher education could live in Saint Petersburg or Moscow, so that there were enough Jewish lawyers and physicians, but a small merchant, for example, had to have permission to live there. That's the reason the Jewish population was primarily in the South, the Ukraine and White Russia. . . .

O: But there was no prejudice against Jews in your family?

W: No, my father didn't have any. There were so many Jews in the party, in the Constitutional Democrats' party. Had he been prejudiced, he could not have belonged to it. In Russia . . . one can't really call it the persecution—the discrimination against Jews had to do with religion, not with blood, as with Hitler. If someone was orthodox, he enjoyed all rights, like anybody else. There were no restrictions of any kind. In Saint Petersburg, there were many Germans. Compared to Saint Petersburg, Odessa was a provincial city, of course. But the nice thing is that it lies on a hill above the sea. From up there, one has a view of the entire harbor and the ships. It was on a *buchta*, that's the Russian word, I don't know what it is called in German. . . .

O: *Bucht* [bay], of course.

W: *Bucht*. You see, it's actually the German word. . . . In any event, the boys in the lower grades were pretty awful. I recall certain things. . . . We had a French teacher who did not speak Russian perfectly. A student did something and the teacher said, "Go stand in the corner." In the corner, up on the wall, was the picture of a saint. The one thing had nothing to do with the other, of course, but a student wanted to have some fun. He got up, began posturing, and

said to the French teacher, "You must not put God into a corner."
And the teacher, who did not know the customs, said, "Well, then, go
stand in the other corner."

O: And you were always a model student?

W: Well, in the second and third year, I was mediocre, later I was
good. I even received an award, you know, with the inscription To
the Successful. But from that time on, I didn't have all that much
success in life.

O: And you had no friends?

W: In the lower grades, I did, but somehow that came to an end.

O: And your sister?

W: That was probably the bad thing in my situation, that my sister
had no girl friends. She had none at all. So I grew up without having
any contact with girls. The only one was a certain Natasha, a
daughter of a descendant of Dostoevski. My sister was sort of friends
with her. And she was ugly, you know. But otherwise she didn't
really have friends. I remember I was supposed to take German
lessons—I was already at the age of puberty—and the sister of this
Hasselblad would give me lessons. And I was looking forward to this
and was interested—here's a woman, a girl, and so on. . . .

My mother had a very jealous nature, and when she heard a girl
. . . out of the question! I was very annoyed about it, I recall. I told
myself, if you completely exclude me from better women, I'll look for
servant girls. I still remember that I was annoyed. I said that out of
a feeling of revenge, you might say.

You can see that my mother was to blame there. Mother allowed
no women around us, no young women. Suppose she had given me
lessons, would that have been so terrible? It's really abnormal. No,
the brother had to come, not the sister.

O: Was the sister your age?

W: She was a little older. But she was still young, and quite pretty, I
believe. And I had been looking forward to it. That whole situation
is something I was pushed into, in a manner of speaking. By my
sister and because my mother was jealous and because my sister had
no girl friends. There was no one.

O: There's one other thing I would like to know. Did you ever have
real homosexual relations?

W: Of course not, never. But since you bring it up, I happen to remember something. In Russia, the Armenians were known as homosexuals. I was told that when one went to a bathhouse in the Caucasus, they asked, do you want a woman or a boy? When I was a student in Odessa, there was an Armenian. His name was Murato. He was a good-looking person but had disquieting eyes. Very strange eyes. That was so beautiful about him.

There was a small group of us students, and this Murato was one of us. Once, he said to me, "You know, after the performance, we are all visiting S. P. That was an actor in Odessa who was a known homosexual. I also told Freud about this. S. P. you see, like my initials. S. P. is mentioned in his text. Murato said, "We are all going to see S. P." I knew right away what he meant. One day, I was at the university to attend a lecture. All the seats were taken except for one next to this Murato. I sat down there. Suddenly, he takes my hand and starts pressing it. That was supposed to be a test. I immediately distanced myself.

O: You had no experiences in school?

W: No, in school I never heard about anything going on. In Odessa, there wasn't much homosexuality, much less than abroad. Only in the Caucasus, the Armenians. There were also a few Armenians in school, but I am convinced that none of them was homosexual.

Then there's something else. I had a second experience. But please, I'm not certain. I was going to Paris, there was another gentleman in the compartment. I stretched out and fell asleep in the corner by the window. Then he stepped up to the window and placed his foot close to mine. I didn't know what to do, should I push his foot away? So I pretended to be asleep. Then he played with my knee, but finally he stopped. It must have been a sort of hint. He wanted to see how I would react.

O: And what Freud writes about your homosexual tendencies . . .

W: Subconscious, of course. For Freud, all relations between men are homosexual.

O: It's probably true that every human being is naturally bisexual.

W: But homosexuals are relatively rare.

O: The educational barriers are very strong.

W: And, well (*laughs*), I don't know whether I should tell you about this.

O: Why not?

W: Walking up to strange women and talking to them. At the tailor's I talked to a woman and didn't think that she could find out my name there. And she did find out my name from the tailor and that I work for the Municipal Insurance, and then she called me on the phone. And that's how we became acquainted.

O: And you still are today?

W: Well, yes.

O: So that's your lady friend?

W: That's the lady friend. You see, one has to pay for everything.

O: It's an irony of fate. Freud writes that you always had a special relationship to your tailors.

W: It's an irony of fate.

O: And she called you on the phone?

W: I should have told her immediately, "Conversations aren't allowed here." But I thought, I have no one, and so on. Very well, so let's meet. You see how the whole thing started, and then she became ill, and now I am in trouble.

O: It's really very funny. I apologize for laughing.

W: Yes, it's funny.

Therese

WOLF-MAN: I was going to ask, do you still plan to write something about me?

OBHOLZER: That depends on how much more you tell me.

W: Well, you see, I am at an advanced age, and I have had enough of all these things. Besides, I am at an age where it is natural for a person to get tired, and where everything is too much. When I die, you can write about me. I simply ask you that nothing be published while I am alive. Because then I would come into conflict . . . And I wrote Gardiner that you stopped. You have to understand, I cannot do otherwise.

O: All right. . . .

W: I don't know what one should do, the whole thing all over again. These interviews with you, they degenerate into a kind of psychoanalysis, don't they, and I've been through so many analyses.

O: And you have enough now?

W: I don't feel like any more.

O: I can understand that.

W: Yes, I have enough of analysis (*pause*). Something occurred to me in connection with Dostoevski. Actually all of Dostoevski is an illustration of Schopenhauer's world as idea. His heroes do not act in their own interest or as their class would dictate but according to their own ideas, which are often quite odd and absurd. Do you still remember *The Possessed?* There's a certain Stavrogin in it who clamps his teeth on the governor's earlobe. And another time, he hears him say, "No one leads me by the nose." And he gets up, takes him by the nose, and leads him through the room. Those are ideas that sound unrealistic. . . . Everything this Stavrogin does he does only to prove to himself time and again how great a man he is, that he is capable of enduring all sorts of things. When he is slapped in the face, for example, he does nothing. What benefit does he or anyone else derive from this? So, the entire world is transformed into an imagined world, that's why it has such an unreal effect, and because there's also so much in it that's subconscious and not described by others, it is so interesting.

Something else struck me. Do you remember how this novel, *The Possessed,* ends? This Verhovensky, who lives at the house of the general's widow, must always live according to her whims and always do what she demands because he has nothing, no pension, nothing. And in the long run, he can't stand it and goes away, takes the train. And then, after the first station, he doesn't know where to go, catches a cold, becomes feverish, and the general's widow appears on the scene with physicians.

Actually, that's the very same thing Tolstoi did. He even died like that. He and his secretary took a train and went off, no one knows why, to what purpose, or where to. After the first station, he had to get out because he had caught a cold and become feverish. His wife was notified and she came, full of reproaches, naturally, about what he had done to her, running off like that. And then he dies. He dies exactly like this Verhovensky. That's never been noticed by anyone, at least I haven't read that anyone drew a parallel.

O: But every writer creates the world as idea.

W: Yes, more or less. But most of them write in a way that is closer to reality, I feel, more understandable. They have fewer absurd ideas. He marries an impossible person, this Stavrogin, a mad person, a crazy girl, don't you see. Those are all actions that overleap reality, as it were. Of course, other writers also describe the world as idea but not as radically as Dostoevski.

O: Couldn't one draw a parallel to Freud? Doesn't he also describe persons according to his idea rather than to reality?

W: Well, Freud had a very high regard for Dostoevski. I don't know whether you know that. He esteemed him much more highly than Tolstoi, although Tolstoi is just as famous as Dostoevski. But the descriptions of people correspond more closely to actual conditions in Tolstoi. When this Anna Karenina kills herself, for example, she has a specific reason, because she is excluded from society. Everybody understands that. But in Dostoevski, there are often situations where one asks oneself, how did this fellow come to have that idea? There is a scene, for example, I don't remember where, someone wants to shoot himself but the moment is decided by another person. Suddenly, one hears a shot and the person has shot himself, although he had no reason to shoot himself.

O: In any event, after your sister killed herself, you became depressed again. But you had recovered satisfactorily from the gonorrhea.

W: Yes, when my sister killed herself, I was overcome by a terrible depression. . . .

O: And you went to various sanatoria in Germany.

W: Yes, it was similar to what Thomas Mann describes in *The Magic Mountain*. I think you find that in a review of my book. It really was as if one lived with others in a pension. They either used hypnosis or treatment by natural remedies. But I wasn't really susceptible to hypnosis. I remember that a physician in a sanatorium once went through that hocus-pocus and then left the room on tiptoe and so on, but I didn't fall asleep. This is how it is: I allow myself to be influenced by others, but it is difficult to hypnotize me. I don't fall asleep. It's curious, isn't it? A person who needs advice is suddenly not susceptible to hypnosis. It's an odd situation.

O: But when you attended the university in Saint Petersburg after graduating from the gymnasium, you write that you saw a physician who hypnotized you. And that helped you temporarily.

W: Ah yes, in Saint Petersburg.

O: And he hypnotized you.

W: Yes, yes, that was Bekhterev, a well-known psychiatrist. He wanted the money my parents donated after my sister's death for his institute, but they gave it to the hospital in Odessa. But Bekhterev didn't help, I didn't fall asleep. The next day, I felt better, less so the day after that, and the third day the effect was gone.

Well, psychiatrists before Freud barely bothered with the psychological. I remember one of them whom my mother called to the house several times. And I spoke with him at length and in some detail. In the room we were in, there was an armchair with springs so you could lean back. Well, I was talking about my states with a great deal of enthusiasm. Suddenly, he gets up and asks how the armchair works. That's how little interest they had. The armchair interested him more than the patient.

Among the earlier psychiatrists, it was the rule that they did not go into the substance of people's complaints. It was thought that there was some physical malfunctioning that could be cured by baths or things like that. That was false, of course, and in that respect, Freud brought something new.

O: But before Freud you saw Kraepelin.

W: Yes, that was in Munich, where I got to know Therese. It was in a sanatorium in Neuwittelsbach, near Munich, about ten minutes' walk from Nymphenburg Castle. He came there. And I recall that my uncle arrived from Italy. He didn't speak German but Kraepelin spoke Italian. And Kraepelin told him that my illness was an illness of the will, a weak will, you know. Well, that was because of Therese. And the people in the sanatorium, when they discovered that I had fallen in love with her, they said: "You won't get anywhere, she is so conscientious, she won't start anything with a man. All your efforts are pointless." That's what I was told. And then it turned out differently after all.

What it was, she had been married before and had a daughter, Else, you know, and the marriage had been a failure. Now she took refuge in the idea that she wanted to help the sick and had ideals that women ordinarily do not have. Particularly when you consider that she was so beautiful. It is really astonishing that she took that job in the sanatorium. It didn't fit. Well, and then there was me, she didn't want to have anything to do with me but then she changed her mind and came, wrote again, no longer wanted to have anything to do with me, and wanted to stick to that decision. Then that wasn't possible any more, apparently, nothing gave her pleasure any more, and she left the sanatorium.

O: Why was Kraepelin against your marrying Therese?

W: Well, someone arrives in a sanatorium and suddenly he wants to get married, and it's not a suitable match. At least according to the ideas of the time, you know, *mésalliance,* that sort of thing. I have already told you that he said to my uncle that my illness was an illness of the will and concerning Therese, he said that I should get over it. That's how I could become well, that it was precisely the right moment. Freud saw that differently. And my interest in Therese, he thought that was some . . . what did they call it, a manic state, you know.

O: And you think Kraepelin didn't accept a *mésalliance*. . . .

W: Yes, he probably felt it was crazy because I was Russian, after all. It wasn't a suitable match.

O: You mean he shared the prejudices of your class?

W: Yes, of course.

O: And what about Therese's first marriage?

W: That was something else again. You can imagine the sort of relationship that was. Later, when we were in Russia and the war had broken out, it was impossible to send money to Germany. I said to her, "Can't you write to Else's father and ask him for help?" She was indignant, she said, "That you should suggest a thing like that to me, that scoundrel. . . ." You see, she didn't even want to do that because there was an enmity.

O: Why?

W: Then Else died, she went to Germany by herself, I followed. At the time, we still hoped that she might be saved. We wanted to go to Switzerland. But then the physician said, "It's pointless now, it's hopeless," and two or three weeks later, she died.

O: Why didn't you take Else with you to Russia?

W: Well, at first I didn't take Therese either. When the war broke out, she was in Munich and I was in Odessa.

O: Yes, and then she came to Russia. But she could have brought Else along.

W: That idea didn't really occur to anyone. That could have been done, of course. But you see, it was very difficult at the time to get an entry permit. Travel between the two countries had stopped completely. And people didn't think that the war would last that long. They thought it would last a few months but not four years. And Else was in school in Munich and lived at her uncle's in Munich. She was left with Therese's brother, that's all. Therese also reproached me, she blamed herself that she had gone to Russia and left Else behind. . . .

O: What was Therese's maiden name?

W: Keller.

O: And her first husband's name?

W (*pause*): Let's not discuss that.

O: Why is this so unpleasant for you?

W: It isn't pleasant.

O: Did you ever get to know this man?

W: No, she no longer had anything to do with him.

O: You never got to know the man and yet this first marriage is such an unpleasant matter for you?

W: Yes, I found it unpleasant.

O: But she was already divorced when you came to know her?

W: Yes, she was already divorced.

O: Why do you find it so unpleasant?

W (*pause*): A cigarette (*offers a cigarette*)

O: How old was Therese when you got to know her?

W: Well, you know, my wife was a good deal older than I.

O: How many years?

W: I believe she lied about her age.

O: You mean she never told you the actual year she was born?

W: I think what she said at the time was that she was eight years older. So it's at least eight years, perhaps it was nine. It's not known, precisely. Because when she came to Russia, she said she had lost her papers. When I got to know her, she said that she was twenty-eight, and I was twenty.

O: In the beginning, there was such a curious vacillation with Therese.

W: Well, that was her fault, not mine. She kept writing me farewell letters.

O: Reading your book, one is surprised that suddenly, as you arrive in this sanatorium, you act so aggressively. Before then, you always had depression and weren't at all well. One would really expect you to be quite shy.

W: That's true, but Freud said that it was the breakthrough to the woman.

O: What is that supposed to mean? Judging by what you write earlier, one expects you to be shy.

W: I was active.

O: And suddenly you are so active.

W: You are right, it isn't altogether understandable.

O: You simply walk into her room. . . . And then this odd vacillation. Why did she keep writing that she wanted to break things off?

W: Perhaps she was afraid of having a child. Later, when she visited me in Berlin, she told me that she had had a miscarriage. I had never concerned myself with such matters. That was stupid. That's something I should have thought about, shouldn't I?

O: And you never did?

W: I never did. I wanted to possess her, that's all. But you are quite right, it is curious that a patient who tends to be weak and depressed should suddenly become so energetic. I was really very energetic. It seems that there are times people feel one way, and there are others when they feel differently.

O: And the miscarriage . . . The child was yours?

W: Yes.

O: Was it a miscarriage or an abortion?

W: She said she had had a miscarriage.

O: And you hadn't known that she was pregnant?

W: She hadn't said anything to me. She didn't tell me until later. Then I left.

O: And in what month did she have the miscarriage?

W: I don't know. But it must have been quite late because she told me that the child had resembled her. It only had my eyes, my light eyes. So it must already have had some kind of shape. I took no interest in it at the time. There was nothing there.

O: Was it a boy or a girl?

W: A boy, I believe.

O: Did she have the miscarriage at home or in a hospital?

W: I think it was at home. She said she had picked up something heavy and that had caused the miscarriage.

O: Was she still working at the sanatorium?

W: Yes.

O: And they noticed that she was pregnant?

W: She never mentioned that they noticed. She said it was a miscarriage.

O: And she didn't tell you anything at the time?

W: No, she didn't write, nothing.

O: Strange, don't you find?

W: She said she had lifted something heavy and had a miscarriage. That's all I can say.

O: But at the very beginning she cannot have been pregnant yet, and still there was this vacillation.

W: No, that wasn't until later, when I was already gone. And when I was in the Schlachtensee sanatorium, I saw her from time to time. And when I broke with her in Berlin, she said to me that earlier . . . No, I think she only told me later. In Berlin, she didn't say anything. . . . And what about the will? What's your view?

O: You mean, was a mistake made in your upbringing?

W: There is really no such concept as "will" in Freud. For Freud, will is drive. But actually, it is the opposite, it is the capacity to repress the drive and to do what one considers rational. Which would mean that drive does not equal will. And here's something else: when I left Therese, my uncle wanted to be helpful. He gave me an address in Odessa that I did not know. Society women came and went there. I met a very pretty lady there; she was a Jewess. Once, I was taking a walk with my uncle in the park. Suddenly, we see this lady with a little boy or girl, he looks at her and says, "Look at this woman, that's magnificent, a truly beautiful woman." And I say, "I was with that woman at the address you gave me four weeks ago."

Later, this procuress told me, "Your uncle keeps wanting to meet this woman, but she doesn't want him and says she wants to meet with you." And I saw her a few times. That was the one thing that just occurred to me, and the other is this: before Therese came to Vienna—that wasn't until two years later—I also went around with women. I told Drosnes he should find out if there was something in Vienna like that procuress in Odessa. He inquired and told me, "There's something like it." It was quite nearby, in the Wipplinger-strasse.

I went there. An older woman opens the door and says, "Do you want to stay with my niece, with Ter?" Her name was also Theresa. I said, "I'll have to have a look first." The niece comes out, pretty as a picture, in her early twenties. So I went there for a time. A while later, I was walking along the Kärntnerstrasse one day. Suddenly, I see this Ter coming toward me. Made up. Wearing a splendid fur coat. And alongside her a tall, handsome man, also very elegantly dressed. I almost did not recognize her. Well, I said good day and walked on.

She left the man, came after me, and said, "You know, I am at the operetta now, why don't you visit me? I still live with my aunt." But

I never went back. I simply wanted to tell you so that you see how careful I was. It never occurred to me that something like what actually happened would happen to me, that I would fall into the hands of a woman who constantly demands money. . . .

O: I don't quite follow. What did they procure? What kinds of women did they procure?

W: Society woman. Not prostitutes but prostitutes in secret, if you will.

O: I see.

W: They were real ladies and nobody knew that about them.

O: You paid them.

W: Yes, yes, a fair amount, actually. At the time, those were trivial sums for me. Everything was different then. . . .

O: And Therese knew that you had other women?

W: Well no. There was only one thing that happened that made her jealous. She had a cousin whom she always described as the black sheep in the family. She told me that she supposedly had an affair with a Count Thun, this Liesl. Here's what happened one day: I see a woman on the street and she has . . . actually, as I think back, she didn't look that much like Therese. But something about her struck me, and I thought that must be the girl. . . .

I walked up to her and started talking, and said, "Aren't you Therese's cousin?" And she said, "No, no, I am not the cousin," and so on. Well, I talked to her for a few moments and then, just to be polite, I say, "Perhaps we'll run into each other again." And then she told Therese extravagant stories about me, that I wanted to start an affair with her. . . .

O: So it was the cousin after all?

W: That was the cousin. So she got really jealous. What a time that was! But later it stopped.

O: And when did all this happen?

W: When I was seeing Freud. It must have been during the time when she had not yet moved in with me. At first, Freud wouldn't let me see her and two years passed until he did. And she didn't come immediately but stayed on in Munich for a while longer.

O: And the cousin was in Vienna?

W: She kept moving back and forth the whole time from Munich to Vienna, and from Vienna to Munich.

O: And you recognized her without ever having seen her before?

W: I guessed that it was the cousin.

O: Had you seen a photo?

W: No, I had not seen a photo. Although the resemblance wasn't great, some feature must have been similar because I recognized her. I have a picture of Therese. I must show it to you sometime, she looks like an actress in it. She asked me if I would permit her to go to a ball in Munich. I said, "I have nothing against it." She went to balls and then she sent me that picture. She looks as if she were out to turn a few heads.

There was something else about that cousin. She told Therese that I wanted to start an affair with her, and no letters came. I wrote, and got no answer. I told Freud, "Something's up, she isn't answering." And Freud didn't want to acknowledge that, of course, and said, "You are just imagining things." But it continued, I heard nothing from her. I said, "Look, it's been three weeks now since I've received a letter." So he gave his consent for me to go to Munich. Well, I went. When I rang the bell, the maid, her name was Maria, opened the door and wanted to shut it in my face. So I put my foot in the door and went in. And we had a reconciliation. She wanted to stop seeing me altogether.

O: Because of the cousin?

W: Because of the cousin.

O: And later, when you were in Russia with Therese . . .

W: After the treatment it was all right because Therese was a decent human being. Had it been another woman, the treatment would not have been that successful, of course. She had certain difficulties when she started the quarrel with my mother.

O: Why?

W: Well, there was considerable enmity between my mother and Therese. This enmity was Therese's fault. Nothing suited her; she wanted everything different. That's the reason I could not have my mother live with me until after Therese's death. It bothered her that my mother was so attached to her relatives and not to us. That was Therese's idea. Her relatives were the most important thing to my mother, you understand, but I was never really that aware of it.

Due to the quarrel with my mother, the fortune was lost because I couldn't discuss anything with my mother. . . . And she was constantly with her relatives, and those relatives naturally also turned away from me. So it was an awkward situation. During the winter, in 1914–15, I was in Moscow with Therese, preparing for the examination. . . .

O: Therese was jealous of your mother.

W: I'd say so. You see it correctly.

O: But your mother also had a prejudice against Therese.

W: Of course. My mother did not like my having married Therese.

O: Because it was a *mésalliance?*

W: Of course. She was a nurse—that's a lower class. But you see how it is when a mother is jealous of her daughter-in-law, and vice versa. My mother was always jealous. My father said that he was unfamiliar with that emotion. But she had reason. . . .

O: And a woman after your mother's heart, what would she have been like?

W: Rich, for one thing.

O: Did you ever get to know one?

W: Things didn't get that far. And Therese sensed her rejection. She was very much attached to her mother, to her parents. She wanted my mother to act toward her as her own mother did. And that was a wish that could not be fulfilled. There were always difficulties with Therese. I remember some details. She was such a petite bourgeoise, she had entirely different ideas. When she came to Russia, she had her own maid, of course, who could not be kept working later than eight o'clock at night. That always caused disputes. The other girls were jealous. . . .

O: You find that petit bourgeois?

W: No, no, not that, exactly. But she could not adapt. And a German on top of everything else. Perhaps she also sensed the rejection. Don't forget, the war broke out at that time and there was this hatred of the Germans. And so it was disadvantageous that she was German, although she was not persecuted on that account. Married to me, she was Russian, after all. There were signs in restaurants, We Ask You Not to Speak German. That wasn't such a terrible insult, after all.

You know, in Russia, things Nordic were adored long before Hitler came. They unearthed that old name Igor, for example. The persecution of the Jews and the enthusiasm for what was Nordic, that was quite similar, only on a smaller scale.

O: When was that?

W: Before the First World War. It was only during the war that this terrible hatred of the Germans arose. There were many Germans living in Russia who were industrious and capable. Besides, Normans and Germans were two different things for the Russians. A Norman tribe conquered Russia. They were called Varangians. And the English were good at stirring up emotions against the Germans. It's only because of the war that things turned out this way. Otherwise, everything would have been different. One cannot say in what way, but I believe Russia would have become a parliamentary democracy. All parties were for the war, including the Cadet party (Constitutional Democratic party), to which my father belonged. Only the Bolsheviks were against the war, that's the reason for their success. . . .

I must tell you this story: actually, I took no interest in politics, only in painting and literature. But after the revolution, when Kerenski came to power, I thought, well now, I will have to join the Cadet party. Kerenski was the chairman of the Cadet party. They accepted me right away because my father had played such an important role in that party. They immediately elected me to the committee. Every week, there were social evenings. People actually didn't discuss politics a lot. There was music and dancing. I used to go.

I told you about Stavrogin before, who always did those strange things. Who, according to Dostoevski, constantly wants to prove that he can do everything. I resemble him a little. I do something in order to prove that I can do it. Once done, that's it, I don't go on. It's enough for me to know, I can do that, then I drop it. Of course, with painting it isn't that way, but then painting is a hobby. In the Cadet party, there were young men who gave lectures. And I had the idea that I should also give one. I had to prove to myself that I could give a lecture too, although previously I had not felt any need to. Freud thought I should take up economics. He said that if he had not become a psychoanalyst, that's what he would have done. But he wouldn't have gone far. You can see for yourself, all those economic experts nowadays don't know what to say.

So, I picked a subject, some economic matter, and gave a lecture. There were a few hundred in the audience. It cost me a great deal to speak before so many people. Well, in any event, it was a great success. I recall, there was a certain Grossfeld, a well-educated lawyer who said, "I heard that you gave a splendid talk." Now those people thought they could show me off. And I was given the assignment to go to a provincial town and to give talks there. I went but did not prepare anything. In a word, it was enough for me to have had such a success once in my life. Otherwise, I didn't care about politics.

And here's something else that comes back to me. In the Cadet party, there was a Prince Trubetskoi. I heard him give a talk, he discussed the revolution. And he said: "Compare the French and the Russian revolutions. Four months have already passed"—Kerenski was still in power—"and nothing has happened to anyone, no one has come to the slightest harm. How peaceful the Russian people are." He called attention to the executions in France and so on. "And that's the way it will remain," he said.

I went home in a horse-drawn carriage and asked the coachman about his attitude toward the revolution. He said—Kerenski was still in power at the time, there were no executions or anything—he said, "A great deal of blood will be spilled." I was surprised and said, "Why, four months have come and gone and nothing has happened to anyone." He says, "It's got to be that way," You see, he was right, he knew more.

O: Was he a Bolshevik?

W: No, he was quite apolitical. The peasants were not Bolsheviks, generally speaking. The peasants wanted the estates to be split up so that they could become the owners, but they didn't want the kolkhozes. The peasants weren't for the Bolsheviks. He was a completely uneducated peasant. Why he had that feeling . . . But you see, his prophecy was correct. Isn't that odd? He had grasped it better than the scholar who thought everything was well, and that that's the way it would continue. And the peasant knew that things would change.

O: And even at that time it did not occur to the ruling class that it would not retain its privileges forever?

W: No one foresaw that. Look, had there been no war, Bolshevism would never have come. I am convinced of that. The war was the purest madness. The liberals, who weren't socialists yet but only democrats, were also for the war. Lenin grasped things correctly. I have read that he said before the war that he did not believe that Czar Nicholas and Emperor Franz Josef would do them the favor of starting a war. That was also a stupidity in the program of the liberals, wasn't it, this war to a victorious end.

It was obvious that victory was out of the question. The soldiers were flooding back. It was completely blind. According to the view of the time, it was unpatriotic to conclude peace. Solzhenitsyn has written quite correctly that Russia promised the Allies to continue the war to final victory. But he quite rightly wrote that we had not promised to commit suicide. And it was suicide. Something more stupid cannot be imagined, to keep talking of a victorious conclusion as everything collapses around you.

O: It was the same thing with Hitler.

W: All right, but Hitler wasn't in his right mind. But those were more or less sane individuals . . . so blind . . .

O: Let's get back to Therese.

W: This is the way it was with Therese: Freud said I was looking for something inferior because she was only a nurse, although people thought highly of her in the sanatorium. There were difficulties, but Freud said I had looked for something inferior and had received something very good, you see, because she was a very decent human being.

O: Was it on your account that she left the sanatorium?

W: To begin with, it's apparent that she no longer enjoyed it after what had happened between us. In the second place—I wasn't going to write this—I also sent her money.

O: When you separated from her, did you give her money? And did she take it?

W: She took it. And with that money, she bought the pension.

O: I was wondering where she had got that money. She cannot have earned it as a nurse.

W: The money came from me. You see, I always felt that I was not the man to spend enormous sums of money on women and ruin himself that way. With the women I knew, two or three times, no such sums were involved. But here's something I still want to say— my father put restrictions on my inheritance because he was afraid I would fall under the influence of a woman who would steal from me.

My father had a mistress who wrote me letters directly after he died. I threw the letters away.

O: Your father had a mistress? And your mother knew?

W: Yes, she knew. This is the way it was: my mother had ordered a box in the theater and was told that it had already been assigned to someone. My father had taken it for his mistress. That's the way it became known. I never saw her, but she must really have robbed him.

O: And what did your mother say?

W: The relationship between my mother and him was no longer good because he was unfaithful. And my mother was a very jealous woman. Actually, I wanted to tell you something else. My father restricted my inheritance until I reached twenty-eight because he was afraid that I might fall into the hands of such a robber. And I always felt, that's not a danger for me. I never thought that I . . . let's call her Luise, that I would become involved in such an affair with this Luise.

When my father died, I had a lawyer, he was a Jew. And my mother had a lawyer, a Pole, a wealthy landowner. Once, I visited my lawyer's wife with mine. Normally, Therese didn't want to go anywhere. They lived in the house of a businessman who owned a perfumery. His name was Audersky; he was also a Pole. And his wife looked like this Luise.

In any event, when I and my wife visited the lawyer's wife, we became acquainted with this Mrs. Audersky. Well, I found her quite attractive and occasionally ran into her in town. I'd greet her and walk a little with her. Of course, I did not feel like starting something with her because it was too risky. And lo and behold, Therese had barely left Odessa because of Else when this Audersky woman writes me a letter. She is in financial straits. She wanted money, of course.

You see, I found that woman attractive, but I tore up that letter and did not go to see her. That I would come to this is something I had never believed, because I did not have the inclination. And now I fall into the hands of such an impossible person. Well, one of these days I'll have to tell you about this Luise, how everything developed. Another time . . .

O: As regards Therese, that no one supposedly noticed that she was suffering from something. Don't your analysts have any theories about that suicide?

W: Not really.

O: They can't explain it?

W: I remember that I told Mack something about Therese at the time. "Therese," she said, "what do I care about Therese? You are my patient! It's you I have to consider." That's an unacceptable point of view, isn't it?

O: Was Therese still alive?

W: Yes, it was during that nose business.

O: Well, that's the view of the Freudians and people are getting away from it these days. Today, they also concern themselves with the family or with the couple if that's what it is.

W: That's the way it should be, of course. For if I am dependent on Therese, she must also deal with Therese and not say, that isn't my patient.

O: The orthodox Freudians don't do that. That's another school.

W: That's the better way. Of course, I don't know what else that school stands for. But in this matter, they are right, that one involves the others because the sick person depends on those other people. One cannot exclude them and say, "That isn't my patient." Well, Mack helped me and I wrote as much. But then there was the death of my wife. If that hadn't happened, things would have continued to be bearable. But then I committed so many stupidities, you know, because of that complex. I could have picked some other woman. This Luise was completely unsuitable. It's through her that I spoiled everything for myself.

O: That cannot be altogether so. You spent so much time with Freud, and then you were with Mack, that was a long time before the death of your wife.

W: All right, that's your point of view, and I agree. If Freud had helped me, had really helped me, and if it had been a perfect cure, I would not have found myself in that situation with this Luise. This sister complex should have been eradicated long before. And you see, it wasn't.

O: In any case, it's very odd that Therese killed herself and that you weren't aware of anything. There's something fishy. It's impossible that someone should kill herself and the people around her be completely unaware.

W: What do you mean?

O: You lived with this woman, she kills herself, and you don't notice a thing. That strikes me as quite improbable.

W: Why?

O: One should have noticed something.

W: On the contrary, when I went away at the time, I had the impression that she was feeling better. She was perfectly normal; there was nothing out of the way.

O: But she must have been dissatisfied for years.

W: Don't forget, that was the time Hitler came. Perhaps she had some delusions about being Jewish because she looked so southern. She told me that her grandmother was Spanish, which her brother later denied. But she looked Spanish. And then she told me something, that her mother allegedly had had a relationship with a Jew. I didn't write about that but she told me. And I said, "Well, could you be Jewish? And she answered no, but that was at a different time altogether. It is possible that she worried . . .

O: Her brother knew nothing about this?

W: No, I didn't discuss it with the brother. I only asked if she was Spanish, and he denied it. And when I told her that one could write to her place of birth, Würzburg, and ask for the documents showing that she was Aryan, she got so frightened. . . . The suicide is incomprehensible, conducting oneself as if one didn't have anything in mind. It's incomprehensible.

O: But something like that doesn't develop from one day to the next.

W: Well, she always complained about her health. That's something she also wrote in her farewell letters: "The time will soon come when I will be unable to go on. . . ." Then there was something wrong with her gallbladder. The physician always said that there was nothing wrong with the gallbladder. But finally she did have an examination and the report said that the gallbladder was full of stones. And she said, "I have to have an operation, I can't stand this." And then she started talking about her heart and was constantly preoccupied with her gallbladder, although she had no attacks. But the suicide, that was a fixed idea of hers.

O: The difference in age must have played a role.

W: Well, she would stand before the mirror and say, "I am old and ugly!" I said, "You just imagine that, that's nonsense." But it was useless. She lost all interest in clothes and I said, "Why don't you make yourself a new dress." But she didn't want to make anything. This suicide idea has not been explained.

O: Did you mind being married to a woman who was that much older?

W: She was well preserved, you can see that in the photos.

O: But she was younger then. When she died, she must have been sixty.

W: She did not look old. Yes, that's something I wanted to tell you. That's an intimate matter, what I am telling you now. I wanted Therese, Therese excited me sexually. Sexually, it was the breakthrough to the woman, that's true. But then what? I went away, I came back to her and what did I find? She was broken in health, emaciated like a skeleton.

So now I saw, this woman . . . Freud said it is narcissism, injured narcissism. I didn't accept that. The woman must have loved me, otherwise she wouldn't be in that state. Now that I was back, the first thing was, I marry no woman except Therese, so my narcissism was satisfied; the woman who rejected you, who wrote you that she would not see you again, has become ill because of you. If you had not come, she might have died; she was in a terrible state, so she loves you, so you marry her. And now comes the other thing, the sexual. She was sexual as long as she had energy; then, after she fell into that role—this is a secret I am telling you now—she no longer excited me sexually.

O: When she was so emaciated?

W: When she was so emaciated and ill because of me, she . . . She was the strong woman, she rejected me. I was no longer an element—that was the premise, wasn't it—and now it was difficult. I forced myself . . . And it was true of her, too. And when there was intercourse, she never made herself a little prettier or anything like that, no, she put on her worst clothes. You see, and that was the bad thing now, this is a secret, what I am telling you, now I looked for the sexual in other women. I loved her, and with other women it was the sexual thing. But that has nothing to do with her suicide. Hitler had something to do with her suicide. . . . You see, going through something like what I went through with the suicide, another person cannot grasp it, the impression it makes and the effects it has.

O: That's true, of course.

W: That also affects my relationship with this Luise.

O: How so?

W: Because it was a terrible shock.

O: You mean that now you give in more easily because you are afraid that she will also kill herself?

W: Of course. Then she imagined that business about her gallbladder. Stones, it said in the report, that was a terrible scare for her. She said, "I won't survive this, another operation." Earlier, she had had her appendix out—the best professor in Vienna did it—and after the operation it got much worse.

She imagined she was incapable of going on living. And this idea, I am old and ugly, took hold. She gave no indication whatever that she was going to do something like that. There was no reason. I mean, if there had been a quarrel, or jealousy. But there was nothing, that's what's so absurd. There was a thought in her farewell letters—I mention a letter in my memoirs. It's always the same thing. The same thing in all the letters: I won't go on much longer in any event, now it is better; she spares me the terrible end. She is not capable of going on living.

I can bring you the letters one of these days. One can't make head or tail of them. She wasn't that ill. But suicide seemed something grandiose to her. She always said, "Bad people don't kill themselves." And even earlier, there was shooting on the street once, and she said, "If they'd only hit me." Well, the loss of the fortune and the reduced circumstances. Don't forget, she reproached herself on account of Else, that she died. Then she marries a wealthy person, and faces total ruin once again.

O: Why didn't you send Therese to a psychoanalyst?

W: But she didn't feel ill psychologically.

O: Your wife found it difficult to establish contact, she wanted to go nowhere and isolated herself more and more. Isn't that a sign that there was something wrong?

W: I don't know. I noticed nothing. Perhaps there was a life there that I knew nothing about. And the protest against my mother, she was very consistent in that. Weakness of the will didn't exist for her. She had no need of an authority.

O: But her interests narrowed more and more; she only cared about money.

W: Yes, but she would never have gone to a psychoanalyst. She didn't feel the need.

O: Did you suggest it to her?

W: No. I knew she was against it. If she was ill, it was an illness psychoanalysis could not cure. One must feel that one needs help, that one cannot manage by oneself. She never had that feeling. When someone kills himself . . . If there is such a thing as a death instinct, Therese had it. She always extolled suicide as something very beautiful and right. Like a glorious heroic act. And when the money was devalued, she blamed herself perhaps because I had always wanted to buy something. I think it is difficult to define the state in which a person kills himself.

O: You believe there is such a thing as a death instinct?

W: As far as I have observed, psychoanalysts no longer believe in the death instinct. And I don't either, really. I just think that conditions can be such that one prefers disappearing. But I don't believe that it is an instinct. The instinct of self-preservation may be stronger or weaker, but it exists. . . .

O: And you think that psychoanalysis is only for someone . . .

W: . . . who is looking for help. And that was never the case with Therese. Freud said that she was perfectly all right psychologically and that only physical illnesses need be considered in her case.

O: Oh yes? You sent her to see Freud? Why?

W: I don't remember. I had probably told him that there were dishonesties. And he also said, "I can see that she did not conduct herself properly in Russia."

O: When was that?

W: A few years before her death. Five or six years before. Mack said, "That's where the professor was very badly mistaken . . ."

O: About Therese?

W: . . . and was amazed that she had succeeded in convincing him that she was all right psychologically.

O: And that wasn't Mack's view?

W: No, she said, "You were married to a crazy woman for twenty-five years."

O: Mack said that when Therese died?

W: Yes.

O: And what reasons did she give?

W: The suicide was proof, as it were, that she wasn't normal. Well, those quarrels with my mother really weren't normal. But you see, the case of my sister is even less comprehensible than Therese. . . . In the case of my wife, it was real hypochondria that she was so ill. She wasn't ill at all. She imagined she was ill, that she wouldn't live much longer, and so on. . . .

The Sister Complex

WOLF-MAN: Just now, as I was coming here in the taxi, a Russian proverb came to my mind: From the great nobleman to the ridiculous is but one step. I don't believe you have that proverb in German.

OBHOLZER: Not that I know of.

W: I kept thinking of it when I read: Pushkin for Tough Guys. Pushkin would turn in his grave if he read that. Then I thought of his poems—of one, I'll translate it for you: "The comrade believes that the glorious star will rise, Russia will awaken, and from the fragments of autocratic absolutism our names will be written . . ." And now they put on a bottle of liquor Pushkin for Tough Men. It's ridiculous, isn't it? I'll admit that there are "Mozart balls," but that isn't so striking, it's restrained. . . . "Mozart balls."

By the way, Dr. E. felt that I should continue my memoirs and write. I said that that wouldn't suit Gardiner. Everything tells me that she wants to be my only patron. She wrote me that when my book came out, a Russian woman wrote her from Paris, in Russian. You know, even S. said that she could have had a Xerox made and sent it to me so that I might find out what that woman wrote in Russian.

Perhaps it was a wealthy woman who wanted to invite me to come to Paris. It could have been a wealthy émigrée. The Russians didn't go in for psychoanalysis. And if a Russian woman took an interest in it, she must have been educated. In any event, she should have sent me that. And she didn't. You can see the reason. She didn't want another woman to enter the picture. I won't write a word about you. I asked her what sort of letter it was and she said that she was so forward.

O: Who? The Russian woman?

W: Yes.

O: But that's no reason . . .

W: It's obvious that she doesn't want someone else to write about me.

O: I understand that. It's human.

W: E. judges differently. He wrote me that he does not object to what you are doing.

O: You mentioned once that he also tapes your conversations. One would not expect him not to mind our conversations.

W: Apparently he doesn't. . . . And besides, what he tapes won't be published for I don't know how long . . . fifty years.

O: But he won't be alive then.

W: Yes, precisely, when he's no longer alive. He said it had been stipulated that Freud's patients would be questioned, and it is the practice of the Freud archive where he works that it won't be published until later.

O: Well, he's a physician, so things are more difficult for him. The obligations of the doctor/patient relationship aren't binding on me and the basis of our relationship is different. Yet I find E.'s attitude impressive.

W: That he is so objective. . . . Well, I have to tell you what shows him in a good light and what doesn't, don't I? He said that the truth is important. But Gardiner understood it differently. What has been written has been written, and that's that.

O: But E. may believe that the truth is on his tapes.

W: He does not seem to be that petty. All right now, I'll be perfectly frank with you. What you told me once, that you had gonorrhea, you did that very skillfully. That's how you get a certain identification on my side, identification with you. And on the other hand, it somehow freed me of that prohibition. I am much too old, of course, for that to have any practical consequences, you understand? If I were twenty or thirty years younger, that might be the cure. . . .

You understand? Because we are equals in that respect. You tell me something that actually shows you in an unfavorable light. You trust me. That should have happened earlier, you understand? So, here's my conclusion: Knowledge and memory, knowledge and interpretation, aren't enough. There must be some additional experience. And that experience didn't occur. Or, if you wish, we might say it came but it was already too late. That you had this idea . . . Another woman doesn't talk about that sort of thing. But you told me that story about the gonorrhea, didn't you?

O: Yes, but why shouldn't I tell you?

W: Very well, that's the way you are, but others think differently. There's something not the way it should be. This is the way it was: Therese died and she wrote in her farewell letter: "Marry a decent woman and go to Sister"—I forget her name—"and seek her advice, and don't become attached to some slut because that could be the end of you." She had understood the important thing.

O: That you feel drawn to sluts?

W: Yes, she understood that that's where the danger lies. When I am friends with a decent woman, I can marry and live in some fashion. But there's nothing to be done with a slut. Because sluts . . . either they demand money from you all the time or who knows what. . . . Well, and that's what happened, and so I find myself in an awful situation with this friend. Should I tell you about it?

O: Why not? But in what way is she a slut?

W: Isn't it being a slut when the woman gets married and tells me nothing about it?

O: What? She got married . . .

W: She got married and told me nothing about it and kept coming to see me the whole time. Had she said that she had got married, I would have stopped seeing her. But then she divorced him. All right, *slut,* what does *slut* mean? The word isn't attractive. Couldn't we find a better one, one that isn't so offensive?

Twice I associated with impossible women, and with the first, things turned out all right. I even wrote about it, I was lucky, I got away from her, but I was stupid and gave that material to a certain Cermak, who was a friend of mine and with whom I then had a falling out. And I can hardly call him on the phone now and ask, "Do you still have that material?" I thought I'd give it to you. S. also advised against it; I shouldn't take any steps. It happened ten years ago. But I could tell you about it briefly. Luckily, things turned out all right. You'll see how everything is chance. And then I got involved with this other one and I can't get away from her because the woman has nothing. She has no pension, no health insurance, and she is ill. . . . There's something wrong with her heart, he has angina pectoris, there is something the matter with her kidneys, with her gallbladder, and she has diabetes. What can you do? And now she says she has cancer. I don't know if it's true, of course.

And she constantly torments me with reproaches and wants me to marry her. One cannot marry this woman, she is a serious psychopath. I don't even know what I should talk to her about. It's always the same thing that interests her. We pass a house and she says, "I wouldn't mind having a house like that. . . ." She makes demands that are altogether absurd, and she has no health insurance, no pension, is ill, and I have been her lover for twenty-five years, as it were. I only see her on Sundays. The whole relationship is crazy and impossible. It is a catastrophe, the whole thing. There've been times when I've wished they'd take me to America. But they don't want to. And anyway, what would I do in America?

O: You want to go to America because of this woman?

W: Well yes, because of this woman, because it's impossible.

O: And the man she married?

W: But she has had two divorces!

O: And she doesn't get anything from those men?

W: Nothing. She is so clever, when people are standing in line at the movies or the theater for tickets, she simply walks up and says, "I ordered tickets," and they give them to her. You'd think she's really clever. She has no interests, nothing. She says she has read a great deal. But then I saw what was on her shelves, it isn't true. She is only interested in material things, and she has no health insurance. . . . I must tell you this, you must have an overview. . . .

O: But when she got married, you could have separated from her.

W: But she didn't tell me until she was divorced again.

O: But she changed her name.

W: She came to me and told me nothing. I don't know how long that marriage lasted. In any event, she was already divorced again when she told me the name, the new name.

O: And in spite of that she visited you?

W: She came to my place in spite of it.

O: And demanded money from you?

W: Not at that time. But with this book, I made a terrible mistake. I earned some money from it and gave her a great deal.

O: But she doesn't know where you got the money?

W: No, she knows nothing about the book. And I am not going to tell her either, otherwise she will think it pays millions. She says to me, "Curt Jurgens gave his wife such and such an amount. You would not have done that." . . . Constant reproaches. Everything is my fault. I never had any idea that there are people like that, women who are so impossible in every sense.

O: Of course there are.

W: E. writes, "Let her scold, let her rage, what of it?" It's easy for him to talk. . . . But if that woman is constantly causing scandals like one time . . . We were quarreling on the street and people were already calling the police—that sort of thing is unacceptable. Perhaps you could give me some advice. S. once said, "Men are stupid."

O: There's only one advice one can give, and that is that you dissociate yourself from that woman.

W: S. says that if it didn't work back then when I broke with her and then took up with her again, there's no hope that it can be ended now. I told Gardiner that and she said, although she doesn't know much about this story—I only told her that there's a woman who pursues me with demands—that S. shouldn't have said that. One cannot assert, "He made up with her once, so now he'll have to stay with that woman for the rest of his life."

O: Gardiner is right there.

W: She is right. But he always said, "It'll work out, it'll work out." Well, it's embarrassing to me too. I see him now. I pay nothing. And he is a very nice fellow.

O: S.?

W: Yes. But he said, "If it didn't work back then, it won't change now." There were a few occasions when I could have broken with her. But this idea that S. expressed, that this is the way it has to remain, prevented me. Instead of doing me some good, psychoanalysts did me harm. Please, I am telling you this confidentially, it is . . . I see S. and then E. arrives and does psychoanalysis with me for three weeks, surely that's . . . What about transference in a situation like that? There must be transference on the part of the patient. That must be the father complex. But when he is given advice by ten people, it is the way it once said in the newspaper: "Does relying on others mean that one is truly forsaken?"

O: What does E. tell you to do?

W: I wrote him that the two of us get together. And he said I should go to your place.

O: E. said that?

W: Yes. Of course, I no longer write Gardiner anything because I realize that there's something that doesn't suit her.

O: And S.?

W: In the end, he felt it was a diversion for me, talking to you. But Gardiner is against it. I am not going to write her anything more about you.

O: And what does E. say about your lady friend?

W: That's a relevant question. What does E. say? I think S. hit the nail on the head. E: "Now we can have a heart to heart talk, that's good, everything is all right." S. said about that, "He thinks you are healthier than you are." That was the theory, that Freud had cured me 100 percent. You see, my memoirs, the entire book is based on that. And that's why Gardiner recommended that I write memoirs. To show the world how Freud had cured a seriously ill person. And then the reviews of this book: "The Wolf-Man lost contact with other human beings." That's all false too. Contact was never lost. On the contrary, contact with others was too close, everything turned into conflict. It's all false.

Well, well, going to America . . . who would take me, who would bother with me? It costs money, doesn't it? At first E. wrote, I still have the letter: "Friends in America will do everything for the Wolf-Man and if he absolutely insists on coming to America, he can come to America. But I don't know whether he will feel good." Well, I showed him the letter and he said, "That's a fantasy."

O: You don't know English and the strange environment. . . .

W: Yes, of course, it was a fantasy. But here's what E. thinks: I should act like a normal person. A healthy person would perhaps have the strength to finally break with that woman. But it isn't much, a few hours on Sundays, E. says, let her rant and rave, I should put up with all of that. What's so terrible about it? But where is it all going to end?

O: What was it that attracted you about that woman? Did she have such a strong sexual attraction for you?

W: She had sexual attraction. And the absurd thing is that the sexual attraction wasn't really all that strong.

O: Oh?

W: In the beginning, perhaps, but then it decreased. In any event, this woman is . . . How am I to describe it to you? This woman is always ready to quarrel. That's her element. To slander, to berate others, to feel the victim . . . that all kinds of injustices were perpetrated against her. And everywhere she goes she must have her way. Even in restaurants: her portion is so small, the person at the next table had a larger one. Then she has a heart ailment and says, "The air is bad." Or, "It smells of mothballs, that coat hanging there, it smells of mothballs." She can't stand it, the window has to be opened. But the waiter says, "We can't do that, there are other people here, there's a draft. . . ."

I cannot describe to you how awful this woman is. There's nothing you can talk to her about. And what should I talk to her about? I once told her that an acquaintance of mine had two positions, one in a ministry, another in a literary society. The society didn't care for his views and didn't want him to do anything, but he was paid regardless. The amounts weren't large. I simply tell you this because of that woman. She said immediately, "One should print that in the newspaper." Such an injustice. The fellow doesn't do anything. There's nothing you can say to her, she immediately starts threatening.

O: How terrible.

W: Now you see, you understand me. I knew you'd understand me. Men don't understand it.

O: Who doesn't understand it?

W: Men don't understand because they adopt a purely male point of view. What does S. say? "You are not obliged to give her anything. You don't owe her anything whatever. She is not a small child, after all. She got involved with you, that's her business." And as regards the pension . . . Well, you see, I am not a member of the Social Democratic party, but my views are rather socialist. Because I tell myself: of course it is unjust that some have money and others don't. How can one take the opposite position? It's not possible. But you see, S. is a count, and E. is well off. Those people don't understand.

But you, a woman, will perhaps understand: I feel a certain obligation, because I have been with this woman for such a long time. And she really is ill, isn't she? But the terrible thing is, one cannot talk to this woman. She wanted to report me to the police. She will make her case public—this injustice, this terrible viciousness, what I did to her because I was so old and she still so young. The public must hear about this; it must be shown on television. What do you say to such a woman? You can't talk to her. I sit there like an idiot and keep my mouth shut. And she says, "You are having another one of your spells."

O: What sort of spells?

W: A depression.

O: I see.

W: One cannot explain to her what a depression is. And she's not really stupid. No, she isn't stupid. But she has such a closed mind, you know, in the small circle in which she moves; she can function only in this small circle. She can go to the window and say, "I ordered tickets," and in fact she never did. She's very good at things like that. She went to a business school although it was nothing more than a secondary school. But it is called *Akademie,* so she's an academician, of course, and her mother also told me how talented she is and so on, and so well educated, you understand. But one cannot talk to that woman. Whatever one says, her immediate comment is, "That should be brought to public notice." So, what's your opinion?

O: It's completely crazy, mad.

W: Well, and what does S. say? "A serious psychopath with paranoid ideas." Wherever she goes, she feels persecuted. She feels disadvantaged by fate.

O: Was she always like that?

W: No, she wasn't like that at first. But now she's sixty. She looks much younger, in spite of all her illnesses. She goes to the movies, and on top of that, she insists on going to the theater, the Raimundtheater.

O: Does she go alone?

W: Alone. I got out of the habit. Well, she is ill, deathly ill is her every other word. I merely told you so that you get a feel for the kind of person I am close to. I don't know how I'll get out of it. But I still have to tell you about the first one, my first experience. Is it already late?

O: No.

W: I don't want to leave so soon, otherwise we won't make any progress. I described my first experience, but I turned it over to this Cermak fellow. We have drifted so far apart, there would be no point in looking him up. He would say, "Now you need me and want a reconciliation." He has written a book that he even sent to Roosevelt's wife. Well, he was a dreamer!

O: What does he do?

W: He's a writer. But he has written only this one book and it was not successful. He had to pay part of the costs. Here's what happened: there was a certain Countess Saint Quentin in the Cottage.* She came from Odessa although it is an Austrian family. The father had a position as director of an industrial enterprise in Odessa and that's why she grew up in Russia. They speak Russian like Russians. There are two sisters. And then there was also a brother who was a big Nazi and who died in an accident, no one knows how. During the war, he was in a plane, and when the plane landed, he was gone. No one knows how he could have fallen out of that plane. A very odd affair. This Saint Quentin woman, in any event, said after my wife's death that she would introduce me to this Cermak because his wife had also killed herself. He was the only person who understood something about those things.

O: When did his wife kill herself?

W: Much earlier, ten years earlier.

O: And this Saint Quentin thought that because both women had killed themselves . . .

W: Yes, that he would feel sympathy.

O: Did he?

---

* A sanatorium in Vienna.

W: He understood immediately. He had gone through it and he warned me. He warned me hundreds of times. Because he also became ill and also became the slave of a woman. Unfortunately, I didn't take his advice. But he was interesting to talk to. The most important thing for him was to be successful with women. He considered that more important than anything else. He was tall, and had a rather good figure. He wasn't handsome, but he was lucky with women. And those states that occur after a suicide, he somehow judged them correctly.

He told me how he fell into that slavish dependence on a woman. And it lasted until he caught her with another man, and then it passed. And the second time, he was married to a French woman who owned a café in the 1st District. He was constantly unfaithful to her and involved with all sorts of women. It was a marriage of convenience because the woman was wealthy. She was the proprietress of this café. During the war, people didn't have enough to eat. Occasionally, when I went there, she would make me something to eat. Then she must have found out because she kept complaining that she wanted to be repatriated. Back to France. But then there was a reconciliation, I believe. I'll quickly tell you the whole story, it went on for a few years but ended well. . . .

O: And that was during the war?

W: That's the life I led after the death of my wife. Nothing but stupidities. And now I find myself with this impossible person on my hands.

O: She was the first woman after the death of Therese?

W: After the death of Therese, there was a woman, a very young girl. I can bring you a picture of her if you like. She was pretty, blonde and pretty. And it ended well. Chance intervened so that I could get rid of her. But she was ten times better than this one. And then I got involved with this woman. And all because of my carelessness and my stupidity.

I saw this woman at the tailor's. You know that the tailor played an important role in my life. Normally, when I spoke to a strange woman—I am speaking very frankly to you—and then went to a hotel with her, I didn't give her my name or address. And that's something I should have thought of, that I was at the tailor's and that he knew my name and address. And that didn't occur to me, you see. She was made up, blonde—no, dyed blonde—I found her fairly attractive. And I waited outside until she came out and then we went to a café and her mother joined us. What can I tell you?

O: She went to bed with you right away?

W: She went to bed right away. I knew a hotel. Today, when I walk past that hotel, I feel sick. The hotel in which I started something with this woman! My God, it's terrible! Here I sit and don't know what to do about this woman. We agreed that I would leave a letter in a nearby café when we would meet again. If she had not known my address, I would just have gone two or three times, that would have been enough. Suddenly, she calls me on the phone.

O: At the insurance company?

W: At the insurance company. And the first one, she also called. I felt so embarrassed because the doorman told me that she had brought something for me because it was so difficult getting food. In any case, I thought, very well, I have no one. . . . I should have said right away: "Please don't call me. Private conversations aren't allowed here," and I should have put down the receiver then and there. And I didn't do that. So she arranged that we would see each other every two or three weeks, and I went to the hotel with her. And that was all there was to that liaison. Not at first. Until things changed completely and I spent Sundays with her, and so on. Well, I have to tell you the whole story so you get the detail. I'll have to tell you that.

O: Did it never bother you that when you went to bed with a woman, she'd take money from you?

W: I found it normal.

O: You thought there was nothing wrong with it?

W: She has nothing. She has to live, after all.

O: I find the whole thing strange, I must admit. . . . The least I would have expected from analysis is that it would free you of this tie to primitive women.

W: Well, you can see that Freud did not free me.

O: That's really the least one would expect, that you would find a woman that suits you.

W: You see, my wife guessed it. She wrote it in her farewell letter. I must say, talking to you is not the same thing as talking to S. He has less time for me. . . . Then this woman also has a cleanliness complex. The fuss she makes if there's a spot someplace or it smells of mothballs. . . . Surely that's the least, that I should have been rid of that complex, don't you think?

O: I'd say so.

W: The least one would have expected! He did not cure me of that complex. On the contrary. Because I put such stress on the sexual . . .

O: You mean you did that?

W: Well, of course, Freud praised the sexual to the skies. He extolled the sexual.

O: Why do you say that? I don't understand.

W: Look, it's not possible to give sexual things free rein. You can see by my example what that leads to.

O: How so? Did you give your sexual drives such free rein?

W: Pretty much so.

O: Really? I wonder. I don't really have that impression.

W: Well, perhaps it was harmless from a modern point of view. . . .

O: You seem to believe that there is a difference as regards the sexual between an intellectual woman and a more primitive one, a slut, say.

W: But that was the false idea!

O: It's completely false.

W: That was due to the sister complex. You said quite correctly that I should at the very least have been cured of that. It ruins one's entire life. One becomes involved with impossible women and has to put up with everything that goes along with that. And for someone who is neurotic to begin with, it's the worst thing there is. That's something I want to tell you about now. Do we have the time?

O: Of course.

W: You agree, don't you, that it would be embarrassing for me to call this Cermak on the phone and say, "Do you still have it?" Then he'll say, "Now you need me, now you call me." And I must admit, had I followed his advice, none of this would have happened.

O: How so? Did he know your friend?

W: He did not know her, but he warned me. I'll tell you: it was a girl, early twenties, pretty. And she didn't look like a prostitute. Was simply dressed. Everything. I walked up to her and started talking. She went to the hotel with me. And then we agreed that I would write her when I wanted to see her again. I did not give her my address. But apparently I did later, after all. In any event, I met her once or twice a month, and everything would have been fine. It didn't cost much and she was nice and there was sexual satisfaction too. Everything would have been all right.

Well, I started committing stupidities again. I went on vacation. . . . It was November or December when I first met her. Then, the following spring, I went on vacation and thought, why not go on vacation with this girl? I suggested it to her and we went to Neusiedler Lake. I felt right away, you did something really stupid that you and this girl . . .

O: But why?

W: She was modest. Suddenly, she started making demands, buying things. . . . She was completely uneducated and primitive but had, oddly enough, some understanding of literature. In the afternoon, she ordered wine to be brought up to the room and read, always read books. I don't know whether you know that novel of Goncharov's, it is one of the best Russian novels. . . .

O: By whom?.

W: The writer's name is Goncharov. He wrote a book in which he describes a man called Oblomov who owns an estate, lives only in his imagination, and is incapable of doing anything whatever. Actually, this novel—it's called *Oblomov*—is rather boring because nothing happens. He then courts a woman, but there is a German who wants to prevent the marriage and who is energetic and rational. I think it's the only Russian novel in which a German is glorified. Well, the German marries the woman; he's in love with her. But the entire book has no action, so one needs a certain literary understanding. Well, just imagine—it's a thick book—she liked it. She understood.

But then there was this money business. She constantly wanted money. Though compared to what this person is costing me now, those were ridiculous amounts. She had an illegitimate son in Yugoslavia for whom she needed money. For the son. At least the purpose was decent. She always said, "Fifty schillings," and another fifty the following week. In those days, money was still worth more and I had saved a little.

We knew a captain with whom both of us were good friends. Of course, being a captain, he was very conservative, but that didn't bother me. He was wild about the Nazis and then the Nazis marched in, he came to me and said, "You can rest assured now. No one will take this place away from you," although no one had tried. He was enthusiastic, as I say. But he didn't join the party. And what was the consequence? He wasn't promoted, of course. He came to dinner fairly frequently and conducted himself in such a way that one thought he would be arrested at any moment. That's how much of a Nazi enemy he became, for personal reasons.

I told you about this—Gretl was her name—about this Gretl. Gretl Falland. I'd say to her, "What a beautiful name you have." And she'd tell me that she had been called a Gothic type. Well, probably blonde and Nordic. The captain said: "You'll never get rid of her. She'll stick with you all your life!" It looked like that, but it turned out all right. In any case, I saw, my God, there's not much you can do with this woman. You committed a stupidity. And then I put an end to it, as it were.

O: And what did she say?

W: I find that funny. It didn't suit her, of course. In any event, I had understood that this couldn't go on indefinitely and had decided to leave her. Before that, I had rented a room for her in Vienna. Although they weren't large amounts, they weren't inconsequential for me. I threatened her with the police. Then she came back one more time, I believe that was the last time. That didn't suit my housekeeper, who had had hopes that I would marry her.

O: Tiny? She had hopes?

W: Yes, she did, that I would marry her. She never said anything. But my mother told me that she wanted to kill herself because of this Gretl. But she didn't say anything to me. In any event, it was a tragedy for Tiny. Gretl at least had some understanding for my paintings.

O: And your present friend doesn't?

W: None whatever. On the contrary. She reproached me for showing her paintings after intercourse. Awful.

O: Funny.

W: I don't know, perhaps there's a desire in me to get involved with crazy women. I don't know what's behind it. In any event, this is the way it ended with Gretl: I get a letter . . . You know, the things she'd tell me at times, I'd think she wasn't normal. She told me, for example, that she was standing on a bridge once, looking into the water. A man came up to her and asked, "What's wrong?" She: "I have no money." He gave her 100 schillings and walked on. You know who that man was? It was . . . I don't remember the name, a well-known composer. I thought to myself, all that sounds rather odd. . . .

Suddenly I get a letter, from where? From the hospital for venereal diseases in Klosterneuburg. Here's what she wrote me: "I am ill and am having a malaria treatment (*laughs*). But when I get well, I am going to work, I know that." I thought to myself, very well, we'll see what you'll do. Whether you will work the way you have been working up to this time.

O: She was a regular prostitute?

W: No, she was no prostitute, she was a knitter.

O: Oh?

W: She didn't even live in Vienna but somewhere nearby.

O: A little while ago, you said something. . . . And she immediately went to the hotel with you. . . .

W: No, she was no prostitute. She just went with me. That doesn't mean that she had to be a prostitute. She was a knitter, she knitted. I went to the hospital for venereal diseases. She had written that she was there for a malaria treatment, but I knew what was what. You know, the malaria treatment for syphilis. And I am supposed to send her money.

Another person would have had no pity for the woman. I cannot be that way. I couldn't make myself say at the time, all right, she has venereal disease and so on, I won't send her anything. I felt sorry for her and went out to Klosterneuburg. Of course, the advice I had been given up to that moment had been perfectly correct, that I break off with her.

O: Cermak advised that?

W: Cermak had had a very similar experience after the death of his wife. He fell under the influence of a woman who wasn't from the lower classes, she was a teacher even, the daughter of a professor, but she was unfaithful to him. And the moment he discovered that she was unfaithful, he could no longer do without her. Otherwise, he was really a rather energetic individual. But you see that suicide has certain consequences. Why could he before? Why could he before? You see, there's a connection somewhere.

What was to be done? I felt sorry for Gretl. I wanted to visit her. So I went out there. The nurse said to me, "She had forged identification papers, her name isn't Gretl Falland but Karoline Müller." Then the nurse said . . . you see how important it is, giving the right advice at the right time. The nurse saved me from her. She said, "Don't concern yourself any further with that Müller woman." That made such an impression on me that I thought, perhaps it is better if you don't visit her. I thought, I'll talk to the physician. So I ask the nurse, "Can I see the doctor?" She says: "Yes, but he's in Vienna. He is in charge of a clinic. I can give you the address." She gave me the address and I went to see him.

And he was enthusiastic about Gretl. He says to me: "Yes, you know, that's a decent family, the father is a worker. She's just the blacksheep in the family. We want to make a decent human being of her," and so on. "She's in good hands here, we'll take care of her." I say, "I rented a room for her." He says: "Don't keep it. This is much more important, don't interfere. Don't send her money. You needn't concern yourself. We'll make a decent human being of her."

When he talked like that, I thought, all right, I might spoil everything. I sent no money and heard nothing further from her. And then, many years later, I see her in a pharmacy in Währingerstrasse. She was lowering the blinds, this Gretl or Karoline, she was lowering the blinds. I talked to her and we agreed to meet in a café. I met her and she told me what she was doing and that she was working in that pharmacy. And her son was also taking care of her, and that I should come visit her sometime and have a look at the paintings.

O: She painted?

W: No, my paintings.

O: You had given them to her?

W: I had given them to her and she had given one of them to the head nurse because she had liked it so much. And she still had the other paintings, and I should visit her. We agreed on a time and she told me that there was a man who wanted to marry her but that he wasn't working and that she wanted to leave him. And the son was grown up and helping her. So she had become a decent woman.

O: Did you see her again?

W: I said, "I'll come see you and look at the paintings." Then I thought, perhaps it's better I don't go, and I didn't. So I've told you a story, you see, I was lucky that time. And then I get involved with a woman, that one . . . this first episode, it's a very interesting thing how, through chance . . . and it is chance that the physician took care of her. She had made an impression on him, he spoke enthusiastically about her, and she was pretty.

You drew the right conclusion, which the psychoanalysts don't want to do. They don't want to recognize it. I said to E: "Look, what a sad end." And what does it mean, I've been completely cured? And he said, "But what do you want, you are cured." But that's something one cannot expect of any physician, that he cures one forever. Then he said that so many years had already passed and that I was already so old, and that the one thing had nothing to do with the other. But when we thing logically, we have to agree with what you said: at the very least, I should have been freed of the complex. With Therese, Freud said, I had looked for something bad because she was no more than a nurse, and that I had received something very good because she was a decent person. I would never have believed that I would end like this. And now I fell into the hands of such an impossible individual. And the terrible thing is . . . this Gretl told me, she was very much against the Nazis. . . . She said once, "The only good party is the Communist party." But she also said, "it's just red rabble." What was I about to tell you?

O: What Gretl had said.

W: Yes, well, she was very much against the Nazis. But it seems she did become friends with some Nazi, a Nazi official. And then she told me about another girl who was in touch with the French or the English and it was discovered somehow. And then she said, "She did all that for finery."

O: For what?

W: For finery. You see, that's the most terrible thing about this woman, that she is so much interested in finery. She demands money for her health and then she buys clothes. And yet she is sixty years old and hates old women. It seems she feels she's a teenager. So this Gretl said, "Everything because of finery, because of clothes." And I can see in the case of Luise what it means when a woman really goes after that sort of thing. Gretl didn't do that. She dressed simply, and the money was for the son. That was understandable. But this one? What does she need all that money for?

O: She's forever buying clothes?

W: Now she has lost weight. And altering things costs more than buying them new.

O: And you go along with all that?

W: As you see, unfortunately. But I don't know how it's all going to end.

O: Can you afford it?

W: I got money from the book.

O: And all the money you got . . . you spent nothing on yourself, you gave it all to your friend?

W: Only she benefited, really. I was so restless at home, and so I gave her the money. I did make that mistake.

O: But she is never satisfied?

W: No, never. And now it's always the same thing: "What am I going to do when you die?" And I console her. E. sends me small amounts of money for her.

O: He sends you money? For what?

W: For that woman.

O: He helps you for humanitarian reasons, or did you give him something for the archive?

W: I gave him quite a few of my paintings.

O: And the archive pays for them, or does E. pay out of his own pocket?

W: The archive.

O: Regularly?

W: Yes.

O: So you actually get a kind of pension from the Freud archive.

W: . . . which does me no good, it's for the woman. If they sent it to me, and I kept it, I could live quite well.

O: But surely you cannot blame the archive. It's your fault.

W: Of course it isn't the fault of the archive. I depend on them financially because I couldn't give her that much from my pension. Whatever view I take of it, it's a terrible situation, you can see that everything is full of conflict. And that also influences how I feel. This dependence on America, whether E. sends it, isn't pleasant either. I depend on question marks. How long will he continue sending something? How long can I continue giving that woman something?

O: And Luise knows about this?

W: She knows about the archive. I haven't told her anything about the book. But begging isn't pleasant either. And it is not a pleasant feeling that they send me something because they feel compassion for the woman.

O: Will she get something after your death?

W: I'm uncertain. At times, E. says one thing, at others another. So a dependence on E. has arisen, and so it drags on. And I receive free treatment. A whole number of dependencies arise, and that's harmful, of course. It harms the ego, I'd say.

O: The motive is incomprehensible to me. What interest would they have in keeping you dependent?

W: That's easy to understand. E. wants to keep track of the case that has become so famous—Freud's most famous case—and see how it ends.

O: And you are actually given the money for allowing yourself to be observed as long as you live?

W: He helped me with that money for Luise. He meant well; one cannot really reproach him. But it wasn't reasonable. Either one is in treatment or the treatment is over and one must leave the person alone. Contradictions also develop. E. has one opinion, S. another, and Gardiner a third. . . . One becomes involved in a labyrinth of dependencies that contradict each other.

O: What interest does S. have, for example, in seeing you once a week?

W: E. asked him to, and he wants to keep on the good side of the archive. So he took it on. Perhaps he'll also write something, I don't know. . . .

O: A few years back, he asked 200 or 250 schillings per hour.

W: You don't say. . . . Didn't you tell me once I should marry Luise?

O: Me? I don't remember. Do you think that she would be more likely then to get money after your death?

W: No, but she can't ask for more than that I marry her.

O: That's true.

W: But marrying such an individual is difficult when one doesn't get along with the person, cannot talk, cannot agree, yet is married. Then one has even more obligations. As things are now, I have no legal obligations. And these eternal quarrels . . .

O: That's risky. Now you want to marry after all?

W: But you said once . . .

O: One could consider it as a theoretical possibility: Suppose you did marry?

W: Well, after all, marrying someone, there are additional responsibilities that the person will then take advantage of. She is someone who stops at nothing.

But there isn't enough money. She tells me about the increase in prices, and keeps talking about inflation. Everything is becoming more expensive, one has to spend every penny. I tell you, it's a martyrdom. The woman always wants to have her way. When the window is open, it must be closed because there's a draft. When it is closed, it must be opened because she is suffocating, she is getting no air. And the coat smells of mothballs. She is forever making demands. She constantly wants something and nothing one does suits her.

O: Do you ever take her anywhere?

W: But of course. We go to the movies.

O: Aren't you embarrassed when she behaves like that?

W: Of course. What should I do? I am in a situation . . . I will really have to tell you sometime how it all started. Because you, being a woman, think differently, perhaps. . . . But you see, I committed one stupidity after the other. And it can all be attributed to the sister complex. Gardiner ignored all these matters—not that I told her all that much. Toward the end, I said something to her and she answered: "Well, you don't speak English. America is not for you. Germany is the only place." Whom should I go to in Germany? So, I told you the story that turned out well. She never got in touch with me again, and had money for the son. Not for finery. But a woman who is ill, has no insurance, and wants to be dressed in the latest fashion besides, is terrible.

O: It seems she always found men who financed her.

W: Well, she was married twice. And she probably had men besides. She had a heart ailment from childhood on; she didn't have to do gymnastics at school. And the Nazis also let her go because of her heart. But if she can go to the movies and the theater in the evening, she can't be all that ill.

O: She has to parade her clothes. And she sometimes comes to your apartment?

W: It's unnatural, of course, that I really don't want her to come. She used to come fairly often. Sometimes I went to see her, when her mother was still alive. She still reproaches me for that. "People said I was a slut because you came." I ruined her reputation. She's the most beautiful and most proper woman in all Vienna. You see, there's megalomania on top of everything else. What was bad was this: pus had formed in her teeth, so her teeth were pulled, and suddenly she really did have something wrong with her heart. She could hardly walk. Since that time, it's been ten years now, she hasn't visited me because she couldn't climb the stairs. But she could come now because her heart has improved. But I don't want her to. What should I do with her? That offends her, of course. . . . I cannot explain to her what a depression is, she doesn't understand it. Depressions are something wealthy people have, people who are well off.

O: She has no depressions?

W: Then she's proud, too: "I am not nervous, my hand doesn't shake." . . . She has the idea that you must be a fool to have depressions. . . . An entirely primitive idea. And that kind of thing happens to someone whose psychological condition causes him difficulties. . . . Such a person is the most unsuitable and the most impossible you can imagine. Something less suitable than this woman is impossible to imagine.

Sexuality, Money, Masochism

WOLF-MAN: Please, so I don't forget, I don't have your local telephone number. I only have the number of your paper (*pulls a slip of paper from his breast pocket*). If you will be so kind and write down your telephone number. Something might come up. Now, with winter about to set in . . . Next time, we'll have to discuss how we are going to do it. Because that friend of mine became very ill ten years ago. Since that time, she no longer visits me. She would like to, but I don't let her in. But she threatens that she'll come. But it isn't likely that she will.

OBHOLZER: She threatens she'll come?

W: Yes, she threatens. She is unhappy that I don't invite her. It's understandable, wouldn't you say? I have to tell you about these things, otherwise you won't know what situation I'm in. What a story. You know, in Russia, the father's name is added. And Tolstoi wrote a theory how this Ivan Ilyich feels, and how he has the feeling that everything in life was for nothing. A sad affair, certainly. . . . So that's your phone number! Thank you. There might be a day when I'll be unable to come. You have associated yourself with a wreck and have to bear the consequences.

What I wanted to say, you won't discuss this affair concerning my friend, my private affair, with anyone, of course. I confided it to you; it is a very disagreeable matter. It was carelessness on my part, of course, that I started speaking to this woman. Now you see what has developed. It was a stupidity, and that's what annoys me. And once, I had completely broken with her, and then I ran into her, and it started again. There was a reconciliation, and there shouldn't have been. But that cannot be helped now. What to do?

O: After so many years, it's difficult, of course.

W: Yes, because it's been going on for so many years and because she is ill, those are two things . . .

O: And what is she to do when you are no longer alive?

W: That's another problem, of course. We can discuss that problem another time. Perhaps you can give me some advice.

O: What should I advise you?

W: Well, perhaps when I tell you about this in greater detail. You still know too little.

O: When you were being treated by Freud and he kept coming back to sexuality, didn't that put you off? Surely that wasn't customary in your family.

W: The point of psychoanalysis is that one should not suppress one's drives. That must please everyone. It's disburdening, to an extent.

O: And you found it perfectly normal to discuss sexual problems with a physician?

W: Why not? You and I discuss them too.

O: Well, it's almost sixty years later. In 1910, things were different.

W: It impressed me. It was revolutionary. I had a colleague at the office, a certain Captain Leta, a first-rate mathematician. When one visited him, he would always give one a problem to solve. He knew Einstein's theory of relativity well. He was of Hungarian descent, his father was the adjutant of Emperor Franz Josef's brother, the younger brother, his name was Viktor Ludwig or Ludwig Viktor, and he was homosexual. He was at the central baths once and wanted to start something with a boy, and Emperor Franz Joseph heard about it. He was reduced in rank and then went to live somewhere in Ischl. But this Captain Leta—since we are discussing sexual matters now—was always ill. Walking was difficult for him. Then he died miserably of cancer. He once gave me his medical history to read. It said, "Syphilis in 1911." But there was no sign of it when you looked at him. That really is the disease I have always feared most. I don't know, for a while there was no venereal disease in Vienna, and then it came back.

O: Yes, but the percentage is very small. You said that Freud made you less inhibited, that Freud was in favor of one's being less inhibited.

W: The whole doctrine is based on the assumption that one gets a neurosis through repression. That allows the inference that one should impose no restraints on oneself.

O: When I asked you in what way you became less inhibited, you said, "Well, compared to today, it wasn't all that much."

W: Of course, naturally.

O: And what ideas did people have before? Were you really not supposed to go to bed with someone or to masturbate? What were the ideas, and in what sense did you become less inhibited.

W: You see that I talked to women and went to hotels with them.

O: And one really shouldn't do that?

W: One really shouldn't do that.

O: What was permitted?

W: It's difficult to say. One had to decide for oneself. You see, in the past, there was the veto, no sexual intercourse. When I came to Vienna, a brochure—a publication of the State Medical Insurance—came to my attention which said, "Avoid extramarital intercourse." There was a drawing of a woman sitting there, crying bitterly. It seems she contracted a disease. I still remember that picture. It said, "If you don't avoid it, you'll get ill." That's about the way it was. At the time, those diseases were quite widespread.

O: And what was the attitude toward masturbation?

W: Well, my God, people said that one became insane, that it is very dangerous, that it is harmful. And when I first saw Freud, he said, "Well, that's an exaggeration. It isn't that serious."

O: Did Freud advocate masturbation?

W: No, no, that's putting it too strongly. He viewed it as harmless. But it was generally considered to be dangerous. It has been said about Gogol that he indulged in masturbation to such an extent that he died of it. I've heard that there was a movie about him on television and that it said that he had syphilis. I find that difficult to believe because in Russia, people said that he died of masturbation. I don't know, of course, what really happened. Allegedly, he had no relations whatever with women.

O: And this sentence of yours that Mack quotes, is that sentence

correct or not? She writes that you said, "Of course, I only masturbated regularly on the big holidays."[1]

W: I have no idea what that is supposed to mean.

O: But that's what she writes.

W: That I said that?

O: Yes, "Of course, I only masturbated on the big holidays."

W: No such thing. That would be stupid. What does that have to do
with holidays?

O: She writes that you felt a special way about holidays.

W: Well, she was fantasizing. There's no such thing, what silliness.
Mack also invented things occasionally.

O: So you take no responsibility for this sentence?

W: No, I cannot have said something like that.

O: Yet that's what she writes. Didn't you read it?

W: No, I don't remember. What she wrote there is stupid.

O: How so? I found it quite funny.

W: It's absurd (*laughs*).

O: Why? What if you did?

W: When I was seeing her, I was with Therese. I had no need to
masturbate.

O: What do you mean? There are people who masturbate nonetheless.

W: But that's primarily young people who haven't had the courage
to go to a woman or haven't had the opportunity.

O: One also finds it among couples. It isn't that unusual.

W: What is your attitude toward all these things? Group sex, and so
on?

O: I don't think it's for me.

W: I discussed it with Gardiner. And she said at the time, "Well,
that's nothing important. It's the reaction of puritan America."

O: I would probably be too inhibited.

W: Well, of course, you would have to be quite uninhibited. In my
time, it would have been almost impossible. Nowadays, it's a matter
of course.

O: I wouldn't go that far.

---

1. Muriel Gardiner, ed., *The Wolf-Man: With the Case of the Wolf-Man by Sigmund
Freud* (New York: Basic Books, 1971), p. 270.

W: I don't know, of course, but judging by what people write . . .

O: Well, the papers . . .

W: Now one hears less. For a while, it was the fashion.

O: And how do you feel about it?

W: I think I'd feel the way you do. I have too many inhibitions. There are certain inhibitions one should have.

O: And you only read now what Mack wrote about you?

W: Yes, yes. Before, it was published only in medical journals. I can't say that I find it pleasant that my acquaintances or some of my acquaintances should have read that.

O: What Mack writes?

W: What Mack writes and what Freud writes.

O: Well, what Freud writes—that you observed the coitus of your parents and so on—that's not so bad. What Freud wrote is perfectly sustainable, I think, the story of your childhood. As far as Mack is concerned, I don't find it quite correct that she published it. It's about you as an adult.

W: She wrote that when Freud was still alive?

O: Yes, it was published in a journal in the late twenties.

W: It only appeared in specialized periodicals.

O: Yes, but now it has been published together with your memoirs.

W: Well, and what Gardiner writes isn't so bad. She doesn't write much, after all. At first, I thought that my memoirs would appear as memoirs, without the case histories. It was Gardiner's idea. She thought that if only my memoirs were printed, no one would buy the book. In any event, if it were only my memoirs, it would not have been so unpleasant. That everyone reads those case histories . . . But there is nothing to be done about it now. I had to do what Gardiner thought best. But as it is, it's really complicated because there are these meetings—what Gardiner writes, then Freud's text and Mack's and my memoirs—it's a bit confusing. Well, what of it, and perhaps Freud's text . . . But the whole thing leaves one unsatisfied, somehow.

O: To get back to sexuality: Freud says somewhere that you preferred a certain position during intercourse, the one from behind . . .

W: Well, that was no absolute, you know . . .

O: . . . that you enjoyed it less in other positions.

W: But that also depends on the woman, how she is built. There are women where it is only possible from the front. That's happened to me.

O: There are women like that?

W: Yes. It depends on whether the vagina is more toward the front or toward the rear.

O: I see. In any event, Freud writes, "He was walking through the village which formed part of their estate, when he saw a peasant girl kneeling by the pond and employed in washing clothes in it . . ."[2]

W: Yes, I remember something of the sort, but that isn't correct, that has nothing to do with washing.

O: Well, perhaps it was something else. In any case, he thought that you involuntarily fall in love when you come across something like that. And "even his final choice of object, which played such an important part in his life, is shown by its details (though they cannot be adduced here) to have been dependent upon the same condition. . . ."[3]

W: That's incorrect.

O: How so?

W: No, it's incorrect.

O: Then why does Freud write it?

W: With Therese, if you insist on details, the first coitus was that she sat on top of me.

O: That would be the precise opposite. . . .

W: I ask myself the following: Are we sitting in judgment on psychoanalysis? (*laughs*)

O: You know, truth . . .

W: Well, that's why I come to see you, because I tell myself, truth is really the most important thing. And E. said the same thing. And my experience involves something general, not something personal. So one can take the position which E. took, that one must write the truth. In any case, you show more understanding than S. and E.

O: I am not a psychoanalyst.

W: You see, there's nothing psychoanalysts can do either. You said yourself that the sister complex at least should have disappeared. But it didn't.

O: Yes.

2. Ibid., p. 234.
3. Ibid., p. 235.

W: Now, as regards what Gardiner writes, they made a showpiece of me. The book is really intended to prove that psychoanalysts can cure such a serious case. . . . Well, it certainly helped me. Transference, what is transference? It is trust, and you can have transference without psychoanalysis. All human relations can somehow be traced back to it. Except that for Freud and psychoanalysis, it is supposed to be the means of curing people. . . . My cousin—I have a picture of him, I can't find it. An interesting photo. In it, he wears his hair long and looks like a genius. This cousin told me the following story: There was someone who imagined he had a watch inside his chest. He walked around all day long saying ticktock, ticktock. He is the clock, you understand. Finally, a physician comes, goes through a few manipulations, and suddenly—he does it so skillfully that the other one doesn't notice anything—he has a watch in his hand and says: "You see, you did have a watch in there, and I made you well. Here it is." The man got well.

And a few years later, the physician runs into this now healthy person and believes that he can be told everything. And he says: "Do you know how I cured you? I pretended that I was taking a watch out of your chest. And the other one says, "I see." And goes home, sits down, and starts again, ticktock, ticktock. My sister thought it was a joke, that it wasn't possible. I asked S, "Do you believe something like that is possible?" He says: "Yes, it is. You can cure someone in that way." This allows one to draw the following conclusion: Perhaps Freud also put things together and cured people through his constructs. . . .

Yet it is really astonishing how little one advances. Even with psychoanalysis, one doesn't get anywhere. Even S. said that, that psychoanalysis has hardly made any progress since the death of Freud. Every science develops, and I don't know whether the assertion that one unconsciously enjoys tormenting oneself isn't to be blamed.

O: What do you mean?

W: Well, you know, Freud says that when you get into an unpleasant situation, very well, you are suffering, you have depressions, and so on. But along with that, you get a certain satisfaction, a masochistic satisfaction. So that's also a point which hasn't been entirely cleared up. Because when I say—you feel good, it is a state, you feel bad, that is another, so we have feelings of happiness, good mood, bad mood, and depressions—those are different states. But when one says that in a bad state there is a satisfaction in the subconscious, one really abandons logic.

And that's what Schopenhauer means: The principle of reason does not apply to man. Man can be good in one respect and bad in another, and you get into a logical contradiction. That's the way it is in part with Freud's psychology. However bad you may feel, you are told, well, there is satisfaction in the subconscious. That means the difference stops. In logic, we have *tertium non datur,* there is no third possibility. Either *a* equals *b,* or it doesn't equal *b,* but if *a* equals *b* at one time and not at another, you don't know what's what. I don't know if you understand what I mean.

O: Is there satisfaction now, in your opinion, or not?

W: Well, you see, I am not omniscient (*laughs*). I can't say, but I don't think so. Because logic comes to a halt, and when logic comes to a halt, you cannot have a science. But this *tertium non datur,* there is no third possibility . . . actually, there is a third something, because you can feel good and you can feel bad and you can feel bad and feel satisfaction. The one cancels the other. . . . Gardiner once sent a colleague to see me who wanted me to confirm that I had adopted psychoanalysis as a kind of religion.

O: And you did?

W: No, I did not, because I did not want to get involved with that. It is difficult to answer that, that I adopted it as a religion. But it certainly is something like that. When one believes in a doctrine, it is like a religion. Take the communists . . .

O: And you believe psychoanalysis is like a religion?

W: I think so. Take people like E. who are unshakably convinced that all of it is true. It doesn't bother him that there is a contradiction. For example, masochistic satisfaction. . . . Much in psychoanalysis has been replaced by different formulations which sound scientific at least. *Love-hate,* that's what people called it, didn't they, but the psychoanalysts say *ambivalence.*

Well, what difference whether I say *love-hate* or *ambivalence*? On the contrary, *love-hate* is much better. *Ambivalence* is watered down; it's a term you use when the differences are smaller. *Ambivalence* is much weaker than *hatred* and *love.* Russian has a great many proverbs, and most of the proverbs come from the people, are folk wisdom. There's one proverb, for example, which, in translation, goes like this: It's only one step from love to hatred. That describes these states very well. And take Dostoevski. He actually talks a great deal about love-hate. Psychoanalysis really has nothing to say about it except that it gives one satisfaction. But that's no help. . . .

Psychoanalysts are a problem, no doubt about it. They aren't getting anywhere. They should at least advance a step or so. But it is always the same. They only go by what Freud discovered. By those principles and symbols, and they aren't getting beyond that. I read about Lenin, that his success was due to the fact that he was always in tune with the times. He said, for example, "All power to the Soviets." Two months later, he said, "That's no longer relevant, times have changed. We will accomplish nothing if we keep doing the same thing." But the psychoanalysts forever do the same thing. They make no progress. Today, I am more critical of psychoanalysis, as you have noticed. Do you feel more positive about it?

O: Your story doesn't precisely encourage me.

W: Doesn't precisely encourage . . . Here's what I thought: in analysis, the analyst puts the patient back into his childhood. And he experiences everything as a child. But that doesn't mean that the suffering has to pass. That's the important question: Must it pass when one remembers something? This question has not really been answered. In any event, the disciples of psychoanalysis should not have laid hold of me after Freud.

O: You mean they should have left you alone?

W: Yes, because I would have acted more independently. This outside interference has not had a good effect.

O: But you were an adult. All that happened after the Second World War. And one doesn't consider that an adult can be influenced to that degree.

W: But you see how deeply I was influenced by Freud. . . .

O: But that was so long ago.

W: These transferences rest on an erroneous assumption. If one considers someone who is no father as father, or a woman who is no sister as sister, the end result cannot be good. Those are misperceptions of reality. There is a Latvian proverb: "You won't make much headway with another's mind," or something of the sort. The Latvians are a small people and it surprises me that they have such rational ideas, that one cannot get anywhere with someone else's mind. And in psychoanalysis, you live more or less through another's mind. And that is the danger of psychoanalysis, that one is dependent on the decisions of others who are not competent and knowledgeable but who believe that they know everything and can guide one just because they are psychoanalysts.

I just happen to remember, I once told Freud a joke that I had heard in Russia. And he laughed. He really enjoyed it because the joke was so antireligious. Here's the joke: Some children are playing with muck, and an adult says, "My God, what are you doing?" The children explain that they are building a church, and the adult starts scolding them and finally says, "All right, a church. But where is the priest?" And one of the children answers, "Well, there wasn't enough muck for him." Freud liked that a lot. And now, you know, he and all of psychoanalysis are being blamed for the very thing for which he blamed religion, that it is nothing but a faith, isn't that right?

O: So you assume that the transference to Freud has persisted to this day?

W: I believe that this physician whom Gardiner sent may have been right. He presented things as if I had adopted psychoanalysis as a religion. He said that because I had been so religious as a child, transference had played an important role in my life. And perhaps it really is true that the considerable improvement is traceable to transference. But psychoanalysis is complicated. Who can make definitive and official statements? The effect was salutary, in any event. But it was not a complete cure.

O: And do you still believe in psychoanalysis?

W: I no longer believe in anything.

O: Nothing at all?

W: All right, I believe in transference. I am of the opinion, of course, that improvement can be made by transference. You see, I had a conflict with my father, internal, not external. My father dies and Freud says to me, "You were lucky that your father died, otherwise you would never have become well." So he meant, if my father had not died, I would not have managed the transference to him. You see what significance he attributed to transference. And for present-day psychoanalysis, that doesn't exist. Otherwise, E. would not explain all sorts of things to me when he knows that I am seeing S. Those two might conceivably contradict each other, after all. Whom is one to believe?

Anyway, that's something Freud always emphasized: "The most favorable thing in your situation is that you are still so young. Psychoanalysis cannot be used on older people." How can I transfer to some individual when I am twice his age? That's supposed to be my father? It's impossible. And Freud himself said that he had a woman patient—I don't know, was she seventy or sixty . . . and he said: "Psychoanalysis is no use here, but I console her a little because she is afraid of going out on the street. She thinks she'll be run over." He said that himself. I believe both of us look at the thing rather critically. I think you originally thought that you would ask me questions and that we would do the whole thing in a series of interviews. But I am doing with you what I did with Freud. I tell you what comes to mind.

O: That doesn't matter.

W: It doesn't matter. Not all that much is going to come to mind.

O: I don't think you can say that.

W: In any case, what one has to say is, either it helped or it didn't help. When someone gets radiation treatment against cancer and then dies of cancer, one cannot say that he was cured. And what E. says isn't true. He says it helped at the time but that one cannot expect it to help up to a very advanced age. That's no point of view.

O: But with cancer, a new tumor can develop.

W: I think it's difficult to compare that to psychoanalysis. What new element is supposed to come in? According to Freud, everything is already contained in childhood.

O: That's true of course.

W: What is less good about psychoanalysis is that one gets used to living according to another person's guidance. I would say that psychoanalysis weakens the ego. It may perhaps relieve the id somewhat, but the ego suffers because it submits to an authority. Don't you agree?

O: But according to Freudian theory, it shouldn't be that way. The patient himself is to have the possibility of discovering what is best for him.

W: Then there's the father complex. The psychoanalyst is the father figure.

O: But that is only an object of projection. That doesn't mean that this father figure always tells one what to do.

W: Well, there's faith behind it. . . . According to the theory, one would have to be completely free, uninfluenced. . . . Psychoanalysis should really enable one to live without a father figure. But what actually happens is that one goes on living with the father figure.

O: There are patients who get rather furious with the analyst after analysis and no longer want to have anything to do with him. That obviously wasn't true in your case.

W: No, I took the faith with me.

O: After this second education which psychoanalysis is among other things, the patient should become an adult.

W: Yes, that's how it should be. But transference creates certain difficulties, a certain misperception of reality, and one pays for that.

O: Your main problem was and continues to be women.

W: You see the problem: On the one hand, I was hypochondriacal about gonorrhea, and then there were the women. You once said that I had been lucky with women. But I couldn't exploit that luck. One of these days, I'll show you the photos of the women with whom I could easily have had an affair. But that sister complex ruined my entire life.

O: You keep being taken in by women to whom you have to give money.

W: But with this Mrs. Audersky, I still had money then, and could have done something with her and I didn't. But you see, the daughter of my acquaintance also seduced this boy—I told you about that—and he's perfectly normal. You were quite right when you said that I should at least have been freed of this complex.

O: Today, it is generally thought that it is not any specific sexual childhood experience but the family, the family situation, the relations between parents and children that cause neuroses.

W: Quite right. You see, when you repress something in childhood, it means that you did not wish to put up with unpleasantness. It is a step away from reality. As Freud said, the madman drops reality. Some neurotics distort this reality; they know how things are but don't feel that way. That is the inability to put up with life as it is. You have criminals on one side, neurotics on the other.

Steckel is supposed to have said, "The neurotic is a criminal who doesn't have the courage to commit the crime." The neurotic doesn't kill the other person but becomes ill and cannot bear it. And if you repress in childhood, you will always have the tendency to repress in some way when you find yourself in a disagreeable situation.

O: But everyone does that, everyone represses what he doesn't like. That's nothing special.

W: It's a question of degree. If Freud had really cured me, I would not have been stuck with this woman. That's a sort of disease.

O: He probably didn't correctly diagnose this problem.

W: What do you mean?

O: That Freud did not see your relations with women for what they were.

W: So it seems.

O: He obviously thought that being married to Therese, you would be all right.

W: Well, yes, as long as she was alive.

O: And probably it's asking too much that he should have foreseen all that happened.

W: If I had never met that woman, everything would have continued until my death. But that was a mistake. You know, this slut complex, this sister complex, and so on. I happened to get stuck with that one and she is an impossible person, a serious psychopath, and there's nothing you can discuss with her because she will fantasize. And she believes in her fantasies. So a conversation is impossible— logic, that sort of thing. . . . Well, overcoming this inhibition led to this catastrophe.

O: What do you mean? Overcoming this inhibition? That a man has a woman friend with whom he goes to bed must be the most natural thing in the world. That doesn't require getting rid of an inhibition.

W: What else should I have done?

O: When you say that you lost your sexual inhibition and therefore became friends with this Luise . . .

W: Why do I walk up to this woman and start talking to her at the tailor's when I know that she can find out my address? There you have the mistake I made, which is costing me so much.

O: What would be your ideal? To live as a bachelor? To have no relations with women?

W: Either one gets to know a woman with whom one can also somehow communicate spiritually, or one should forever go from one woman to the next so that one doesn't get stuck with any one.

O: And you think change would be better?

W: I should have followed that recipe. Either you find someone— then everything is fine. But if you find no one, it's best . . . My friend, this captain, also gave me this advice: "See to it that you keep moving from one woman to the next." And I followed it. And then I got stuck with this one, that's the tragedy. I don't know what to do with this woman. She has no medical insurance, she has no pension, and I am supposed to marry her. That's what I keep hearing every time I see her—marry, marry, marry, it's awful. . . . She even begrudges it when someone in my house puts the milk outside my door.

O: Why?

W: "Why don't you go downstairs yourself? You can go downstairs yourself." Well, she's afraid that I might establish contact with that person. . . . Here's what this woman is capable of: when we were still seeing each other more often, she went to the Café Aida and asked a man to go up to my apartment, a total stranger, who was to tell me that I should come to the café. What do you say to that? She had the nerve to ask a total stranger to go to my apartment. That's completely unacceptable. . . .

O: And did he?

W: He did.

O: And did you go to the café?

W: Yes, I did. . . . But to whom would it occur to do something like that, to go that far? That woman will do anything, that's what's so terrible. Or she starts talking about my wife, "Why didn't you have an autopsy performed?" Nothing could have been clearer. The Emergency Medical Services came and discovered without any doubt that it had been the gas. The gas had been turned on, and she had sat in front of it, that's what the death certificate stated. It's obvious. Listening to her, you would think I killed my wife because I did not insist on an autopsy. So she starts accusing me. I only tell you that as a shining example, how she is ready for any slander.

Therese's suicide came during the worst possible time. Had I been younger, it would have been better, and had I been older, it would also have been better. But everything really happened at the most unfavorable moment, and so I committed stupidities and had bad luck. I was lucky with this Gretl. And I should have concluded from that that it isn't so easy with women. . . . With this Luise, that I met her again, the probability was zero. I ran into her in the 4th District and she lives in the 17th. And I ran into her at the most unfavorable moment. One month earlier, it would not have been dangerous, and one month later, it would not have been dangerous either. But it was dangerous on that day. So I run into her in the 4th District and the story begins all over. So you see the kind of thing that happens in life, the most unlikely things happen. . . . For a while, she said that she didn't wish to marry me because I had found her too inferior and that she would marry someone else. But then she came and said, "Now I am supposed to marry someone I don't love. . . .

O: But you she loves?

W: Supposedly. . . . She loves me because I am Russian.

O: What impresses her so much about that?

W: That the Russians are the most powerful.

O: Luise seems to come from a rather wretched background.

W: "Wretched" isn't saying enough. I'll tell you a little about Luise. Her father was with the police, first as a patrolman, then in the administration. Her mother came from Moravia, as far as I remember; they had a farm. But although she has those leftist sympathies, she started telling me about her mother's blue blood.

O: Was she an only child?

W: No, there was an older sister who died of a brain tumor.

O: So Luise is a younger sister.

W: Yes. The grandfather owned a circus and there's also some Gypsy blood, she told me.

O: You have a weakness for women like that.

W: Like what?

O: Spaniards and Gypsies.

W: It's romantic. But this romanticism is hard on the nerves. On Sundays, she tells me that what I give her for the month isn't nearly enough. She starves all week and on Sundays eats to make up for that. For dinner, she orders soup, meat, twice the ordinary portion of vegetables. And coffee. She really stuffs herself, doesn't she? I'm in a quandary, I can't cancel those Sundays.

O: You pay for all that?

W: Then there are her demands: give, give. She examines my wallet to see how much money is in it. And then I have to give her a few hundred. All the things she needs, testing her blood for sugar, her teeth . . .

O: And in the evening she has another meal?

W: Well yes. What do you mean evenings? Just one hour after lunch, she wants something. She orders . . . what do you call it?

O: Pastry?

W: Not pastry. Meat again, things like that.

O: She must be awfully fat.

W: She was, she lost weight. Now, her clothes no longer fit, she needs new ones.

O: And her illnesses, what are the symptoms? Does she look ill? What form does it take?

W: There aren't any apparent symptoms.

O: Her appearance is normal?

W: It is. I once had an acquaintance who said that someone who has those wrinkles, those deep lines along the sides of the mouth, won't live long. She had those lines, but they disappeared.

O: So she gets younger and younger.

W: Yes, she gets younger.

O: But if one can tell nothing, are you sure that she really has those illnesses?

W: She probably does.

O: But you aren't sure?

W: I have no proof.

O: Perhaps she just tells you she does.

W: No, no, it's probably true. Back then, when she became so ill, she really did have a very hard time walking. But that got better. But these illnesses wear me out. When someone is ill, one cannot deal with her as one would a healthy person.

O: She probably realized a long time ago that you feel that way. . . . Those illnesses are probably just a ruse. You say she can go to the movies.

W: Well yes, she goes to the movies and she goes to the theater.

O: It's probably all a fairy tale.

W: No, no, she probably really is ill.

O: In any event, your relations to women aren't altogether normal. There's something amiss.

W: That's because of my sister. This seduction in my childhood is something abnormal. Although in the case of my acquaintance, her son, who was perhaps six at the time, the cousin came for a visit and played with his member and said, "How prettily it hangs from his behind." But it was different in my case. My sister proceeded systematically.

O: Actually, I don't believe that your sister explains everything. Your mother or your nanny must also play a role.

W: The nanny was an old woman.

O: You always felt drawn to simple women.

W: Yes, but Therese was a decent human being, whereas this woman . . .

O: Emotional relations are learned, just like other things. I believe that you learned emotional relations to simple women from your nanny.

W: Freud didn't express that idea, and it was not a sexual relation.

O: But mother-child relations are also sexual.

W: Freud didn't bring that up. There's nothing about that in the case history. That's your idea, that I—because I was close to this Nanja, that I am therefore more interested in simpler women. Freud explained it through my sister, that it was incest.

O: And you tend to believe Freud's thesis?

W: In this matter, I think he's right.

O: And the whole atmosphere, that one gives women money, there's less of that today, I believe. And the milieu with the nanny, and so on.

W: It was very strange in my case. There was the sister, there was this Nanja, there was the governess. On the estate, you were cut off from other impressions. In the city, one meets people. But one was confined to this narrow sphere. But if you don't subscribe to Freud's view, why do you want to write about this?

O: But it isn't absolutely necessary to espouse Freud's ideas to write about it.

W: The will, in any case. The concept of "will" disappears in Freud. For Freud, the will is really a drive. Yet the will is actually the opposite of a drive. The will is the suppression of the drive by rational insight. Kraepelin said that my illness was an illness of the will. I told that to E. and he said: "On the contrary, you have a strong will. You set a good many people in motion, Gardiner, and me. . . ." What do you say? Surely that's false. If I had a strong will, I would never have become involved in this situation with this woman. . . . You can see, I have no will. She nips all will in the bud.

O: I wouldn't say that you had a strong will either, to be honest. Something must have gone wrong in your upbringing.

W: Perhaps it is an innate shortcoming.

O: A pedagogic error, I should think.

W: Freud confuses will and instinct. But he also said this: "After psychoanalysis, one has the chance to become well, it's like a ticket. Whether one makes use of it depends on the will." So there *is* such a thing as free will. You see, there's a contradiction. All of a sudden, one has to want to, and the whole time he confuses will and drive.

O: That's where psychoanalysis makes it easy for itself. If the patient is not cured, one simply says that he didn't wish to be cured; the resistance was too great.

W: That's very true. As a psychoanalyst, one would have to say that when all links have been uncovered, the patient must become well. But not that it depends on whether one wants to or not.

O: Besides, it is the nature of neurosis that one does not want what is rational.

W: That's the core of the matter. You can see it in my case: I want to be with this woman although I know that she brings me no joy. On the contrary, she costs money.

O: Or, that one understands that one is doing something wrong but cannot change. . . .

W: You see how clumsy E. is: "You are afraid of this woman, you are afraid of castration." That's the sort of thing he tells me. . . .

O: What does he mean by it?

W: If one has an excessive fear which is unfounded, it seems that it must always be castration if it's a man. That's nonsense. You said, quite correctly, it's the nature of all neuroses that one knows that something should not be but cannot help oneself. All of psychoanalysis collapses. Are you a believer or no?

O: I cannot answer with a simple yes or no. At the time Freud lived, much was trailblazing. But as a method for curing people, it doesn't seem practicable.

W: It's the will, don't you see. Had I been able to deal with the conflict with Therese, had I gone to her although the physicians were against it, that would have been the right thing. But as it is, I took the detour via Freud. That was a weakness.

O: It's odd all right, when someone is in love . . .

W: He acts on his own, he needs no advisor.

O: And you did not have the courage to act against the physicians, against your family.

W: That's a fairly healthy thought, I think. . . .

O: And then, the money . . . Perhaps Freud didn't realize that you always gave the women money. Perhaps he didn't understand what was involved there.

W: He probably did not understand what that meant. He did not take note of it.

O: And it was perfectly natural at the time that when one lives with a woman or is married to one, she lives off you.

W: But you see, when you walk down the street and see a woman you like, you want to go to a hotel with this woman. You know that that's possible only if you give her something.

O: Yes, but the mere idea. It strikes me as completely out of any context that I should go with someone who says to me on the street, "Come to a hotel with me, I'll pay you."

W: All right, you are a decent woman.

O: What does that mean, decent woman? But if I am to go to bed with someone, I do it because I enjoy it. I don't ask for money.

W: That's your standpoint. But it isn't Luise's.

O: When women go to bed with you for money, it's suspicious. Surely that's the way it's always been. Did Freud know that you went with women and paid them?

W: Yes, of course.

O: And he thought it was all right?

W: Perfectly. When I was his patient, I also speculated. The money complex. He said I didn't have the right attitude toward money. And then he said I should study economics. But that's a discipline that doesn't interest me in the least. It's funny that I should now be having these money problems. And he said, "Very well, if you don't study economics, I don't know how you are going to deal with your money complex." And you can see, it's true that my greatest conflict now has to do with money.

O: But if you receive money every month, surely you get along?

W: That's not a problem.

O: Money in connection with women . . .

W: Yes, something isn't right there. This is the way it is with the past. This is how I imagine it: A change can occur when one experiences something that refutes what one has become used to. But memory by itself, I believe, is no use. According to Freud, remembering is enough. But I doubt that. I believe a turn can come through an experience. But it must be experienced in reality, not just in one's mind, not just as idea. That isn't enough.

O: That's one of the most modern views in psychiatry, by the way.

W: I could give an example: that gonorrhea episode. When you tell me that you had gonorrhea, it is something one experiences. That the other person is so frank. That is an experience that can change things. Normally, a woman wouldn't say a thing like that. That is a unique situation, in any event, and such things can bring a complete change. That's just an example. But to remember something isn't enough. The element of experience is lacking. And that's really the reason I don't believe in psychoanalysis.

By the way, Gardiner is supposed to arrive here in November, the end of November. . . . Well, this is the farewell hour. I always find it so difficult to leave you. It is a human experience. And at home, I'm alone once more.

The Insurance Employee

WOLF-MAN: Yes, Gardiner was here. I saw her and she told me that someone had written another letter to the Fischer Verlag to send on to me. It seems she noticed that I wasn't going to go along with the Russian woman at the time. I don't know, of course, perhaps it was a good thing that she turned her down right away. Perhaps I would have had nothing but trouble with that woman. . . .

OBHOLZER: But you would not have been obliged to answer the letter.

W: This time she did not open the letter. Someone had written to the Fischer Verlag and since they don't have my address, they sent it on to Gardiner. I met Gardiner in the café. Well, she had forgotten to bring the letter along. . . .

O: It was in America?

W: No, she had forgotten it here, in the hotel. She said she'd send it Thursday. I had seen her on Wednesday, so I should have received the letter on Friday but I didn't. I called an acquaintance who knows her husband. He said he would talk to her. She did not mail the letter until Saturday, at the Main Post Office. So I got it yesterday.

O: And from whom was it?

W: Guess!

O: From the Russian woman in France.

W: No. I also thought, perhaps it is from the Russian woman. But it is from another lady.

O: What sort of lady?

W: It's occurred to me that one should form a syndicate of all these women and they would have to make contributions.

O: To whom?

W: To Luise. In any case, I got it yesterday. She has an old Germanic given name—I don't want to mention it now, nor the family name.

O: Do you know the lady?

W: No, I don't know her. It's a place near Hamburg somewhere, I've been told. Here's what she writes: "Your book came out such a long time ago, I am afraid you may have died in the meantime. But should my letter reach you, I would like it to bring you some happiness. . . ." Then she goes on to say that her father was born in the same year as I although in April, which is the dangerous month. Luise was also born in April, those are rams, right, they aren't very pleasant.

Her father resembled me when he was younger. She must have a father complex. Then she writes that our lives are similar in many ways because the period or, as she puts it, the cultural sphere, is the same. That's rather interesting. It seems that at an earlier time, there was a great deal of similarity between the north-German and the south-Russian cultural spheres. She writes that it was similar, so it must have been similar. She goes on to say, and I quote: "Your sad face during the occupation of Vienna by the Nazis made a deep impression on me. I would like nothing better than to pay you a visit in Vienna. But because that is impossible, I would like to send you my greetings." Signature.

So, tell me, what should I do? I showed the letter to S. and he said, "The woman seems rather high-strung." The handwriting is quite extraordinary, one has to guess at the letters. So, what is your opinion? To become famous is easy, to be famous difficult. . . .

O: You think so? What did S. say?

W: Well, "Tell her not to come. Thank her for the kind words, and write that you wish to remain incognito and that it's therefore impossible for her to visit you—something on that order." I just remembered that Emperor Augustus is supposed to have said that every human being must play a role in life. Not a stupid comment, actually. It is through fate, often through trivia, that a role is imposed on one for which one was never destined. Now I must play the role of this little star.

O: But that's not the worst role.

W: But why this letter? I can't have her come here. What should I do with this woman? If I did not have the other one, I would have written that she should come, that we'd go to the theater. But I am stuck with this other person.

O: Did she write what she does or what she does for a living?

W: No idea.

O: Or how old she is? Nothing at all?

W: Nothing. She should have sent a photo to let me know at least what she looks like. That Russian woman now, that would be a different matter. As émigrée or as Russian, one might assume that she would want to take care of one. She should have sent me that. But this, what am I supposed to do with this?

O: That's always a problem when you don't know who the person is.

W: One doesn't know who it is and what she really wants.

O: The letter isn't clear on that point.

W: It isn't. The other one, being Russian and an émigrée . . . Who knows if these inferences are correct. Perhaps she thought, he's making money from the book.

O: One doesn't know.

W: It's probable, even.

O: Surely not, you cannot impute that to everyone.

W: One doesn't know, but it looked as if she were genuinely interested, because she wrote in Russian. But there is nothing I can do with this one. What do you think.

O: If you were in a position to establish contact with her and, if you didn't like her, to break off that contact again, that would be all right. But you find that difficult.

W: It would be difficult for me. You know me by now.

O: And maybe she is ill or who knows what, and then you have two.

W: Perhaps she really is ill and poorly situated.

O: Did she say whether she was married?

W: No. But this phrase—"if it is not possible"—suggests that she is thinking of another woman. Why otherwise would it not be possible? It is possible. She can come anytime. The only obstacle would be my being married or having a friend. That might cause difficulties.

O: But since that is true of all women, one can assume that she is looking for a man. According to everything you have told me, that was true of almost all the women you became acquainted with in the course of time. All ultimately wanted to establish relations with you.

W: Well, perhaps not get married but some kind of liaison.

O: On the other hand, should you wish to leave Vienna, this might be a way of getting to Germany.

W: I have thought of that. Gardiner did say, "America is out of the question for you; you don't speak English." But if this woman reads a book like that, she must have some sort of education. A simple woman would not read a book like that.

O: Did she say something about the book?

W: She said that the book had made an impression on her and that I was sad during the Nazi period. Why she put that in, I don't know. But you can see that she is high-strung, somehow—the handwriting alone, you know.

O: Is that right?

W: Curious, so unrestrained, strokes, fantastic transformations of letters. . . . But, you see, if I wanted to get out of Vienna, it's a problem. Then the women would have to support me. She would have to be a wealthy person. One is in their hands, more or less.

O: But you have your pension.

W: I would have to give up the apartment. Leave for a completely unknown environment. And I don't even know whether she really wants me. She wants to come here for a few days. Whether she wants me to come there is something she didn't mention. It would mean thrusting oneself on her.

O: No one can make the decision for you whether to answer her or not.

W: It's too dangerous to become involved. What am I going to do with this one? I find myself in a very unpleasant situation, without help. What use are those pretty letters and pretty words which really don't do me any good? With the Russian, that's something one could have tried. As émigrée, she might feel some kind of obligation, but a German, from northern Germany, a wholly unknown woman. . . . The only thing I don't understand is this: she knows my age but she writes as if I were forty or fifty. Then the letter would be understandable. She is looking for a man, what else. But at such an age, what can you do?

O: You mean your age?

W: My age. But as you see, that doesn't keep her back.

O: There are women who hope for a father-daughter relationship.

W: She's already comparing me to her father.
O: Precisely. But such a relationship isn't really what is wanted.
W: Of course. The relationship is not right. You are quite correct.
O: It is not a relationship where the two have equal rights.
W: What role should one play as father?
O: Vis-à-vis Luise, you also play a sort of father role.
W: That's perfectly natural.
O: But it doesn't seem to make you very happy.
W: As you can see, it isn't pleasant to play such a role. One should learn that from experience alone. But if the woman is old, it's no fun either.
O: Why? I don't understand. That depends on the woman.
W: It is an unknown X. It's too much of a risk.
O: If she writes that her father was born in the same year you were, you can figure out that she must be around sixty.
W: Something like that, sixty or close to sixty.
O: About as old as Luise.
W: Yes, if Luise didn't exist, I could easily write, "Come, we can talk, we can go to the movies." But since I am stuck with that one, she'll make scenes. . . . I have no choice but to write that I thank her . . .
O: Since you see Luise only on Sundays, you would be free the other days.
W: S. advises against experiments. And one doesn't know where the whole thing will lead.
O: Of course, there's no way of knowing ahead of time.
W: You don't drink coffee?
O: I drink apple juice. I'll be awake all night if I drink coffee at this time of day. By the way, you knew Ernest Jones, didn't you?
W: I see I left my hearing aid at home. Last year, I could still hear everything and this year, it's become worse. Everything is becoming very laborious; it's very unpleasant. You speak fairly loud, after all.
O: I said, you knew Ernest Jones.
W: I beg your pardon?
O: Ernest Jones, do you know him?
W: No.
O: He's an Englishman who was with Freud. He also wrote about you.

W: What's his name?

O: Ernest Jones. . . . He writes that he corresponded with you.

W: Ah yes, perhaps it's Lubin. Gardiner once sent me an analyst, and his name was Lubin.

O: No, it isn't Lubin.

W: This Lubin thought I looked on psychoanalysis as a religion.

O: No, it isn't him.

W: I never heard of the other one. Why did he write?

O: This Ernest Jones wrote a Freud biography, three fat volumes. And there's also a chapter about you in this biography. I had it photocopied for you.

W: I see. Thank you.

O: You can take it home with you and read it at your leisure. I would like you to tell me what you think of it. You never heard the name?

W: I beg your pardon? No, no.

O: He says here . . .

W: Well, I'll read it at home. Does he say that he knows me?

O: Yes, it says here, "I am still in regular correspondence with him."[1]

W: Ah, perhaps that's Dr. Sterba. That's the physician with whom I correspond. At Christmas, he always sends me . . .

O: No, Jones is dead. He died in 1958, so that must have been earlier.

W: I wasn't in touch with any psychoanalyst at that time.

O: This Jones is well informed. In your memoirs, you write *Dr. D.* for *Dr. Drosnes,* for example, and he supplies the correct name.

W: There's a certain Dr. Sterba. He is Viennese but went to America. About ten years ago, I was invited to his house. I did not hear from him again. He's someone I know. But that one? And you say he writes that he and I . . .

O: . . . . corresponded.

W: Would you repeat the name once more?

O: Ernest Jones.

W: Ernest Jones. . . .

---

1. Ernest Jones, *The Life and Work of Sigmund Freud,* 3 vols. (New York: Basic Books, 1953–57), 2: 273.

O: He was an Englishman and studied with Freud in Vienna around the time of the First World War.

W: Wait a moment, Freud had a patient who was an Englishman. I don't remember his name. In any case he introduced me to him, I recall now. He was a very elegant man, opulently and elegantly dressed, and I visited him two or three times. But he had another name. What was his name? Johnson, you said Johnson?

O: Jones.

W: Jones, no, that wasn't his name.

O: In any case, this Jones wrote three fat volumes about Freud in which he presents all the information that could be got hold of. And allegedly he also correponded with you and put various questions to you that were worked into a chapter.

W: Well, I'll read it at home, perhaps it will come back to me. Kirle was his name, the one I mentioned just now, who was so elegant.

O: He was a patient?

W: I don't know. Either he was a patient or he did a teaching analysis. In any case, I visited him. His apartment was very aristo-cratic; they must have been rich. I think I saw him once or twice, then I never heard from him again. But his name was Kirle.

O: That was in the twenties?

W: Yes, in '22 or '23, or even earlier.

O: Jones, that must have been later. I imagine that he asked you those questions sometime between 1950 and 1958.

W: Wait a moment, perhaps in '55.

O: That's possible, yes.

W: In 1955, there was a physician from Switzerland . . .

O: And what was his name?

W: Wein or Weiner, something like that, I believe, but not Jones. And he wanted people to make a drawing from childhood, I think.

O: That was probably the Rorschach test. That was invented by a Swiss psychiatrist.

W: I don't believe it's a key. That was a waste of time that I did that. You did something with color or ink, and then it was assembled and he interpreted it.

O: And he visited you?

W: No, I was on vacation and he came there. It was on the German border, near Salzburg. He stayed for one or two days. But that was through E., and he was from Switzerland. I think he's also died in the meantime.

O: Jones is also dead.

W: Well, if he says that he spoke with me.

O: No, he doesn't say that. He writes that he corresponded with you.

W: But that's something I should remember. Perhaps he confuses me with someone else.

O: I don't think so.

W: I don't remember. There was that fellow from Switzerland, and then that Kirle. And then there was a married woman—English, I believe—Strachey. I think she's a writer or he is a writer.

O: James Strachey is the editor of the standard edition of Freud's works.

W: What is he, a psychoanalyst?

O: I think so.

W: His wife, I remember her, a typical Englishwoman, slow and cool, quite pretty. I gave her lessons for a while.

O: When was that?

W: In the twenties, but not for very long. I gave Gardiner lessons for years. But she remembers nothing. At the time, I saw her first husband, she was divorced from him, and then she married an Englishman.

O: But she married that fellow Buttinger.

W: Yes, but before that she was married to an American who was much older than she. I believe it was very brief. And then she married an Englishman who was younger than she, and who studied music. I don't know where he disappeared to. He also took lessons from me. What was his name now? Well, Gardiner, of course. I think that Buttinger worked for the *Arbeiterzeitung,* like you.

O: No, he didn't.

W: I think he came into conflict with the Social Democrats. He criticized the position of the Social Democrats toward Hitler. And then he wrote that book, *Am Beispiel Österreichs.* I own a copy.

O: Before the Nazis occupied Austria, he was the leader of the Socialist party, which was illegal at the time. He had to live underground and Gardiner supposedly helped him a lot in those days.

W: I think he is a little younger than she, at least he looks younger.

O: And you, did you have any dealings with the Nazis?

W: There was something involving the son of Freud. I made his acquaintance. In the beginning, I worked for the Anglo-Danubian-Lloyd, and Freud's oldest son was there, his name was Martin.

O: As an employee?

W: No, no he was a lawyer and had something to do with bank loans. I remember he once gave a talk which was called "The Morality of Interest Rates" (*laughs*).

O: Really?

W: Well, I don't hink he was any great genius, Freud's son. Hasn't he also died in the meantime?

O: Martin Freud? Yes, I believe he has.

W: We had a tax matter at the insurance company. There was a publishing house on Berggasse. Not in the house where Freud lived, you know, but a few doors down toward Währingerstrasse. There was a publishing house then and Freud's son ran it.

O: Wasn't that the Psychoanalytischer Verlag?

W: Yes, the Psychoanalytischer Verlag. At the time the Nazis came, I thought, I'll get those tax documents from him. I went there; everything was quiet. But the doorman saw that I wanted to see Freud and he called the Nazis.

O: You didn't know that that's what he was doing?

W: No, I didn't. He gave me the documents and I left. Suddenly, I see some fifty men with rifles in the front yard. They immediately arrested me and took me back to Freud. I sat there and a Nazi watched as if he thought I wanted to run away. I wouldn't run away. They were some sort of volunteers. . . .

O: What year was that?

W: Well, in '38, when Hitler came.

O: Before Therese's death?

W: Yes, before. Well, and Freud, Freud's son, conducted himself impeccably. He showed no fear. He simply said that doctor so and so, the superior of those men, would be there in a few moments. I don't know what sort of official he was. Apparently he knew those people. "He will come and I will show him that it is a tax document." And quite soon, after half an hour, a Nazi functionary arrived, and I showed him the document. "You see, this is a tax matter," Martin Freud said. "Dr. P. had given it to me." And so they let me go.

O: And that was all?

W: No, I was also arrested by them once.

O: And everyone that came to see Freud was arrested?

W: I imagine. When I arrived, no one was there, and suddenly there were fifty armed individuals.

O: That was because of Freud?

W: Yes, because of Freud, because they were opposed to psychoanalysis. I don't know what they thought. But Freud, Freud's son, conducted himself very courageously, although the situation was not pleasant. I was surprised that he did not seem to mind. And this official, the superior of those men, also conducted himself quite properly. And I went home.

O: Did they know that you were a former patient?

W: No, and they didn't ask either. He simply looked to make sure that it really was a tax document. It was a matter that had nothing to do with Freud's father.

O: Did you have close contact with Martin Freud, or was it just professional?

W: We did some loan business and somehow he also worked for Anglo-Danubian-Lloyd. But otherwise I had nothing to do with him.

O: You were against the Nazis?

W: Well, I was stateless at the time, and that was fortunate because I did not have to go into the army. Someone once came to see me and started hinting around.

O: A Nazi?

W: Well, a man started talking. Then I showed him my father's picture. He said: "I must tell you frankly that I have been ordered to determine whether you are of Jewish descent. But I see the picture of your father—he looks like a czar." And he left. Once, I received a summons and had to go to the police. There were other immigrants there and one addressed us, saying that it was a sign of a special trust that they talked to us at all. Then he said that we should report as interpreters.

O: As volunteers?

W: One should sign, saying one agrees to being used as an interpreter. There were perhaps ten Russians there who twisted and turned, trying to wriggle out of it. But only one got away without signing. All the others signed, including me. One of them presented things in such a way that the place where he worked would collapse if he were drafted, and that that would be a catastrophe for the German Reich. Well, he didn't have to sign, but all the others did.

For a while, nothing happened, but suddenly I received a summons. I had been appointed interpreter. Do you realize how Russians feel about interpreters? They are traitors. "Well," I said, "I am so old and sick," and so on, and started whining. And the official said, "Very well, we'll let it go, we'll get someone younger." I managed to get away and could go home. But actually it was a very dangerous business.

O: Would you have had to go to Russia?

W: I would have had to go into the army and the Russians would have shot me immediately for being a traitor. It was very dangerous. But I succeeded in fending it off and heard nothing further. They could have forced me. It so happened that I ran into decent people.

O: You were lucky.

W: I was lucky that they took my name off the list.

O: So you see, you were lucky for once, and you always say you've never had anything but bad luck.

W: Yes well, of course, sometimes I did have luck. The worst thing that ever happened to me is this business with Luise. That finished me. And I don't know how to get out of it.

O: And then you worked at the insurance company for thirty years although you had not been brought up to do any kind of work. How do you explain having been able to keep it up? How do you account for the fact that you stood it?

W: I just did.

O: It's a cliché, of course, but so many Russian émigrés are taxi drivers or work in nightclubs. You chose such a bourgeois profession. It's surprising that you managed to survive as an insurance employee.

W: Well, I was lucky there too. I describe in my book how a student got me an interview with Ehrenzweig, who was the god of the insurance industry. When he said no suit will be brought, none was. He was always the ultimate authority. And it was through his sister that I got the job at the insurance company. I didn't actually want to work for an insurance company. I had never found that appealing.

I would much rather have worked in a bank, although I probably wouldn't have cared for that either. When I see them counting money, I think I would never have been able to learn that. They are real artists, aren't they? But I did really want to work in a bank. I imagined one could speculate there, become rich. But he had no connection with banks, insurance. Then I got a letter from Schlesinger, from Director General Schlesinger. He was the sales manager of Elementar Phönix, an important man. So I went there. . . .

I was disappointed because I had thought, a bank, that's something. But insurance, I didn't care for it, it seemed such a bureaucratic and boring place where nothing ever happened, while a bank, you have the stock market, the prices of the shares. So I went and got the job. I went and they pretended not to know what to do with me. I sat there all winter long without anything to do. Of course, it's possible that I would have been even more unsuitable in a bank.

O: Yes, but that you stuck it out for such a long time, that's the surprising thing. Those regular office hours day after day. Do you think that's the influence of Freud? You certainly didn't get that at home.

W: I attended the gymnasium. One had to force oneself there too. That stays with you. Had I been educated wholly at home, had I never attended the gymnasium, I might not have managed. It was no great pleasure, going to the gymnasium every day.

O: You mean it has something to do with your education?

W: I think so. I had to learn languages. In the beginning, I had tutors, then I attended the gymnasium. That's a certain discipline. In any case, what should I have done? As long as Therese was alive, there was some sort of base but now . . .

I remember when the Russians arrested me. Actually, they didn't arrest me. I was told, "You weren't arrested, you were stopped." So I was stopped. And I said that my father had had an estate in White Russia. I said, "The soil was very poor, sand and loam." They started in immediately: "How so? It's excellent soil." They began disputing. . . .

With those Russians, that was a problem. How could I have walked into the Russian sector to paint? They said: "If you had asked us, we would have given you permission to paint. But you made the mistake of not asking." What do they mean, ask? I did not paint the house, I painted the landscape. You couldn't call it a house, it was a few bombed walls. Nothing there. But they were somewhere, far behind those walls. But I didn't know that. . . . For the Russians, it was important that I had not fled but emigrated legally. The French were in Odessa at the time.

The situation I was in when I was arrested—no one knew that I was in the Russian sector. But I must say, they were quite decent. The soldiers said: "It doesn't matter to us, we bring everyone food. We don't care why someone was arrested." They weren't so political. Once before, there was a dangerous situation. That's because I had been terribly careless, I started talking to the Russians. In the house in which I live, they always called me to the door. Once, I was coming home and was going in and two Russians came toward me. And I said in Russian, "What can I do for you?" One of them looks at me and says, "Counterrevolutionary." He could have shot me right then and there, they wouldn't have done a thing to him. At that moment, someone calls outside, "Come here, quickly, quickly, come here!" He looked, and ran off.

O: Where was that, at the door to your house?

W: Yes.

O: Your house? But that wasn't in the Russian sector.

W: It was directly after the end of the war, before the Americans arrived.

O: Of course, the Russians got there first.

W: Then they came once, my mother told me, and asked for me. The concièrge told them that I was in the office. Then I read that the Americans were indignant that the Russians were sticking their noses into every district. But that was only at the beginning. Later, they didn't come any more.

O: The Americans got excited because the Russians were spying in their districts.

W: They did in the beginning. I remember another experience. I come home, and there's an officer there, making a face, scolding. Just as they called the Russians "Ivan," so they called the Germans "Fritz." So he scolds, "Those damned Fritzes, they refuse to give Russian officers apartments!" There were quite a few people standing about, like a herd of sheep. I went up there right away: "What do you want, an apartment?" He says, "I don't want one in this house, I want one next door. Come with me." I went with him, we came to a house and immediately found an empty room, and he calmed down. A few more Russians came and the officer told me to get a bottle of wine.

I went and got the wine. When I come back, the noncommissioned officer says, "It's dangerous, there might be poison in it." "I'll show you there's no poison in it," I said, poured myself a glass, and drank it. So he saw that there was no poison in it. He calmed down and said, "We are going to eat now, why don't you join us." So I said, "Yes, with pleasure" and I ate with them. After we had eaten, he demanded that I get a few more bottles of wine but said that they must not be open. I say: "Where am I going to get bottles like that? Very well, I'll try to get some." He explained: "You know, we are afraid that it might be poison. Tomorrow, when you come here, you must bring unopened bottles." I didn't look for any of course. Where was I to have looked for something like that at that time? I went back once more, but they had already left. I was lucky. I was terribly careless. I spoke to the Russians; I acted as interpreter. Well, nothing happened to me. But we had a physician for a while at the time, for example, who was from Russia but had a German name. He told me that his son also started talking to the Russians. He was warned and finally they took him with them. You see, one has gone through all sorts of things and then one is faced with an enigma with such a stupid woman and doesn't know what to do. It is really . . .

O: Grotesque.

W: Grotesque. And now I gave her 50,000 schillings so she has medical insurance. Just this one item comes to 50,000. . . . Well, it's all very sad. But what should one do, kill oneself? Should one kill onself?

O: That doesn't pay.

W: Sometimes, when I think about all those things, it seems the only way out.

O: It would be a little like going to America.

W: It's less complicated.

O: I find it very complicated, killing oneself. How would you kill yourself?

W: I have gas.

O: Gas, you know, is not what it was in 1938. Today, it's practically impossible to kill yourself with gas. The gas is detoxified.

W: It's detoxified?

O: It used to be fashionable, but today it's hardly possible.

W: It's good that you told me. And one can't get cyanide. This is a nice conversation we are having.

O: Using gas is completely pointless.

W: Then I'm even worse off. Let's change the subject and talk about something more pleasant: I brought you my cemetery number. The grave is at the very beginning, when you start at the church and go down the main walk. . . . Thank you for having told me about the gas.

O: Had you seriously considered it?

W: Yes, but now it's out of the question. Come to think of it, you never read in the papers any more that someone killed himself with gas. One less hope for a tolerable end.

O: Why would you want to kill yourself? You are healthy, you are not yet frail, there's nothing wrong with you. There is no real reason.

W: Well, that's something we'll come back to. Luise . . .

O: Why do you keep giving her money?

W: She has nothing. Am I to let her starve?

O: Yes, but that much?

W: Well, I got something from the book just now. I made the mistake that I gave her too much. Now she is used to it. As regards marriage . . . But to marry someone whom you can't talk to? She invariably rattles off a whole list of reproaches. "Thirty years ago, you gave me so little, you let me starve, you exploited me." And one has to listen to it all. And E. writes, "Put your knowledge of psychoanalysis to use," and so on, and reproaches me besides. As if I were the guilty one.

I don't know what to tell you now. There's a variety of subjects. Take Gardiner, for example, who edited my memoirs. And she herself also wrote a good deal in that book, under the title, "Meetings with the Wolf-Man." Actually, what she writes there doesn't amount to anything. She writes that I have rheumatism. I don't recall having had rheumatism. I had headaches, migraine. That went away completely later. It used to be very severe. There were times when I had to stay away from work and lie down. The things she wrote were really quite trivial, weren't they?

O: Being the editor, she had to write something.

W: She didn't know much. Earlier, she played a role in my life, at the beginning, but not when I was giving her Russian lessons. I remember, she came once, I think it was before Christmas. She rang the bell and brought me cigarettes. I don't know what had come over her. Well, the bell rang, and she said, "I would like to meet your wife." Well, Therese was also a curious person. I don't know if she was jealous of her. In any case, she said that she wouldn't come out. I should say she was ill. So what could I do? The whole thing was very embarrassing to me. And I had to say to her: "I am sorry, but my wife is ill. She cannot see you." That was the only time she made a social call.

But Gardiner did play a role because I met her on the street after my wife's suicide. She helped me a great deal then. When I went to Paris and London, I was able to get over it. And now the situation is this: when I wrote her that you had proposed these interviews, she sent a telegram that I shouldn't do it. That's why I suggested to you: "Go ahead and publish it after my death, it won't matter then. But while I am still alive, I don't want a conflict with Gardiner." Well, Gardiner wrote in these "meetings" that she did not want to be pushed into the role of psychoanalyst. . . .

O: Of advisor. She writes, "It has required all of my ingenuity not to be drawn into the role of advisor."[2]

W: Well, but that's difficult. On the one hand, she wants to write about me, and on the other, she doesn't want to be drawn in. That's why she didn't really know a great deal about me. And I couldn't tell her much. There were only those few times she came to Vienna. And during those few hours I spent with her, I couldn't tell her all that much. There's nothing in that book about my life after the death of my wife. And now I want to clear up this question: Do you want me to tell you more precisely what happened after the death of my wife?

O: Of course.

W: If you now write about what happened after the death of my wife, it's another long story. My wife died in '38. '38, '48, '58, '68—it's already well over thirty years. And nothing has been written about that.

O: Little.

2. Muriel Gardiner, ed., *The Wolf-Man: With the Case of the Wolf-Man by Sigmund Freud* (New York: Basic Books, 1971), p. 360.

W: Except for what Gardiner writes. But that's as good as nothing.

O: It's a little superficial.

W: Well, you see, the death of my wife completely unsettled me. I committed stupidities. And I got myself into a very unpleasant situation with this friend. I should tell you the story at least briefly. I don't know whether you want to write about it. I don't know at all whether it was a good thing that Gardiner encouraged me to write memoirs.

O: Why?

W: Well, you know, Freud was against it.

O: Writing memoirs? I don't understand.

W: It says in the review in a German paper that Freud only wrote the childhood story because a biography cannot be written and is socially not . . .

O: . . . acceptable. All right, but you are in a wholly different position. Being a physician, Freud was obliged to remain silent. He couldn't do it. But you are not obliged to remain silent about yourself—that's a completely different thing.

W: But you see that he was against it.

O: But he regarded himself as a physician.

W: When he became sixty, I believe, and his anniversary was being celebrated, I wanted to write something about him. I told Mack about it at the time and she said, "The professor is against your writing something about him." You see? He was against it.

O: But that need not concern you. It's your personal affair if you want to write something.

W: Gardiner obviously understood it like that.

O: I believe that psychoanalysts wrote all sorts of things on the occasion of his sixtieth birthday.

W: In my memoirs, the Freud chapter, I wrote that while Freud was still alive. I wanted to publish it. But Mack said, "The professor is against it."

O: Freud was always against people writing about him. But that's his problem. If you feel like writing memoirs, Freud cannot keep you from it.

W: Well, I didn't publish it at the time because Mack said he was against it. I gave it to Gardiner. And she wrote me that Anna Freud had said that in her opinion, it was the best thing I had ever written.

O: I don't agree.

W: I beg your pardon?

O: I don't feel that that chapter is the best thing you have written. I much prefer the childhood memories.

W: I believe that that's more important too.

O: The childhood story is much more alive. The text on Freud is so impersonal.

W: Well, I wanted to write something objective.

O: That's the mistake, apparently.

W: (*laughs*): You think so?

O: In my opinion, it's better to be subjective in such matters.

W: I was not objective about the other memories. But, you see, that's also a strange thing. I placed such great value on those memories. Writing them diverted me, and now it seems to me, well, what was the point of all that writing? It would have been better had you thought about how to deal with Luise. I failed there.

O: But you had fun.

W: Yes, at the time I did the writing.

O: And that does something for you, that a book you wrote was published.

W: Well, that's vanity.

O: That's nothing bad!

W: It's nothing bad, but it isn't good, either.

O: Why isn't it good?

W: It is ephemeral, somehow. Initially, one feels satisfaction. Then time passes and one asks oneself, what was the point of it all? Well, now you have set yourself the task of writing about me. I brought you a few pictures. It does seem that I want you to write something.

O: Apparently.

W: Otherwise I wouldn't have brought these pictures. . . .

"I, the most famous case"

WOLF-MAN: You see, I had one problem after another. With my denture, for example. But there's no point in my getting a new one. I have a few very long teeth. It tickles, I cannot bear it. Those teeth would have to be filed down, or pulled.

OBHOLZER: Are those real teeth?

W: In the lower jaw I still have two or three of my teeth. They are enormously long. An acquaintance gave me the address of a dentist. I had been seeing a woman dentist, but she failed me this time. The first time, she did all right, but the second time, she only made a second set of teeth and they didn't turn out right. So now I keep changing back and forth. Sometimes I use one denture, sometimes the other, and neither works right. The one I am wearing today is the least troublesome and it is already fifteen years old. I completely forgot, I brought you back the Jones material.

O: You can keep it, I don't need it.

W: I don't need it either. You can take it, it's in my overcoat.

O: Did you read it?

W: No, no, I noticed that it's all wrong. I gave it to S., who says that Jones wrote a biography of Freud with many mistakes in it. It's false not just about me but about other things as well, I don't know what sort of person he is.

O: You don't know him?

W: Jones? No, I don't know him.

O: But why then does he write that he corresponded with you? Did you see that sentence?

W: Yes, I did. I never exchanged a letter with him.

O: How odd.

W: I did write a letter to this Lubin, I believe. Otherwise, I never corresponded with any psychoanalyst except Dr. E. Oh yes, there was a certain Sterba—they were Viennese, not Jews, but they emigrated to America. I met them, and every year, at Christmas, he sends me a small photo. It's always something to do with the Church. They were in Vienna once, but they didn't get in touch with me.

O: Then you didn't read any of what Jones wrote?

W: Well, I leafed through it and noticed that it is incorrect. The year of my father's death, for example. And how can he write that my father was a lawyer? My father was an honorary judge. Then he writes that I published something. I hadn't published anything at the time. It's incorrect.

O: You had published articles in an insurance periodical.

W: Yes, well . . .

O: Perhaps he means that.

W: Did you read them?

O: No, you told me.

W: Yes, that's true. But he writes that I corresponded with him. I never corresponded with him.

O: Strange.

W: S. says that some of the things he wrote about Freud are also incorrect.

O: That's possible.

W: How can someone write a biography and fantasize like that. I don't understand.

O: It's three fat volumes.

W: But there was no need to write things that are false.

O: There was a great deal of material he had to work through.

W: Well, perhaps he confused things.

O: Perhaps Gardiner told him about you.

W: I don't know, he might have heard things from people. And Drosnes, I think the name Drosnes also occurs in Freud.

O: No, no. And this one comment I find extremely curious. But since you didn't read it, it's difficult . . .

W: Well, it's too much for me.

O: Here is is: "From the age of six he had suffered from obsessive blasphemies against the Almighty, and he initiated the first hour of treatment with the offer to have rectal intercourse with Freud and then to defecate on his head."[1]

W: And what? His head? I don't understand that. What's the last sentence?

O: Yes, it is curious: "He initiated the first hour of treatment with the offer to have rectal intercourse with Freud and then to defecate on his head." In German, it's something like, to have intercourse with him from behind and to shit on his head.

W: No, that may have been something else. When I was lying on this couch, I turned around when Freud said something that especially interested or struck me. And Freud said, "You turn around because you want to show that you have beautiful eyes." Freud said that to me. Of course I stopped doing it so that he wouldn't think I was vain, or what not. Unconsciously, he meant. But that was the only time I turned around. And Freud explained this situation to me like this: He sits at the head end rather than at the foot of the bed because there was a female patient who wanted to seduce him, and she kept raising her skirt. I still remember that. And he said that was why he sat at the head end. . . .

O: You mean Jones simply invented this?

W: Perhaps Freud wrote something . . .

O: Jones quotes a letter to Ferenczi.

W: I cannot remember Freud writing about it. That I turned around was inconsequential, wasn't it? But what that fellow writes, I don't know, it seems to me he doesn't have all his marbles.

O: So you know absolutely nothing about this?

W: No, I know nothing. What does he mean? What does intercourse mean?

O: Having intercourse from behind . . .

W: Homosexually?

O: Yes, homosexually, I imagine.

W: For heaven's sake, what nonsense! But that's . . . to write something like that, I don't know, is that fellow crazy or what, writing such nonsense. He explained it to me, he sits with his back to the couch because he had a female patient and he sat at the foot of

1. Ernest Jones, *The Life and Work of Sigmund Freud*, 3 vols. (New York: Basic Books, 1953–57), 2: 274.

the bed and she did some sort of gymnastics with her feet and wanted to seduce him or God knows what. That's what he told me. But this? Having intercourse from behind, what does that mean? It's nonsense, utter nonsense. That fellow must have a screw loose. How can he write about a lawyer, since that never came up. Where does he get those ideas?

O: I ask myself the same question.

W: S. said that too, that he wrote much that is incorrect. Well, I can provide no explanation.

O: I gave you the text because I was curious about what you would say, since it is about you.

W: Those are delusions. . . . People fantasize. Just as someone wrote that I could not dress myself.

O: Mack, if you please. Jones also mentions that, by the way.

W: Yes, to make it sound better.

O: It does sound interesting.

W: Then Freud's success was all the greater. Well, the mistake E. makes is that he believes that one can do psychoanalysis with an old man. Psychoanalysis is not suitable for an old man—Freud said so himself. He told me the case of a female patient who was, I don't know, seventy or even older. And he said: "What can you do in a case like that? She is afraid of going out on the street, of being run over, and therefore she refuses to go out on the street. Well," he said, "so I console her a little." So he admitted himself that the ability to transfer stops at a certain age and that psychoanalysis apparently no longer works then.

O: And E. doesn't believe that?

W: Apparently not, because he keeps trying to advance analytical explanations for various things. But how can there be any transference, considering that I am twice as old as he is?

O: How old is he?

W: I don't know, late fifties, perhaps a little older. No, I don't believe he's much older.

O: And S.?

W: But you know him. How old can he be?

O: Around seventy, wouldn't you say?

W: I don't think so.

O: Sixty, perhaps.

W: Something like that. You know, having been treated by Freud makes psychoanalysis with others difficult.

O: Aren't they as good?

W: No. And then I was . . . How old was I when I came to Freud in 1910? I was born in '87 . . .

O: Twenty-three.

W: Yes, twenty-three, that was really the right age.

O: Does S. believe there is transference by you to him?

W: I didn't discuss the matter with him in any detail.

O: How long have known him?

W: For years.

O: How did you happen to become his patient?

W: Well, through E. When E. took me to S., S. refused at first. He had no time and so on, and gave me the address of a certain Winterstein. I saw that man a few times and told him that this woman is impossible. And he said, correctly, "Well, we don't really know such women." Who would know a woman like that, I ask you? Only someone who is the slave of such a woman, but otherwise we don't know people like that, he said.

O: This Winterstein?

W: But S. and E. both believe that they understand this woman, that one can work things out with her. And that's the mistake.

O: Why did you stop seeing this Winterstein?

W: That was only temporary. Then he said I should go to S. But this Winterstein understood the matter. He said himself that we know nothing about such individuals. But you also understand that it is impossible to work things out with such people. An argument is simply ignored. . . .

O: Do you still lie on the couch nowadays?

W: No.

O: But if this fellow E. is so orthodox, he should really insist that you stretch out.

W: Well, it isn't so important whether one lies down or not.

O: But one concentrates better.

W: Granted, but E. surely is intelligent enough to . . . No. He is an orthodox psychoanalyst—intelligence is of no use. They are stubborn. They believe one can rid oneself of everything with a few ideas. But the links are much more complicated. In reality, the whole thing looks like a catastrophe. I am in the same state as when I first came to Freud, and Freud is no more.

O: Do you believe that Freud could help you today?

W: No, I don't believe that.

O: Does S. have you tell him your dreams?

W: He doesn't have that much time. But when E. comes and I tell a dream, he interprets as he always has. There would be something to psychoanalysis if psychoanalysts were gods. But they are only human beings, influenced by one thing and another. Why was S. always so supportive in this Luise affair, "It's all right, it's all right." Because he himself has a young wife and the problem old man/young wife was probably not to his liking.

O: Do you know his wife?

W: I was there once and saw a woman and thought it was his daughter. But it was his wife. And he is elderly. The problem existed for him too. So when he sees the same thing in someone else, he tends to see it optimistically somehow and to overlook the dangers. So you see, psychoanalysts are not always clear-sighted either.

And to orient someone so that all he ever consults is a psychoanalyst is also quite wrong. Freud didn't take that position—I must defend him there. He said that once analysis has ended, one should make one's own decisions. But the things they do! He comes from America and discusses those matters with me and sends me to S. and so on, that's all wrong. In a word, there isn't much one can say for psychoanalysis. But E. still believes everything Freud said.

O: Hasn't he developed at all?

W: He hasn't developed at all. S. is more critical. What can possibly be the result when one is treated by three physicians and each of them says something different?

O: But you are only being treated by two.

W: There is E. and S., and Gardiner also to an extent, she also wrote about me. And you are the fourth.

O: I am no analyst.

W: Yes, but we discuss these things.

O: I don't want to analyze you.

W: Very well, but isn't it enough when S. says one thing and Gardiner something else? One becomes completely confused.

There is a Russian proverb which I told S. He liked it. Here's how it goes in German: "When a child has seven nannies, he lacks an eye." That means that when that many persons concern themselves with you, responsibility keeps shifting around. And that is really the situation in which I found myself after Freud's death. Because I don't know whom to believe now.

O: But isn't that in part your own fault because you always ask everyone for advice?

W: Yes, naturally (*laughs*), of course. There's the saying "Does reliance on others mean that one is wholly forsaken?"

O: I find your behavior odd. If something is proposed to me, I ask myself, what do *I* want?

W: Yes, yes, I believe the ego is damaged somehow.

O: Yours?

W: Yes, I think so.

O: You got too used to analysts.

W: The bad thing about an analyst is that one clutches on to him, that, in a manner of speaking, one moves back into childhood and experiences everything as a child because of transference. For a child, every adult is an authority. And he asks everyone, "What do you think, and what do you think?" And then one arrives at no decision.

O: But you cannot remain a patient all your life. There has to come a time when you leave that condition. Why can't you have a relation with E. where the two of you are equals?

W: Well, Freud thought that when one has finished analysis, one should not continue going to an analyst. Yes, and Freud thought that psychoanalysis is a kind of reeducation. But at my age, this transference as father complex no longer comes about. . . .

O: Why must you always remain at this level? You could be friends with this E.

W: But you see, he reproaches me all the time. I am of the opinion that he simply does not understand the situation.

O: You always seek advice from others. Why don't you undertake something on your own? When someone makes a remark, it influences you. When E. says he won't come back, for example, then you can't marry. . . .

W: Marrying, you know, marrying someone with whom one cannot talk rationally . . .

O: If you don't *want* to marry, that's something else again.

W: It's too risky.

O: But this state of indecision doesn't make you happy either.

W: No.

O: In other words, you have no talent for making life pleasant for yourself.

W: That's what E. says, I don't have a talent for finding the right niche for myself.

O: You said just now that psychoanalysis is a sort of reeducation. So Freud really must have reeducated you quite extensively.

W: Apparently not.

O: But it is part of Freudian doctrine that the analyst should give advice only in exceptional situations.

W: That's not what he did.

O: The patient is to discover things for himself.

W: That's not what he did. I already told you that he kept me here. And he said: "You know, if you are short of money or a few garments, that doesn't matter. It's much more important for you to stay and that we treat the residual matters." And that took such a long time that the Red Army marched back into Odessa. . . .

O: Does S. also give advice?

W: Of course he does.

O: And E. too?

W: E. too. E. says, "I hope that you will take my advice this time." That's his idea, you know, that one observes and takes care of the patient to the very end. When he is dead, there's nothing further to be done. As long as he draws breath, he is to do psychoanalysis. Curious, isn't it? What E. doesn't understand is that one's inner strength declines as one gets older.

O: In what sense doesn't he understand it?

W: He doesn't understand it.

O: But it's true of everyone.

W: A fanatic of psychoanalysis. There are people like that.

O: And when you tell E. that analysis at your age is pointless, what does he say?

W: I never said that to him so bluntly. I don't want to offend him, after all. He means well. But this is the way he sees it: he believes one must pursue the patient to his last breath.

O: Every patient?

W: No, not every patient. But when one gets hold of one like me. I am the most famous case. So he must observe me to the very last moment.

O: You got to know E. through Gardiner?

W: Well, Gardiner wrote me that an analyst from the Freud archive in New York wanted to visit me. I thought, there's no harm in that and said I didn't mind. But then someone else came, a certain Lubin, who advanced the theory that I had adopted psychoanalysis as a kind of religion. . . . He may not be altogether mistaken for all I know. This transference played a very major role, I see that now. Although today I am no longer affected by what they say, I used to be.

O: And how did things develop with E.?

W: What developed is that he comes here every year. I don't know why or for what. He is Viennese and emigrated because of the Nazis. There's a psychological association here—after all, Freud worked here in Vienna—perhaps that's why he comes, I don't know. In any event, he does psychoanalysis with me and I don't get anywhere with him. He constantly reproaches me for not taking this or that into consideration.

O: What don't you take into consideration?

W: Freud's doctrines. In his opinion, I do not follow what Freud said.

O: What does E. think you should do?

W: The concrete problem is this Luise business. He finds that I don't conduct myself properly toward her, that I am not energetic enough, that I should not make so much of her unpleasant qualities. S. is not as fanatic a psychoanalyst as E. E. is a *terrible simplificateur*, he simplifies everything, you understand. The whole thing becomes very simple, clear, obvious. You throw her out, you understand—she can make no demands because I am neither married to her nor is there any sort of life partnership. But there are various inhibitions and certain buts, aren't there? Things aren't that simple.

You see, the whole thing is what used to be called a love-hate relationship. And now the analysts dismiss that by calling it an ambivalent attitude. Well, calling it ambivalence doesn't benefit me. On the contrary, the word *ambivalence* makes it harmless somehow, more harmless than it really is. But love-hate is something alogical, there are contradictions there, and they don't get anywhere with logic. Very well, E. writes that everything is really perfectly all right and that only I am at fault because I take things too tragically. Now tell me, how do you see the situation?

O: I also feel that you should have become more accustomed to it. You have been living with this for thirty years. Some people are married, and it's no different.

W: Yes, of course, there are many unhappy marriages.

O: Is there something you want to change?

W: S. always says, "Finding a solution—there are no solutions in life, one has to endure." Well, much in psychoanalysis is farfetched. Castration fear, for example, that's farfetched. I can tell from E.'s letters. He believes in all these things, and then there are those symbols and explanations. They suppress the real picture. He writes, "Put your knowledge of psychoanalysis to work," and re-proaches me besides. I am the guilty one.

When he began sending me money for the woman, I went on a vacation and wanted to paint and climbed a hill, held on to the bushes, and then got a pain in my hands. He said I could not bear the happiness that he helps me and that's why I inflicted that on myself. That's farfetched. After the war, Gardiner sent me a box of chocolates. It was winter; I carried it home. I got something similar and had a professor give me radiation treatment. He explained to me that there is a plate inside the hand that is extremely sensitive in people who no longer work with their hands. And his successor said, "No one knows what the cause of it is." E. knows better, of course: it is joy—I could not bear his helping me—and so masochism enters the picture.

O: Is Gardiner as orthodox as E.?

W: Well, E. is really very orthodox. I read once that Lenin's success is to be ascribed to the fact that he always adapted to the situation and did not start off from a particular position and always say the same thing. But he said, "What we proclaimed two months ago is no longer valid today. Today we must proceed differently." He went along with the times, as it were. He took the changes time brings into consideration. And that's what Dr. E. doesn't do. He insists on those psychoanalytic symbols like castration fear and God knows what else, and always comes back to them. That one gets older, that one sees things differently, that psychoanalysis cannot lead to a successful conclusion when one is older—Freud himself said that, and he ignores it. It is dogma for him and always to be applied. . . .

O: And Gardiner is the same?

W: You see what she wrote about me. She said she did not wish to be drawn into the role of psychoanalyst . . .

O: Of advisor . . .

W: If I write about someone, I must know everything.

O: Or as much as possible. One doesn't discover everything. I don't discover everything either.

W: How so? Surely I told you enough about myself. I don't know what I would have concealed from you. You see, I am afflicted by this unfortunate idea that I entered into a relationship with this woman whom I cannot deal with, and the older I become, the more difficult it gets. That's my problem. And I don't know how to extricate myself. It has already occurred to me to go to America. When she heard that, Gardiner said, "Since you don't speak English, Germany is the only possibility for you." Germany! To whom should I go? To this Mrs. Bulle, I suppose. . . .

O: Did you ever write her?

W: Yes, yes, I turned her down. That's all I need, don't you think? What would I do with her since the other one is jealous.

O: What did you write her?

W: I wrote . . . I also discussed with S. whether to give her his address. But I thought, why? She'll answer, and I'll have to think up something. And S. said, yes, he agrees, but inclines against it—I don't know—something like that. He does not forbid me to send his address if I insist. But he considers it better that I don't. So I wrote her a polite refusal: her kind words had given me much pleasure, but complications would arise and she could probably imagine what was involved. In a word, I don't know whether this proverb exists in German: "The mountain gave birth to a mouse . . ."

O: It's from Horace: "The mountain labored and gave birth to a mouse."

W: . . .much to-do, a lot of fuss, and nothing behind it. A whole mountain is set in motion and all that comes out is a mouse. Well, Gardiner didn't handle the matter correctly. She should not have said that she will not be drawn in. She should have taken more of an interest in my fate.

O: Did you tell her nothing about Luise?

W: I tried several times.

O: And what did she say?

W: She said, "Perhaps one can buy her off." But how can one buy her off? For the issue is, what happens when I die? That's always the question. And E. hinted that the archive would send something, and the last time he was here, he denied it. I no longer know what goes on. Well, things aren't what they used to be in America either; psychoanalysts are earning less now.

O: Because of inflation, or do they also have fewer patients?

W: I think they also have fewer patients. I remember Gardiner's sentence: "Psychoanalysts no longer earn as much as they used to." Perhaps psychoanalysis is no longer so fashionable.

O: There are other therapies that are less expensive. Who can afford that drawn-out treatment?

W: Precisely. I used to be able to, but today I couldn't.

O: People try to find methods that are more workable. . . .

W: Well yes, drugs . . .

O: They may do more harm than good.

W: They don't do any good. One gets used to drugs. And I know from experience—S. always gives me something—that I don't notice much difference whether I take them or not.

O: What does he give you?

W: Different ones. One of them is called Nutrilen—I don't really remember—there were different ones.

O: And what are they for?

W: For a period of time, I was not always in this melancholy state but only now and then, and that's when S. gave me this Trofanil, and that helped. But now it is chronic. And the drugs no longer do anything. They produce this dryness in my mouth, but I got used to that.

O: Then why take it?

W: Well, S. says it is a depression, I am in a state of depression since Tiny . . . I asked S. since when my condition had deteriorated so much and he said, "Actually, it's since Tiny died." You said you also had depressions now and then. What do you do?

O: Nothing, actually. I would hesitate to take drugs. It's useless if you become addicted to them.

W: To sleep, I take Montadon. Have you heard of that one?

O: Is it a barbiturate?

W: I don't know. I'll have to ask S. That's bad, isn't it? I remember that when I arrived in Vienna, there was something in the paper about someone who had killed himself in a hotel and there was a piece of paper on the table that said, "By means of a small dose of Veronal, I depart this vale of tears." Yes well, people took Veronal. My father took Veronal—he died at the age of forty-nine.

O: Have you always suffered from insomnia or is that recent?

W: Now I've actually got used to those drugs.

O: You can't sleep without sleeping pills?

W: I would have to try.

O: How long have you been taking those drugs.

W: For years and years.

O: Ten years, five years?

W: Ten years.

O: Every day?

W: Yes, every day.

O: You can really take it, I must say.

W: Someone else would probably have died. . . . On my last vacation, I was in Tragöss. There were two ladies at my table, one of them, I don't know, almost dying, the other perhaps seventy. I went for walks with the seventy-year-old one. She said that there was something wrong with her foot and that she didn't dare walk alone. There was nothing the matter with her foot. She wanted company. So. I walked with her and we became friends. She wrote poems, played with words. I still recall: "Who has loved, cannot forget, and who loved and has forgotten has forgotten how one loves." Not without skill. Pretty. Another poem had the meaning that the flowers stop blooming when you go. She's probably said that to many men.

I got along with her fairly well. I told her about myself and said—you know Solzhenitsyn—"That's the first circle of hell, what I am telling you," because I had not yet told her anything about Luise. When we traveled back to Vienna, I thought, that woman is so pleasant, I must ask for her address and continue seeing her. It turns out she doesn't live far from Luise.

O: Really?

W: Of all things. Well, I visited her and thought, if she has an apartment, it may be a place where I can escape from Luise. But she only had one room. The entire apartment consisted of a single room and a kitchen. The room was rather nicely furnished. Then I started telling about Luise. She says, "Oh, I know her by sight." They went swimming in the nude and Luise also went there, with her bracelets, she told me, and conducted herself so provocatively. Her behavior was such that the women became scared of looking at her because they thought, either she will say something vulgar or she'll become violent.

You see, that's the impression that woman made on complete strangers. Then I acted improperly. But what was I to do? Tiny, my housekeeper, didn't care for her either. In a word, I stopped seeing her. Because I was also afraid of going there and running into Luise. I went there and complained about Luise and she complained about Luise and we didn't get beyond that. It's different with you: we discuss psychoanalysis and we have common interests. And I wasn't sure what she was really after. The whole thing was a little suspicious.

O: How so?

W (*giggles*): She said something that surprised me. She said when a woman loves a man and so on, and when they have known each other for some time, then the woman can also fulfill the man's particular desires. What is that supposed to mean? I thought is was a little suspicious, those special desires she was talking about. . . .

O: So here we have another woman that fell in love with you.

W: Well, well. Sympathy . . . That's what's so tragic about me. I would have had such opportunities! Better opportunities! And I didn't exploit them and got stuck with an oaf. Luise is an oaf.

O: Well, if it should become necessary to run away from Luise, you can come here whenever you like.

W: Thank you for the offer. Well, I had the idea at the time—I'll be quite frank with you—if I have to run from Luise, I can't run to her; she only has a kitchen and one room. Then she said something about people who were so nice to her. And they gave her an envelope with 1000 schillings inside, as a token of their appreciation. . . .

O: So it's the same old story.

W: Well, she wouldn't be so dangerous. She's a decent person.

O: What did she do for a living?

W: She worked in a store. She is retired. But you see the impression Luise made on her. And E. keeps saying, "She's a harmless psychopath." What does that mean, "harmless psychopath," when there are such quarrels on the street that strangers intervene and call the police. Once, even a radio car came, but fortunately it drove on. That's not a harmless person. Why harmless? And now, Luise has that dog. That's all I needed. In the past, her every other word was, "Those miserable dogs!" They weren't allowed to come close to her because all women have to do with dogs—sexually, you understand. It's disgusting. Now she has bought herself a dog, a small dog, and she feeds him, and that costs money.

O: Why did she buy a dog?

W: Well, you see, the relationship with me is clearly disagreeable for her. What does it mean, "Only on Sundays?" Only on Sundays, and otherwise we don't see each other. You understand. From that point of view, everything is unsatisfactory. One has to admit that. But what am I to do? To be married to her is impossible. Didn't I give her money for her medical insurance? She doesn't know the word *gratitude*. She can only make demands, nothing but demands. Demands and accusations. And on top of that, she's a communist. Not a party member, but by conviction.

O: She isn't religious?

W: She hates the cross like the devil. You can't imagine how much she is against religion. Priests seduce boys. I don't know, of course, how religious you are.

O: I am not religious.

W: You are not religious. She isn't either. Very well, one can be irreligious, but there's no need to have a tantrum every time one sees a priest. But she immediately starts reviling.

O: It seems she berates everybody.

W: For her, life is combat. Where she has a chance to fight, she takes it. And I want peace. There are no greater opposites than these. So, are you placing your apartment at my disposal?

O: Not all of it.

W: But a part.

O: A part.

W: How is one going to get out of this? If you would give me some advice what I should do. Well, let's let that go, later perhaps. S. says she's a serious psychopath.

O: You probably don't want to get away from her at all.

W: That's the question I cannot answer.

O: Freud writes that you have marked masochistic tendencies.

W: You keep mentioning masochism. I have never had women beat me. Real masochists ask women to beat them.

O: There's also a psychological masochism.

W: To get to the present for a change, it's such a complication that this woman is ill. She has a heart ailment, she has diabetes, there's something wrong with her kidneys. So she must not excite herself. She thinks I should endorse everything. Otherwise she excites herself, gets an attack. My hands are tied.

O: You allow those illnesses to intimidate you too much.

W: The stupid thing is that she has no medical insurance.

O: But you said that you had given her money for that insurance.

W: She says it's only limited coverage, but S. says there's no such thing. She claims she can only see a general practicioner, not a specialist. She is trying to tell me it's limited.

O: On the other hand, you have been stringing this woman along for thirty years. She wants to get married. She probably still hopes . . .

W: One cannot marry this woman. Can one marry a woman with whom one cannot talk, who has crazy ideas?

O: Then it would have been better if you had left her.

W: But she doesn't want that either. You see, that's the conflict. Psychoanalysts only deal with wealthy people. The problems of life—what do I live on? do I have medical insurance? do I have a pension?—all these things are of no interest to those people because such questions do not come up in their practice. Now they stand there—I should like to use Luise's vulgar expression—they stand there like a child before a pile of shit.

O: The psychoanalysts?

W: One tells you this, another something else. They really don't take note of any of those things. As long as I was wealthy, everything was different. . . . I'll tell you about that sometimes, as a woman, you can perhaps explain things better to me than the psychoanalysts. Because they represent the male point of view. S., for example: "You owe that woman nothing. You are not married; it's not a partnership for life. You give her money but you don't have to." In that vein. But I say to myself, I've been with that woman for a long time and she is ill, and she has no pension. That oppresses me, of course.

O: I actually share the view that you owe this woman nothing.

W: Now the question is always, "What will I do when you die?" There's no way out.

O: But she wouldn't get a pension all that quickly.

W: No, one would have to be married for ten years. I am not going to live another ten years.

O: There's no way of telling. But then you should marry quickly. Though it is true that there is the question how long you will live.

W: It's obvious that I wouldn't live long under those circumstances.

O: You might no longer want to.

W: Even now, I no longer feel like it. Here's the way it is: I thought I was a progressive person. *Mésalliance* and simple women—those are all prejudices; all human beings are equal. But practically speaking, I see that one cannot get along with a person who does not have a certain level of education. I don't know what to talk to her about. It's forever the same thing: disputes with neighbors, the old Bohemian who doesn't open the windows along the corridor, there's a bad smell there, the air is stale . . . Her interests are so limited. Nothing but constant demands. . . .

O: Does she tell you every Sunday that she wants to get married?

W: Last Sunday she didn't mention it, but the previous Sundays all she talked about was marriage.

O: An what do you say?

W: Nothing.

O: What does she say then?

W: She starts talking about something else. I thought a way out might be if I went to America.

O: One cannot solve problems by running away.

W: That's right. S. says, "You would worry about her."

O: You would have a bad conscience.

W: I have too much of a conscience. Other men do things differently. Her father simply left her mother and did not pay alimony.

O: The parents were married?

W: Yes, they were married and he simply walked out, took a younger woman, and did not pay alimony. That's a reason for treating
men badly, isn't it?

O: So what are you going to do?

W: This is no life any more.

O: But you can't end it either.

W: It's not that simple. Although she is revolutionary in other
respects, it's her view that a man must take care of a woman. The
woman need not do anything. And why this story about her heart?
Her heart isn't as bad as all that, considering that she goes to the
movies and the theater. It can't be as bad as all that. Why didn't she
accept a job? That's the trouble with these women, they don't want
to work. . . . And into that institution?

O: Live there? Did S. suggest that to you?

W: Yes, for some weeks or months—I don't know what he is thinking of.

O: Don't! It would be better to go to an old people's home. I'm
familiar with the Steinhof . . .

W: What is it? Steinhof?

O: Yes, the Vienna Psychiatric Hospital. Why does S. say you
should go there?

W: So that I don't see Luise. She will not be admitted. I could
recuperate from her, he said. But I think that's a mistaken idea.

O: It's a full-fledged insane asylum.

W: I asked him, "Is it an insane asylum?" He said, "No, there are
different sections, there are also sections for people who are not
actually insane." I don't know, of course. But it's a good thing you
warned me.

O: Of course, if you are adventurous and really insist on having that
experience . . .

W: Have you been inside?

O: I once did a newspaper story . . .

W: Well, at the moment there's no necessity, considering the state in
which I find myself. He said if my condition deteriorates, I can come
to him. And when I asked him if he believed that the moment had
arrived, he said no.

O: When did he suggest it?

W: He mentioned it as a possibility. He did not say that I should go now. He simply meant that if my condition deteriorates, that would be a possibility.

O: Compared to the Steinhof, an old people's home would be paradise. I hope you realize that.

W: I wrote my memoirs and my case really became a propaganda piece for psychoanalysis. If you write something now, it will turn into something else.

O: I am after the truth.

W: That's why I showed you the painting in my apartment. What is truth? You remember? E. said I should write what happened after the death of my wife, but I can't. It requires distance. I told him, "That wouldn't suit Gardiner because she had written that I am in good health." E. said, "The main thing is not Gardiner, the main thing is the truth." I told S. and he said, "If everybody told the truth, the world would go out of existence." You see, opinions differ. . . .

O: Gardiner writes rather uncritically and credulously . . .

W: She looks at what Freud accomplished. . . . That she didn't send that letter from that Russian woman! If that woman writes Russian, one should find out what she writes. Gardiner is nice, but one has no idea what these women are like. One doesn't know it about the Russian woman either. She might have said, "Come here, if you are having such difficulties." But I would have to become used to living in France and I don't know what she has in mind. She might have thought that I could do all sorts of things with her, that I was still robust. That would also be a difficult problem. . . . As regards money, because there are always disputes about money with Luise, I thought I might say, "You go ahead and decide what should be spent. I won't concern myself with it." That's how it was with my wife. I gave her money and she spent it as she wished. I had nothing to do with it. But Therese was a decent human being. With that sort of person, you don't know what's in store.

O: Then you may starve because she spends all the money.

W: It might be one's fate that one no longer has anything to eat. It was careless that I gave her all that money. And one cannot even be punished by gas.

O: What does S. say about your suicide ideas?

W: "She isn't worth killing oneself over."

O: And besides, what a disgrace for psychoanalysis—the most famous case kills itself! You cannot do that to them.

W: I have to consider the psychoanalysts.

O: It wouldn't be nice if you did that.

W: The showpiece! Well, next time, I would like to come after the
holidays. I thought January 8 would be best. All the hubbub will be
over by then.

O: How will you be spending the holiday?

W: I am stuck with Luise. She won't let them go by.

O: Will you be seeing her more often than Sundays?

W: Well yes, the first and second Christmas days and New Year's
Eve. I should also visit my acquaintances.

Love/Hate

WOLF-MAN: Just think what a terrible stupidity I committed. I had drunk a glass of wine and so I promised her 50,000 schillings. My mother was already afraid that I would become an alcoholic because my father drank, you know. But I didn't inherit that. I am really neutral toward alcohol. I don't hate drinking; I am indifferent. But I am not used to it. I don't drink. This glass of wine made me careless. I thought, if I give her the money, I'll have peace and quiet. . . . And what happened? The next time, she shows up with a new winter coat with fur trim and with a new fur hat. And this in spite of the fact that she already has a fur hat but a dark one. Now she bought a light-colored one, to go with the coat. In that coat, she looks like a princess. And you can imagine how much I blamed myself and how I told myself, how can you be so stupid as to believe that she would show a little gratitude? She was more unbearable than before. Even more unbearable!

We were at the movies. She simply moved to another seat. Suddenly she was gone. I thought, I'll go home. I don't know where she is. Then a woman walked up to me and said, "There's a woman waiting for you down that side street." Otherwise I wouldn't have found her. I am telling you, I feel as if I were in a Dostoevski novel.
OBHOLZER: You have already given her the money?
W: Unfortunately. Unfortunately I have. And then I almost went mad, of course. What have you done? Now, there's no money left. You have given her all that remained. What this woman is doing to me! Then I thought I was finally becoming rational. And then I had the idea, if you give her the money, you will have no feelings of

remorse. Of course, that's also a thought with which she constantly torments me: "What will happen when you die?" And then this marriage business. But one cannot marry such a woman. It's impossible. Impossible! She understands nothing. Then she tells me that I gave her so little twenty-five years ago. She had been divorced at the time. And the way she talks, it's me that seduced her. How can a man, an old man like myself, do anything at all with such a young woman? It's disgusting. That's the sort of thing she says to me. And I ought to say, you are a pig yourself since you got yourself involved with me. But that woman is incapable of logic. And you see, when I tell E. about all this, he ignores it and gives me advice on how a healthy, rational person should act. But that doesn't do me any good.

O: So it seems.

W: I thought, it would be best if I jump out the window, since I live on the fifth floor. But then I tell myself, if you had given her only thirty thousand, there would be something left over for you. And I say to myself, to kill oneself because of 20,000 schillings isn't worth it. The money isn't worth anything, actually. And that's her argument, money isn't worth anything. That's why she squanders it. When she showed up with that fur, I didn't say anything, of course. That would only have led to a quarrel and recriminations. "You never bought me anything, you never bought me jewelry, you never bought me a fur." You get the idea. We'd only quarrel, and that's pointless. So I said nothing. That fate sent me this person is really vicious. And she's infatuated with Russians.

O: What do you mean?

W: Well, she had an affair with a Russian. And up until now, until recently, she always said, "I love you because you are Russian." That's what she kept saying. You remarked once that I was lucky with women. But my luck is my bad luck with women, it seems. Why I am lucky, I don't know. I am not the type that pleases women. What they prefer are aggressive men with muscles.

O: That may be one type. But another is the precise opposite.

W: All right, now I've told you, at least I got some things off my chest.

O: You must have had pleasant holidays.

W: Terrible I tell you, terrible. I saw her the first Christmas day, the second, New Year's Eve, and yesterday she wanted to celebrate Epiphany on top of that. That's when I said no. Epiphany, that's really my birthday. But if she celebrates my birthday, it's a second celebration of her own. In any event, it's also the wine that doesn't agree with me. I promise things. I must remember that: When you have had some wine, don't discuss these matters.

O: It would be best if you didn't drink at all.

W: Well, when I do drink something, I feel a little easier. But it's not the moment to make decisions. She said that she needs security, she needs money for her teeth and for a kidney test and for X-rays. She has all kinds of illnesses. And with all those illnesses, she goes ahead and buys a fur. She's deathly ill, supposedly. A deathly ill woman doesn't buy things like that. And she wants to go to the theater twice a day—once with me, and then I am to give her money so she can go by herself. I am telling you, the whole thing is a nightmare. It's the purest Dostoevski. Isn't that yet another awful stupidity? But it's not worth killing onself for.

O: You yourself could become ill and need money.

W: There's nothing the matter with me. When she has a fever, she goes out. She demands the same thing of me. When I have a fever, I am also supposed to go out. You know what else is bad? In the past, she didn't bother with politics. No idea about history, of course. She doesn't read, either. Well, she did read but then she saw that life is something else again, and she stopped. Completely uninformed and uneducated. Tabula rasa, one might say. No position on politics. But now she sees movies on television. They are showing the period of serfdom in Russia. Serfdom was abolished in 1861; there hasn't been any since. And the greatest famine occurred after the war. People may have eaten human flesh, I don't know. But she thinks that during my time, the estate owners really lived it up and ate human flesh. How am I to explain to her that it isn't so? She doesn't believe me. Now she tells me these things and believes she has a moral claim, as it were, because here's an émigré and they exploited the people, so why not exploit him in turn? That's a communist, I'm telling you. She isn't in the party. But she wants to play princess.

What kind of communism is that? It's nothing more than envy, that one has nothing oneself. She really understands nothing about the theory, about communist doctrine, what is involved there. But she uses it to accuse one all the time and to arrogate rights to herself. I lost all my money, I worked at the insurance company for thirty years, after all. So nobody can call me an estate owner. That's absurd. She treats me as if I were the owner of a large estate. There are so few communists in Vienna. It's a devilish idea fate had there. Well, I am telling you, it was horrible, those two days. If I marry her, we'll find ourselves in the category, "people before the judge."

O: What do you mean?

W: Because I won't stand it, I'll kill her.

O: You think you would be capable of that?

W: Absolutely. How one gets out of this ambivalence, Freud didn't show. But Dostoevski dealt with the problem. You mustn't forget that it's also a question of race. A Western European can more easily come to terms with things like that than a Russian.

O: Do you believe that?

W: Because with the Russians, the savage instincts are still in the blood, somehow. That's why they cannot come to terms with these things in a normal way. Perhaps the emotional is stronger than among Western Europeans who have been living according to reason for a longer time. You and your husband also didn't see eye to eye when you got your divorce, but you straightened things out somehow. Gardiner, being American, doesn't understand any of this. It's alien to her. Mack might understand me better, but she was also American. Well, sometime I'll have to tell you how it all started. You really don't know anything yet. But I don't want to begin today, it's already quite late.

O: It's only half-past seven.

W: Well, if I tell you, it's a certain relief, like confession, something like that. Perhaps it will help me.

O: It's possible.

W: You see, I can't do that with S. He has his half hour, and that's already a great deal, and so we don't get anywhere. This can only be discussed the way I talk to you, over the course of hours. Well then, should I start?

O: Yes.

W: You said that I had success with women. Why did you say that? I wrote nothing about that.

O: Well . . .

W: It's true, I do have success with them. But I didn't exploit that success, because I had those inhibitions. I must be the one that pays. But how did you get that idea?

O: I inferred it from what you have told me, and then it was simply intuition. I came to visit you once and you weren't at home. There was a woman there who lives on the floor below you, I believe, and she kept asking what I wanted and if there was a message. She was too curious—she really insisted on giving you a message. It seems she was looking for a pretext to establish contact with you. And so I thought, here's another one that's interested in him.

W: Well, you guessed right. An acquaintance of mine—she lives near Schönbrunn—had a girl friend, a good-looking person, and she always told me that her friend was inquiring about me. I could have started something with so many. Then there was another one who always came to see me and who suggested we get married. She wasn't my type. But a good-looking person, Polish. I could have started something with her. But I said, "No, you wouldn't get a pension because there is too much of an age difference between us." She said, "Really"—she came from a good family—"but then we can just live together." Anyone else would have taken her up on that. She was offended. Still, we remained friends. And the one that lives near Schönbrunn—the fuss she made—and I was no longer a young man at the time. Yes, to fall asleep, to fall asleep, and not to live any more . . . I had the greatest difficulties because I did not wish to wreck her marriage. She had children, you understand. I didn't exploit any of that and attached myself to women who were worth nothing. The less the woman was worth, the more she meant to me. Can you understand that?

O: No.

W: I don't understand either. There was something like the sister, some fear of incest, something like that. I think that's true. Do we have time left?

O: Yes, yes.

W: Well, here's the way it was: I saw this woman at the tailor's. She was good-looking, she still is. And it did not occur to me that one cannot simply start talking to a woman there. Ordinarily, when I walked up to women and started talking to them, there was never any risk. Nothing ever happened to me. In Odessa, I went to a hotel once with a woman; then she suddenly calls me at home and says, "I am such and such." You can imagine what a scare that was. But I said, "You are mistaken," and hung up. That happened once, but otherwise I never had any problems. I could not conceive that there would be consequences. And it did not occur to me that she might ask the tailor for my address. So I met her a few times, and then I thought, I won't see her again.

Suddenly, the telephone rings in the office and she's on the line, she got the number from the tailor. I should have said, "Private conversations aren't allowed here," and hung up. But I thought, well, I have no one, and I find her rather attractive. So we met. That was the first mistake. We got together every three weeks or so, we went to the hotel, she didn't demand much. Today, she reproaches me for that: "You didn't pay me anything in those days."

O: Was that the arrangement from the very beginning, that you get together for the sole purpose of going to a hotel . . .

W: Why yes, what's wrong with that?

O: . . . and that she goes to bed with you for money?

W: It's normal for the woman to get paid. It was a small amount, insignificant. And that went on for years. And I got used to it. Then the Russians came. . . .

O: That was during the war?

W: During the Nazi period.

O: So you've known her for more than thirty years.

W: Twenty-five years, that's the difficulty, that it has been going on so long.

O: The war was over in '45.

W: So it's even longer. During the Nazi period, before the Russians came. But it was a superficial relationship; it didn't cost me much. That's what she reproaches me with today, that I had her cheap. And then, when the Russians came, there was no food. I didn't see her at all and thought, the thing is over. I didn't see her for perhaps a year. Once I ran into her and said, "Let's meet," but she didn't come. Once when I was standing in line for bread, I saw her. But I took care that she wouldn't see me. I considered the matter finished.

And then I had that trouble with my hand. Gardiner had sent me a box of chocolates, which I picked up at the post office and carried home. It was winter; I got those pains. I went to a Professor Maier who used radiation. For a while, I had nothing to do with women because is was a hypochondriacal idée fixe of mine—what's the matter with my right hand? I cannot paint any more—the same thing as with my nose, a torment. So I didn't think about women, that's how preoccupied I was with my hand. Finally, I went to the professor and he said, "You needn't come back, it has healed." And I went home and felt great relief: it's all right, you needn't go back. . . .

Now I had to make it my business to reestablish contact with women. To celebrate, I went to the movies—it was a Russian film, what was it called? *Stalingrad!* First, I went to a café and had a look at the women but saw nothing suitable. Then I went to the movies. As I walk home, I see a woman at the streetcar stop on the opposite side of the street. She had a nice figure. I walk over there and who should it be but Luise. Just imagine, the probability was one in one and a half million. We said hello to each other. "Do you want to come back?" That's the way it started again.

And right away, she started: "When do we get married?" I didn't answer. We didn't go to a hotel as in the past but spend Sundays together. We drove to the Old Danube; things went quite well. And that's the way is contined until '54, I believe. We went to the movies and I went to her place. Luise allowed me to come to her place. So she was pretty tame, it was really nothing special. And then, all of a sudden, it was before Christmas '55, we meet and suddenly she makes a fuss on the street, a terrible fuss. I am to marry her, she doesn't want things to go on like that. She got to know someone, she will break off the relationship with me. I was dumbfounded. I thought, why all of a sudden? She had been nice all that time and now, suddenly, this row. She said she would end the relationship in three weeks. I was speechless and did not know what was the matter with this woman. She was wild. . . . What was I to do? Of course, when she told me that she knew an architect, I should have said, well, go on, take off with your architect. Put an end to it. And I remembered that back in Berlin I had left Therese and had later regretted it. So I put up with this flood of insults. I did not know what to do, and we parted.

Well, and then I had a complete breakdown. Suddenly, the whole neurosis was there and despair and not knowing what to do. And suddenly this fear of losing her. In any event, we saw each other again and here's what she said: "Let's begin a three-week period now, and at the end of it, you'll have to make a decision. Either you marry or we put an end to it." I ran into an acquaintance, that Polish woman, who offered to live with me. We were friendly with each other. She also paints. I talked with her and told her that I had not slept at all that night and that I would do this: If I employ her pro forma, she will get health insurance and retirement benefits. I only have to do that for six weeks. Then she can quit and will get those same benefits, provided she keeps paying in a small amount every month.

Well, I thought, Eureka, I found a way out. I go to her and say, "I'll register you." At first, I did not tell her that I would deregister her again. When I said to her that I would register her, she said, good, then she would be taken care of. She has no pension, she had not worked for anyone, she had spent all her time with her mother, and led an entirely private life. So she accepted and I went home and thought, I cannot keep her as a servant forever since I have a house-keeper, Tiny. So I said to her, "I'll register you and then, as soon as possible, I'll deregister you and I'll pay the monthly dues." No, un-der no circumstances! The employment office will come and bother her. That office has nothing whatever to do with it, but she imagined it did. "No," she said, "we agreed on a three-week period. . . ." An ultimatum, in other words. That's when I made the biggest mistake. Suddenly, I thought the world was going to come to an end. I don't know what I was going through. I should have said, "All right, if you don't want to, we'll end it." Because that was nonsensical. The em-ployment office is pleased when one doesn't bother them.

And I said, "Well, then we'll get married." She jumped up in bed, the world was turning. I was still baron at the time, in the mean-time I have lost that title. Reduced in rank. "Mother, mother, the baron is going to marry me, the world is turning," and so on.

O: You said you would marry her?

W: Yes, I don't know how that slipped out. How can one suddenly decide in five minutes that one will get married? It's madness, isn't it? Well, of course, a moment later, I started wondering, my God, what have I done, what have I promised, it's madness. And she, she was in seventh heaven. . . . So it seems she loved me in some way in those days. How happy she was! She wasn't happy because it was such a splendid match.

Then I run into this Cermak, whose wife had also killed herself, and he says to me, "If you marry that woman, you'll turn on the gas tomorrow, I'll give you that in writing." Then I felt that I could not marry her and if someone killed me on the spot, I could not marry her. Impossible. That was on a Saturday. I met Cermak on a Saturday and as I walk home, she suddenly jumps from the streetcar. I am telling you, the whole thing is like a novel. She says, "I was just in Mariahilferstrasse and picked out a scarf for you."
I am thinking, I cannot marry her, I'll have to tell her right away. We go into a café. She: "What's wrong? What is it?" I had to say, "I cannot marry you."

There was an explosion of insults; she jumped up and ran out. I felt sorry for her and followed. She stopped and says, "Well, we are going to do things differently. . . . " She calmed down a little. I say, "we can still go to the ice show." We had agreed that we would go to the ice show. I felt terrible remorse, of course. I had promised marriage to this woman and she had gone and picked out a scarf for me. She was so happy, and suddenly I tell her, "I can't." Terrible guilt feelings. What was I to do?

I went home in the greatest despair and had this idea, an absurd idea—after I had promised to marry her and now didn't want to, and with the idea of employing her, she doesn't want that—I had this idea: I'll sign part of my income over to her. It was about 250 or 300 schillings at the time. I'll sign that over to her. E. had recommended a woman analyst in Vienna and I thought, I'll talk to her and see what she has to say. So I went to her. It was a woman, a woman analyst—the bad thing about transference in psychoanalysis is that one always asks—and that stupid goose, instead of telling me, "Look, don't do something like that; don't assume any obligations. . . . " I have the civil code at home on my table and it says that a promise of marriage is not legally binding. She should have said, "It's not binding, why sign something like that over to her?" I could have paid some compensation or something. And this stupid goose, this psychoanalyst, says to me," I think that's quite a reasonable idea, like paying taxes. . . ."
O: Is she still alive?

W: I think she still exists, a stupid goose. That that tie remains for the rest of one's life is something she didn't consider. It's the most stupid thing one can do. When one puts an end to something, it has to be definitive, but not in such a way that one has obligations toward the woman.

I went to a lawyer with her and obliged myself in writing to pay her a given amount per month. Of course, my psychological condition was very bad. Then I went to a physician, Menninger was his name, not a psychoanalyst but a psychiatrist. When I said something psychoanalytical, he answered, "Who believes that sort of thing?" He was a professor, a nice fellow, died in the meantime. He said to me: "You cannot meet that women in the state you're in. Write her that you cannot see her for the time being. Pay for now as you agreed, in your condition, doubts are the worst thing. You made this arrangement, leave things alone, but you mustn't see her."

Well, I wrote her—she was even tamer—I wrote her that I was ill psychologically and that the neurologist had forbidden me to see her, and I sent her the amount.

Months went by. That had been Christmas, April or May came, my condition was awful. I spent the day in bed, got up around six in the evening, my housekeeper brought me something to eat, I went for a short walk and then back home. That continued for months, one of the most awful states I've ever been in. After three months, suddenly someone knocks on the door. I had paid the money. She comes in, furious: "Such meanness, I want my money, I am waiting for my money, no one takes an interest in me, I have severe bronchitis. . . ." She conducted herself impossibly and I got so furious that I insulted her. You mustn't think that I threatened her, but they were almost threats. "Get out, away with you," I said. In a word, a row.

I thought, why do I send her money? Cermak also said, "What kind of stupidity is this, why did you do that?" And I thought, why did I do it? I asked Cermak about a lawyer and went to him. And this lawyer says: "The promise you gave is not binding, it violates morality. This woman does nothing for you, so you can annul." I asked him, can I pay a lump sum? And he said, "Give her two thousand schillings, that's enough."

My savings were all used up. I had no money, my entire fortune was ten thousand schillings. I said, "Two thousand is too little, I'll give her five." At that moment, I felt relief: perhaps I can get out of this mess. I had the lawyer write her that I was canceling the previous agreement. Either she accepts the lump sum or I'll stop payments. She came to my place, but I always managed to hide in Tiny's room. Then we met at the lawyer's and the lawyer says, "What an odd woman." She had been to see him and he had questioned her some. So we went to the lawyer and in front of the house, she says suddenly, "I am not going up." So what was I to do? I went by myself and told him that she did not want to come up. So he said, "Wait, I'll go downstairs." He goes downstairs and she tells him," I will not discuss this matter with you, I'll only speak with the doctor." So what could he do? He came back up. We went to a café and it began, ten thousand, no, five thousand, ten thousand, no, five thousand, so it went back and forth. Then she started in, "I need someone, I want a human being." I wanted to smooth things over and said, "You will have a human being. When you need something, advice or whatever, you have me." That was already a mortgage, wasn't it. I shouldn't have said "You will have someone." That was the mistake. We left and she walked off a ways, came back, walked away again. . . . "I think I'll accept." "No, I'll think it over," and so on.

We parted and two days later, I call the lawyer and he says, "She's signed." I still have the piece of paper, but it doesn't do me any good. So the matter is settled.

Two days later, a letter from her arrives: "You promised that you would be a human being to me, I need advice about what to do with the money, come to such and such a café." I went, a constant vacillation, we start again, declarations of love, she will forgive and forget and so on. And I had the feeling, if I say yes now, it'll be the end. And I said, "Under no circumstances, no, I refuse." And I went to my acquaintances who live near Schönbrunn, nice people, who said they had adopted me, and suddenly life there seemed awfully boring. What do you say to that? Instead of being glad that everything had worked out so well, I suddenly ruin everything. I want to see her again. Life seems so empty, and I am already waiting for a letter from her. What do you say to that?

Well, E. arrived. I went to him, and said: "Look, I was so furious, I thought I would kill the woman. Now, suddenly, I no longer feel furious and want a reconciliation with her." Anyone else . . . you know, if I had discussed that with some ordinary person, the concièrge, a maid, anybody with an ounce of brains, he would have told me: "Look, everything worked out so well this time, you should be pleased. Walk up to some woman on the street whose looks you like. You've always managed to get women you liked to go to a hotel with you." Everybody would have said that.

And what does he say? You know what he said to me? "You describe the woman as very bad, but she isn't that bad." Because I had written that Freud had reproached me for having described Therese inaccurately. He said: "I cannot forbid you anything because you might blame me later. I leave it to you. I believe it would be better if there were no reconciliation." "I believe . . ." What is that supposed to mean? "I believe it would be better . . ." The next day, I am walking down the street and suddenly she is in front of me. Instead of hanging back—I'd seen her once and hung back—I run up to her and say, "Good day." And she says, "Nothing in life can be repeated. You were so awful to me." We walk on a distance. There is a park in front of the Regina Hotel; we sit down there. Suddenly, she puts her arms around my neck: "Be nice to me again and I'll forget everything." Well, what do you say to that?

This rejection and then "be nice to me," that was such a contrast, it naturally reinforced everything again. A woman who has just finished saying that I had hurt her so much and now wants to go on, and I do too. . . . So I talked to E. after this and he said: "I cannot forbid you anything. So that you don't blame me afterwards." Who is going to blame anyone? And she was so clever, she knew if it were to go on for two days, I wouldn't come again. And so she said, "Day after tomorrow, I am leaving with my mother, you will have to decide tomorrow." How clever of her! Then I saw E. and told him, "I am no longer furious," and he gave me carte blanche, as it were, so I went to the café and then to her place, and knocked. No one at home. So fate was well disposed toward me. I went to another café and thought, what should I do now, they are leaving, perhaps later I'll go back one more time. And then I went back and she was there. And the whole thing started all over. So. To be continued.

O: Did E. already come to Vienna in those days?

W: Yes, after that incident with the Russians. He helped me a great deal because he said to me, "the Russians have no interest whatever in you." But that was the wrong advice. Wait. Where did we stop? That there was a reconciliation. Now we stop.

O: So that was about twenty years ago.

W: Do we have some time left?

O: Yes, yes.

W: I have to collect my thoughts. . . . Shall I continue next time or finish now?

O: I think it's best to do the whole thing in one sitting.

W: It doesn't matter if we finish later today. I prefer it too. How did things continue? I went to Grossgmain. That's where the Polish woman was. And she said: "What have you done? You made up with her? That's madness. There's only one thing you can do now—give as much money as you can, and be steadfast. And if she doesn't want that, make an end of it." Well, I think I gave her two hundred schillings at that time.

A quarrel soon started, she said three hundred, and I two. The money problem started that long ago. I remained firm then, went away, and she pulled me back into the apartment by my jacket, and gave in. At that time, I still had the strength. I did not feel bad, I felt that I was sticking to what I had decided on. The whole thing didn't cost me a whole lot, the relationship was going well. I did not want to spend much, and she already criticized that, she felt it wasn't enough. I'll tell you briefly.

In any case, as I stuck to my guns, I saw that she was becoming hesitant, wanted to leave me, something like that. That was after two years. I went to Hardegg for a vacation and had the feeling that it was coming to an end, that what I gave her wasn't enough for her, that she was going to leave me. I didn't want that, and was afraid that she wouldn't come any more. But she did come and said: "My mother will no longer let you visit us because people talk. Either we meet at your place or I'll have to end it." I talked to the Polish woman and she said, "She's got someone else." I found that idea disagreeable and thought, she can come here, why not after all, why shouldn't she come here. And I said to her, "All right, then you come here." She married again but did not tell me anything. Had she told me that she had got married, that would have been the end, of course. But as it was, me not knowing . . . At that time, she came to my place twice a month, we didn't meet on Sundays at that time. So I was really practically a free man. I said, "Let's go to the movies." Because I was used to going to the movies with her. She said no, didn't go anywhere with me, came, you know, performed the act, and left again. Because she was married. And that's when I committed the greatest stupidity, you see, I said, "Let's go to the movies." She said, "No, I don't have the time, my mother is ill," my mother, and so on. And I say, "Come Sunday," and she came Sunday, and that's how I ruined everything, because now there were those Sundays. I destroyed everything I had built up. Through my own stupidity. What do you say to that?

Then she was divorced, I think the marriage only lasted a few months. She was divorced, and there were those Sundays. Now I was in a tight spot.

O: At the very beginning, when you became acquainted with her, was she married then?

W: She was being divorced. The first husband was a German. At the time, she gave me her papers and I got the Austrian papers for her. It was automatic then that a divorced woman got her Austrian citizenship back. Now we come to the last chapter of the Egyptian captivity, or whatever one wants to call it. . . .

O: It would have been best if you had got married at the very start.

W: Perhaps it would have been better.

O: And later there was another time when you wanted to marry her?

W: Well, we spent Sundays together, and from time to time, she'd start in, "We could have been married long ago." I spoke with Tiny and she said, "That woman doesn't know where she belongs." Even she agreed. E. and S. were against it, of course. But I told them nothing, against their advice, I said to her, "All right, I agree, let's get married." She said: "I am not suited to marriage. I am suited to being a mistress but not a wife; things will stay as they are." And I was even offended.

O: And when did she start talking about marriage again?

W: Just three years ago. Everything was quiet for a long time. And things went quite well. I knew, the main thing is, she doesn't want to get married. At first, I was offended, but then I told myself, thank

God. It went on like that until she got her illnesses. Eleven years ago, something went wrong with her heart. She no longer came to my place. On Sundays, we'd meet somewhere, and in the meantime, her mother died. Before that, she had lived in part on her mother's pension. And then she must have had someone and considered whether she should marry him. I said, "It's all right, I no longer have sexual relations with her, she is ill, it's good if she has someone."

For a while, she said that she didn't want to marry me because I had found her too inferior, but that she would marry someone else. And then she said, "and now I am supposed to marry a man I don't love." That was three years ago. That man left her—she was ill—three years ago the tragedy began all over. Now I have told you the whole story. And she is becoming more and more unbearable. . . .

All right, I am telling you all this because, you see, E. and S. say, "You have no obligations toward her. That's all your imagination, and your masochism." And you, as a woman, what's your view?

O: It's troublesome. I can understand your feeling that you have an obligation. Your story is touching, somehow. You said, "We'll get married," and she was delighted and said, "The baron is marrying me," and then she bought the scarf and was in such good humor . . . If she had been unbearable . . . But she was nice and pleased. . . .

W: You can see all there is behind it. And you weigh these moments, but an S. or an E. doesn't.

O: Have you already told them the story?

W: They ignore it. You as a woman, you know, you have more understanding. You can imagine how embarrassing the whole thing was for me. And you know, that story with Therese and the conflict, and how long that lasted. There are so many unhealed wounds.

O: Why did you say that about getting married?

W: That's what I ask myself: "Why did I say it?" It wasn't necessary, I should have said, "Either you accept my offer of employment or we part company." You see that I did everything wrong.

O: If I understood you correctly, you went to bed with her and that happened afterwards, when you were feeling euphoric.

W: Well, it suddenly seemed to me that the world would collapse if I didn't see her for three weeks. And now we have this débâcle.

O: Now the situation is a mess. In view of that, one can say that

Freud was more rational than your later analysts when he said: "That is the breakthrough to the woman, and you can get married." If he had not said that, you would have had the same débâcle.

W: Of course he acted rationally.

O: But now, after twenty or thirty years of vacillation . . . One doesn't forget that sort of thing. All one can do is either go on with things as they are, or put an end to them. Either one or the other.

W: That's something you understand, that if I marry now, nothing changes; the hatred is there.

O: You cannot forget what she did to you and of course she doesn't forget what you did to her.

W: We have done a great deal to each other.

O: Twenty years of quarrels and disputes cannot be wiped out. And Luise probably feels that she has wasted her life. Her behavior is understandable, somehow.

W: It's understandable that she hates me.

O: That's an exaggeration, perhaps. But another person in her place would have said long ago, "There's nothing to be done with this man; I'm going to look for someone else." Way back then, after the first promise of marriage. But she seems to have qualities similar to yours, being incapable of saying, "This is the end, I won't have anything more to do with this man."

W: If she said that, I would be pleased. I said that about marriage without thinking, and everything would have been all right if I had not said that she should come Sundays. Then she would have come twice a month. . . . And now I have the feeling that I ruined everything for myself, that's what torments me. Everything I did there was a mistake. You say yourself, "There can be no reconciliation."

O: It would be difficult.

W: And for her that is the greatest offense, when one tells her that she isn't normal. She gets mad. She sees everything in black and white, normal and crazy. It's the most unsuitable woman imaginable for a person who is psychologically damaged. And interests, interests, but not this prattle, for heaven's sake, this woman's prattle about what goes on in the house and the portion, the woman at the next table got more . . . that's her only subject.

O: In any case, it seems that when you fall in love with someone, you lose all control.

W: Well, with Therese, things were all right somehow. But there, Freud intervened. Before that, there was enormous confusion as well. But a way out was found. Although there were difficulties, it was bearable somehow. But this woman is unbearable.

O: But she wasn't always unbearable.

W: Not at first. Well, now let's ask the crucial question: What about suicide?

O: Am I supposed to advise you to commit suicide?

W: It's a very critical situation, surely.

O: And you said, jumping out a window . . .

W: What about it?

O: That is . . .

W: No solution?

O: Not really. Wouldn't you be afraid?

W: Of course I would be afraid. I would be afraid that I might go on living as a cripple. That would be worse still. Then I'll think, my God, how happy I ought to have been when I could still walk and move my hands. Now all my limbs are broken and it is worse still. And one can't get cyanide. There was a film about Hitler where they show the last days of the Nazis. He gives each of his associates cyanide and apologizes because he cannot give them a nicer present. In any case, this woman, all she's interested in is robbing me, and she is unbearable. All that's left is hatred and anger.

O: Even if you were to marry now . .

W: No, that's out of the question now. Now she blames me for my age and behaves impossibly. There is such hatred now, ineradicable. It will not change any more, even if I were to marry her ten times over. I give her such sums of money—not even a thank you, she does not even thank me. As little as a year ago, she said, "I love you for being Russian." There was still something there. But now, nothing is left, nothing at all. Now, there's only the finery, you understand, and exploiting me. The way E. sees it, that everything is so simple, that it's nothing but masochism, that's not how it is. There are real facts there that make the whole situation terribly difficult. I can actually feel the hatred, the hatred . . .

O: When you meet?

W: Yes.

O: And why does she meet you?

W: She comes for money.

O: This money, from the very beginning . .

W: Now there's only hatred, in any case.

O: On both sides?

W: You see how she treats me.

O: And you, you hate her also?

W: When she becomes unbearable, yes, I do.

O: And otherwise?

W: Otherwise I don't.

O: But you don't love her either?

W: I no longer know what's what.

A Young Man at Ninety

WOLF-MAN: Yes, she wants money, and then she brings up her illnesses again and then she buys herself another dress. She has only one dress and when she has a second, she wants a third. . . . And then she tells me she has kidney colic and needs to have her kidneys flushed, and that costs thirty schillings. "Give me another five hundred schillings." Where am I to get the money?

OBHOLZER: But you just gave her money at Christmas.

W: A great deal of money. I gave her everything I got from the book.

O: And she's already talking about money again?

W: Constantly. Stones and flushing of the kidneys and this costs this much. That's what I hear constantly. But if she needs those things, she should not buy a second dress. What a terrible person. She used to be modest. So what am I to do with her? She was modest, but I believe she got to know someone who gave her money. Did she have an affair with him or not? I don't know, she was so ill, and he presumably didn't give her the money for nothing. I thought to myself, is she has someone, all the better. But it seems that he spoiled her somehow. She got used to living in high style. And then she kept talking about marriage. And suddenly she came and said, "Am I to marry a man whom I don't love?" Well, what was I to tell her? "You should marry"? That's pointless. But that was the worst, I believe, that she got used to spending money. The whole thing took a very unfavorable turn for me; it took the most unfavorable turn imaginable, the illnesses, the death of the mother, hundreds of illnesses, sugar, heart, kidneys. . . . What else is there? Those are the realities, in any case, the woman is ill, she has sugar, there's something wrong with her heart and her kidneys, she has no medical insurance . . .

O: But she does have medical insurance now.

W: Well, she'll be sixty next birthday, but I don't know if she really paid the money in. Who knows? I can't get her to tell me.

O: Have you asked her?

W: Yes, now I give her 300 schillings each month, the additional payment that has to be made. . . . She said that she got it into her head that she had to have an affair with a twenty-five-year-old and that she fell asleep, but when she was with me she didn't fall asleep. Proof of love! I was still strong enough at that time to fend her off. And then I went to some people who are friends of mine, and suddenly I missed her. How absurd! I went through a lot, it was very difficult. . . . She came, knocked, and I hid in Tiny's room. I managed that, and then I suddenly missed her. Can you understand that?

O: Because you had no one.

W: At that moment, I should have gone to some woman, that would have distracted me. But I thought, I have no money, and did not go to one. Then E. came and I said to him: "She wrote she had been at my place and that I had choked her. She had a mark." I never touched her. She had a mark on her neck and claimed I had choked her. I tell E., "Look, she claims I choked her, but I didn't touch her." That should have shown him what kind of person she is. And he says to me: "Look, I think it's better you don't make up with her. But I don't want you to blame me later because you missed the opportunity." That was the worst thing anyone could have said. Opportunity! He should have said: "You didn't miss a thing. You can always get her."

And now, of course, carte blanche, I went there immediately and she wasn't at home. You see, fate was kindly disposed toward me. I thought, try again; I go, and she's at home and we make up. That was a stupidity that cannot be made good. Although we made up, there was one other moment when I could have acted more wisely.

O: When you were on vacation?

W: Well yes, here's the way it was: I decided that I would give her only a small amount, and that would be it. When I said two hundred, she said three hundred, and so on. But I remained firm, said two hundred, and walked toward the door. She pulled me back inside and agreed. I was very frugal; I had no servant at the time; the pension was small. We went out Sundays, to Grinzing. Now she goes to the theater; at that time, she didn't. I don't know for how long things continued like that. I have tried to determine that, but I don't know in what year it was. It must have been a few years later.

I went on vacation in Hardegg and noticed that something was amiss, that she was dissatisfied, too little money. I went to Hardegg and wondered the whole time whether she would leave me or not. I thought, well, if she doesn't want to, there's nothing to be done. But it didn't suit me. I went back to Vienna and two days later, there's a knock at the door. She's there and says, "I don't care about other men, I'll stay with you," and then she arranged things so that she would come twice a month. You see, that's when she had got married without telling me.

That's the way I should have left it, twice a month, then she wouldn't have bothered me, and would have cost me little. But twice a month wasn't enough for me. I said, "Why don't you come more often?" She used to come every Sunday. I said, "Let's go to the movies," she said, "No, my mother is waiting for me, I can't," and always left very promptly.

And you see where my mistake lies, my mistake is that when I set my mind on something, that's the way it has to be. Headstrong. Why doesn't she go to the movies? She didn't want to go to the movies because she was married.

I had friends . . . The way it was, I have to tell you this also. Sunday. The whole week was all right. Only Sundays I didn't know what to do. What am I going to do Sunday? I went to see the captain I knew from the office. That took care of Sundays. Then that stopped because I noticed that it didn't suit those people that I came Sundays. And I didn't want to go on other days because it was on Sundays that I didn't know what to do. This damned Sunday, that was the most terrible day after my wife's death. When I went to the office, that distracted me, but Sundays were awful. What was I going to do Sundays?

I had this acquaintance, the Polish woman; we painted together; we were good friends. That's where I went Sundays, every Sunday. Tiny cooked a schnitzel, so she didn't have to cook. I got along very

well with her. Polish women are—you know that from operettas—
the most beautiful woman is the Polish one. Polish women are not
the most beautiful women, but they have a special talent for adapt-
ing to men, they do have that. Well, I got along very well with her.
But does the woman need a friend who can only come Sundays? That
was the end.

O: Awful.

W: Isn't it? Now I did not know what to do Sundays. And without
thinking, without considering the consequences, the serious consequences it would have, I say to her, "Why not come Sundays?" It was
my own doing. And she says, enthusiastically, yes. Meantime, she
had got her divorce; now she could come Sundays. Had it been a few
weeks earlier, she would have said no. As it was, it was the most
unfavorable moment, and that's how these stupid Sundays started.
Now Sunday is a day of robbery because she never stops demanding
money.

O: Every Sunday?

W: I need that, give me a few hundred, and then there's this and
that. She does not take any money with her, I have to pay everything. And then she demands the little I have left.

O: And this Polish woman? How about her as a friend for you?

W: She suggested that herself, she even wanted to get married, but I
told her that she would not get a pension, she was so much younger.
Then she said, "We could just live together." I didn't say anything
because I had already started with Luise. Then she got married. I
had not known that I would live this long, and in order to get a
pension, one has to be married for a certain length of time.

O: But this pension, what would it have mattered if you had liked
the woman, and she liked you.

W: There you see the opportunities I would have had. . . .

O: But you said that you got along well with her.

W: I did get along well with that one.

O: I really don't understand why you didn't make friends with her.
And then she found herself someone else?

W: No, she got married.

O: But you were friends.

W: I had no sexual relations with her.

O: Why not?

W: It was more a comradeship.

O: Then how could she have suggested marriage?

W: She did suggest it.

O: Strange. Normally, that doesn't come up until one knows a man better. What did she do for a living?

W: She didn't work. She had money. Her mother had saved much of her wealth.

O: So on top of everything, she had money?

W: She did. At that time, when I had separated from Luise, there was such excitement and everything ended without a hitch—she signed. And then it started all over again. I told myself at the time, I won't give her much money, it will be all right. And I was younger at the time, too. You mustn't forget, I've already celebrated my eighty-eighth birthday or, more accurately, mourned it. At that time, I was twenty years younger. I persisted, I didn't give her that much money. We had a quarrel once and I said, "No, I won't give you that much," and walked out the door, and she actually pulled me back in. I still had the strength to stick it out, and things wouldn't have been so bad if this Sunday business hadn't started.

Then she said, "Too little money," and reduced it to twice a month, and that annoyed me. Why doesn't she want to go to the movies? That's when she got married but without telling me. Had I known she had got married, I would have put an end to it. At the time, the Polish woman came to my place and said . . . Luise had said, "Mother no longer wants me to come," and I said, "Very well, then you come to my place." The Polish woman said, "She probably has a friend," but I found that idea unpleasant and thought, perhaps the mother really doesn't want me to come. And I did not break with her. The situation was that I only saw her twice a month, and that I spent Sundays with the Polish woman. And then she got herself a friend, and suddenly I was alone Sundays. If only Gardiner had sent me those green pills at that time . . .

O: What sort of green pills?

W: Pills that make you feel better. If she had sent them to me at that time, I would have had an excuse. I would have taken a pill on Sundays and painted. When Gardiner did send me the pills, I had already said, "Let's get together on Sundays." That was the mistake. . . .

O: What sort of pills are they? What are they called?
W: Those pills, I don't even know, I'll have to look. It is not hashish although it's a stimulant.
O: Amphetamines, probably.
W: S. says that it's all right to take them once a week. It's weeks now since I have taken any. I took them when I painted. Now I no longer paint.
O: Are they commercially available?
W: You can't get them here but you can in America. But S. says they are harmless if one takes one or two a week. It's a long time since I have taken any; the effect becomes weaker, of course. In any event, then she came Sundays. Before, she had limited it to twice a month because I had given her too little money. And this idea didn't occur to me, be careful, she only comes twice a month now, so you actually accomplished what you were after. Twice a month is no catastrophe. Why? She used to go to the movies with me, why doesn't she want to go? That was a stupid idea I had, why should she go to the movies with me? And then I committed this stupidity and said, "Come Sunday. . . ." And everything I had accomplished was lost again.

But somehow it was manageable as long as she was in good health. But then her mother died and the illnesses came, and she became older too, and crazier as well. And now she is completely crazy. I cannot make clear to her, for example, that I receive a pension from the pension fund and that the *Städtische Versicherung* (Municipal Insurance Company) makes an additional contribution. I have shown her letters; she cannot get it into her head. It says contribution, so I must get a second pension from the municipal insurance company. I cannot convince her that, from the point of view of the insurance company, the contribution is a gift, since they are not obliged to pay it. It is an extra payment, on top of the state pension. She interprets it as a second pension, and an increment on top of that. What can I say? One could kill the woman. Nothing else would do any good.

She claims that I am guilty because I was already so old and started something with a younger woman. In other cases, when men have such a young woman, they rent her an apartment and God knows what else. She says that I attached myself to her, it's all my fault. I can show you letters from which you can tell that she is attached to me. She acts as if I had seduced her. You, as a woman, is it your opinion that I owe her something? Am I guilty, must I marry her? It's her point of view that I must marry her now because I was with her for such a long time and because she was still so young when it started. She should have married a millionaire or some- thing. . . . But E. says, "If you marry that woman, I won't come back." "You don't owe her a dime," S. says. You are a woman. How do you see it?

O: As a woman, I also think that you owe her nothing. I have to agree with that view.

W: She should have considered . . .

O: Of course. In a relationship, each of the partners must have the right to say at any time, "I've had enough." Even when one is married, one can separate and divorce.

W: It's always the same: "What will happen when you die?" We constantly talk about my death. It's not a pleasant subject.

O: You find it unpleasant?

W: Of course it is unpleasant because I don't know what to tell her. E. said once that the archive would help her; another time he said that it's not the business of the archive to help her. I am confused, and she wants to know what will happen to her.

O: She should get retirement benefits.

W: I believe she will. People who have nothing and are over sixty get it. But I don't know what that comes to, I'll inquire one of these days. In any event, she doesn't want to hear about it, it's terrible, a pen- sion after all these years, when you think that Curt Jürgens gave Simone all those millions.

O: The pension is enough to live on although it isn't much, of course. One must admit that she's not in a very pleasant situation. Just think, you are sixty and don't know what to live on.

W: That's the critical thing, that neither S. nor E. can empathize with Luise's situation. They should tell themselves that it is not a very pleasant situation when one knows that one gets a specific amount every month but that all payments will stop after January 1. One has to take that into account. But they ignore that com- pletely. "You owe her nothing; she should be glad she gets anything. She has no rights." It must be admitted that this woman is in a very unpleasant situation. So what am I to do? Go to America? But

Gardiner told me, "Since you don't speak English, America is out of the question." Yet a language is something one could learn, after all. It's probably not easy at my age. But one learns it more easily in the country. She says, "The only place for you is Germany." But to whom should I have gone in Germany? Now, there's at least that woman, but before, there was no one in Germany.

O: You probably wouldn't be able to make up your mind to go to Germany or America in any case.

W: I probably could not make that decision because I would be completely dependent on the people that took me in there. I have known those people in America for decades, that's another kind of relationship. . . . But to be dependent on people one doesn't know at all . . . In any case, you can understand that I might get the idea of escaping to a woman who writes a beautiful letter.

O: You could escape and send Luise some money every month.

W: E. always wants to convince me that I find myself in an excellent situation, that she is a harmless psychopath, that everything is really my fault because I do not properly understand the situation and master it. You see, Gardiner thinks going to Germany would be best. Now there's that woman, at least, but before that letter, there was no one, and there's nothing to be done with this letter. S. thinks I should not make visits under any circumstances whatever.

O: And you have a bad conscience vis-à-vis Luise because you promised to marry her?

W: Not because of the marriage promise. She put it in writing at the time that she renounced all further claims. But sometimes I think, if I were married, perhaps she'd treat me better. What more could she want? But E. and S. say she would not change, married or not. You see, the woman is a serious psychopath and has no proper idea of right and wrong. She is such an egomaniac, she thinks that everything that advantages her is right, and whatever disadvantages her is wrong. With that point of view, marriage is no use either. I also do not believe that she would change.

O: No, I don't think so either.

W: I told her that she would have to treat me differently if I were to marry her. She said, yes, she would show another side of her nature. What do you say to that?

O: That's funny. It means that she knows somehow that she does not show you her most agreeable side.

W: She seems to be aware of it.

O: And she says she would show another side of her nature. Maybe for two weeks but then . . .

W: Sometimes I think, all right, if I married this person, I would not hear those eternal recriminations. But those are false hopes. Such a character does not change. If someone is like that, that one cannot get along with her, then, whether you marry or not, the character remains the same.

O: Have you ever talked to her about it? How she thinks things would be if you were married?

W: I don't want this matter to come up because then she wouldn't let go.

O: But surely she must have understood by this time that you won't marry her.

W: Apparently she still hasn't understood.

O: You mean she's still hopeful.

W: It seems that way, otherwise she wouldn't always be talking about this marriage. Is it true that the gas has been detoxified?

O: Yes.

W: You know that for sure?

O: Yes, I know it for sure.

W: So there would be no point in turning it on?

O: No.

W: With that money, with 50,000 schillings, I did not really have the right. It was unreasonable.

O: But it is also a pleasure to have that much money and to be able to say, "Here, take this fifty thousand."

W: But it was irrational.

O: Not every pleasure is rational.

W: One could say that I cannot suppress the feeling of pleasure inside me when I say, "Take it." Something like that, perhaps. That's a very important point. When she starts wailing, "I am so ill, I need this and that, it costs so much," and I must give her some assurance, I tell myself, this woman loved you once, you must provide some base. When I hear words like that, I become soft. I used to be wealthy and able to afford that sort of thing. But now I no longer can. And although I have been an émigré for decades, I still feel I have the right to make such presents. That's really the thing.

O: I find that quite strange.

W: I want to play the *grand seigneur* although I have nothing.

O: It seems that one can never rid oneself of these things that date back to one's childhood and youth.

W: One was wealthy but lost everything. One really lost it in an improper way; it was simply taken. And in one's subconscious, one thinks perhaps: it's really still yours. If you had gambled everything away, it would be different. But you did nothing, it was taken from you, it's not your fault. It really still belongs to you; in your imagination, it's still yours.

Look at all those émigrés that came. The psychoanalysts said that I had a masochistic trait because I did not regret having lost so much. But that's not true. None of the émigrés really cared. It's something that always surprised me, that they didn't care. Either they imagined it would pass or, as in my case, they thought, one is intelligent and can become wealthy again. Just as money had no importance in the past when there was lots of it, it was of no importance later when one no longer had any.

S. once said, "Men are stupid. They really are stupid." This is my view: women have been suppressed by men, that's true. And so they developed certain qualities, like the Jews. The Jews were suppressed and they naturally sought a way out. Women more easily find a way out.

You see, a student visited me once; he never came back. He had had a very difficult time, looked in the insurance paper and I don't know what all. And how easily you found me!

O: One cannot say that logic is a quality that women developed to any special degree.

W: You found out. Women's intelligence works somewhat faster. I also see that in Luise. Her cleverness dumbfounds one. To walk up to the ticket window and to say, "I ordered tickets," he doesn't remember the name . . . I couldn't do that, but she has the nerve. I think that in women—how shall I say.—that in women the brain has more convolutions and works more quickly. For thinking quickly and thinking slowly also play a role. You can be very intelligent, but if you think slowly, you miss the right moment and it does you no good. You can forget about all that intelligence of yours. And that's something that astonishes me in Luise, how quickly she understands what is useful to her. Well, with this Luise, how would you act if you were in my place?

O: It's difficult for me to put myself in your place.

W: Because you are a woman.

O: Not only for that reason. I am an entirely different human being. I would not have taken that much from anyone.

W: That's it: I put up with too much. And now the situation is like the situation of those teachers whom student's don't respect. It doesn't matter what the teacher does, it's all useless. We had a mathematics teacher in school who even stuttered. But his whole appearance, his manner, were such that people respected him. Toward other teachers, one was condescending, if you will, one gave them nicknames and criticized them. But that one—no nickname, nothing, everybody respected him. He knew how to instill respect in others. It's the same thing with animals and children. And people no longer have respect for me. So the only thing that's really left is to put an end to it all. Because nothing is any use any more. Everything I do, everything I say, is useless. I told S., "Perhaps I'll marry her so that she has health insurance, and then I'll kill myself." And he said, "What, you kill yourself because of her and want to reward her for that?"

O: What does that mean, "reward"? Actually, you reward her every Sunday when you meet her. That's all utter nonsense, to get married and then to kill yourself. I thought she did have health insurance. You gave her the money for it.

W: I don't know if she used it for that. She constantly buys things. I don't know if she really used it for the health insurance. There's no proof. One should have treated that woman completely differently. And I no longer have the strength and am much too old to get away from her. That's the conclusion I reach. If I am not to see her, someone in America must take me in. Perhaps I can come to some understanding with this Mrs. Bulle. But I don't know, her sympathies might not extend that far.

O: But you don't know her at all. You cannot demand from an utterly unknown woman that she take you in.

W: Yes, but she wrote as if . . .

O: Perhaps her apartment also has just one room.

W: I don't think so.

O: And it will be the same as with Luise.

W: So you share S.'s and E.'s point of view that I have the moral right, as it were, to break off relations with her and to not give her anything more and to let her rot.

O: Legally, you have that right.

W: I would have to be married, or at least she would have to be my life companion.

O: You know yourself that it's idle, speculating about the legal aspects. The legal situation is irrelevant.

W: There is the Roman proverb: *Summum ius, summa iniuria.*

O: You have been associated with this woman for thirty years. It is like a marriage for all intents and purposes, even if you don't live together. And in a marriage, it also happens that people no longer get along with each other.

W: Yes, when one ignores the legal aspect, it is something like a marriage.

O: You won't manage it, so why discuss it. Otherwise you would have left her long ago.

W: Well, something will have to be done because the time will come when I have no money left and am unable to pay the rent and have to kill myself. Someone once said that things would quiet down when I got older. But with me, nothing has quieted down.

I have often thought about Dostoevski and his novel *The Brothers Karamazov.* I have felt that I really represented all three brothers. I am Alyosha; I am Ivan, who discusses; and I am Dmitri, who develops great passions. And that's a very difficult thing, of course. In Dostoevski, you see that everyone is satisfied with his qualities. Dmitri is a passionate individual, dominated primarily by his feelings. The other thinks, the third searches for the truth. But in me, the three personalities are combined in one person. I constantly search for the truth and understand nothing clearly, in spite of my age. And the passions are there too, of course not the libidinous ones, you understand, but hatred and affection and dislike, everything is really as in a young man. It really ought to have a different form. Isn't that strange? And I don't know how to explain that. You cannot explain it by national character. In Dostoevski's novel, you realize, these three personalities are distinct. But all these qualities in a single person, down to a very advanced age, is a little odd.

O: You must not forget that in a novel, the different qualities have to be presented in different individuals. Otherwise it would be impossible to write, it would be too difficult.

W: People would become a little confused as they do in my case, right?

O: It is evidently an illusion to believe that as one becomes older, one becomes—how shall I put it—wiser and more serene.

W: But generally it is true that older people become calmer, lie in bed. That's not just an illusion.

O: You think not? I don't know that many older people. Perhaps it's just commonly believed and not really so.

W: Well, my mother lived to be eighty-nine years old. She was pretty calm. With me, everything is confused, everything has become disorderly, as it were. The Polish woman says that it was a weakness of mine that I went to see Freud. Well, I have no choice but to try various things: there's America, there's Mrs. Bulle, there's jumping out the window.

O: If you jump out the window, you won't be able to try anything else. That'll be final.

W: You cannot imagine what a torture these Sundays are. The Polish woman is perfectly right: every Sunday is the ascent of Mont Blanc. I must exert such strength when I am with that person. My hearing is bad, for example, so she could really speak a little louder. But she speaks softly because speaking louder is too much of an effort for her. And what she says, forever the same things, it's so uninteresting: what the old Bohemian woman did, she doesn't open the window, and men come to visit her daughter. This impossible gossip, I don't know, this one says this, the other that. I should have known you earlier when I was still younger.

O: Whom?

W: You! You would be the right woman for me. When I see that poor parrot on the chain, I feel sorry for it. It sits there, it's no different from locking up a human being. That it gives this woman pleasure to see that animal sitting in its cage is beyond me.

O: She has a parrot in her apartment?

W: Yes, in her apartment, and then the dog, a kind of Great Dane, it's so big; when one arrives it barks for ten minutes and has to be taken to another room. She used to have three cages with parrots. Yes, well, having a dog, buying perfume, being without health insurance, the whole situation is pure madness. Through my carelessness I got myself into a bad situation and, I must admit, through my own stupidity. You remember Gorki's "Night Asylum?" There is a baron who doesn't know how he happens to find himself among all those people. That's the way I feel: What is it that brought you and this woman together?

I have to spend hours sitting with her. In the past, she never went to the theater, but now—it is the purest madness—now we go to the theater together and at night, she goes by herself, to the Raimundtheater. She's seen *Frau Luna* four times.

O: How awful. Do you always go to the theater on Sundays?

W: Yes, in the afternoon. She also wanted me to come with her in the evenings, but I refused. She isn't all that old, she could look for someone. Why doesn't she look for someone?

O: But really, it's probably not so easy at sixty.

W: There are enough men in Vienna.

O: In that age group it's probably very difficult; the men were all killed in the war. There are few men in that age group, I think.

W: That's what's so tragic. She says the same thing, that there are no men.

O: That's true, too. They were all in the war and the survivors are in firm hands.

W: But you also had a man.

O: What do you mean, a man? I am not yet sixty, there are enough men my age. That's another generation.

W: I see. You mean that in Luise's generation especially . . .

O: I was born in 1943.

W: My God! The war was already over then.

O: No, that was still during the war.

W: That was still during the war.

O: What's your relationship with your tailor these days?

W: He is very nice. He made the suit I'm wearing. He says, "If you need something, come see me—a button sewn on . . ."

O: You don't know how to sew on a button? What does your tailor say to that?

W: I ask him, "What do I owe you?" He says, "Either three schillings, or nothing."

O: That's very cheap, really.

W: He even wanted to make me a present of a jacket, but it didn't fit. Actually, if everything were as Gardiner describes it, my condition should be entirely different. And that surprises me and I ask myself: How is it that she doesn't see that everything is different from what she wrote? That it doesn't bother her. It should bother her; she should know in what a bad psychological state I am. She surely knows that from E.; he must have told her.

O: But you said that you didn't tell her a great deal about Luise.

W: No, I didn't. She said, "Perhaps you can buy her off with a certain sum of money." I answered, 'It would have to be a very large sum." She would have to be able to live on it. Gardiner wrote that someone identified with me and that he wanted a picture of me. But the moment money comes up, there's a sudden silence. Well, there's the archive, of course. I read that to you the last time I was here. What I read to you was the answer to a letter from S. to E. in which he asked whether those so-called American friends would be willing to take me in.

O: You didn't read anything to me.

W: E. wrote that he did not have the means to support me there. Didn't I read that to you?

O: No.

W: Well, I can tell you. He does not have the means to support me. The only thing he can do is find me a place to live in New York, and therapy. He would treat me. But he really believes that if I went to Switzerland or Germany, because of my—how does he put it?— "considerable adroitness" . . . I don't know where the adroitness would be. What does he mean, adroitness? It's true, I did succeed in getting away from the Russians and before that, in Rumania, when I had left Russia, when the French did not accept the foreign currency. I did succeed in a few things. But at my age, what great adroitness can there be? In any case, he writes that he believes that in view of my considerable adroitness, I would make new friends. That's a fantasy. One doesn't make friends at my age.

O: It's difficult, you are right there.

W: But what annoys me is this: I never gave Gardiner as many paintings as the last time. And that time, of all times, I get no money for them. I remember that once, a long time ago, I painted a picture of our pond in Russia and through an acquaintance, a painter, I sold it to the minstry. I got seven thousand schillings for it. That was a considerable sum in those days.

O: Here, in Vienna?

W: Yes, it's somewhere here in Vienna, at a ministry. My acquaintance, this painter, had the idea that one should give the painting a musical designation, so I scribbled a few notes on it. And the official at the ministry said: "What's the painting called? You cannot simply writes notes on it." So I said, *"Russian Landscape* is the title of it." That was a purchase to support artists. I no longer paint outside. It's too difficult. And pastel is not real painting, it's dust, and doesn't keep.

In any event, Gardiner is a wealthy woman. She could have sent me the money and then taken up the matter with the bank. Don't you agree? When all is said and done, it is through me that she became famous. She said so herself.

O: She said that?

W: Yes, she has a name now.

O: And she didn't before?

W: Before, she wasn't known as a psychoanalyst. She did pedagogy. But then all sorts of people wrote her because of me, and Fischer Verlag sent her Mrs. Bulle's letter. She really could send me those few dollars.

O: Did you inquire about the money here?

W: Yes, she asked me again, in this letter, she asked me again whether I had received the money. So what does one do in a case like that? One sends those few dollars. She is a millionairess, a wealthy woman. Nothing happens. I keep looking in the mailbox, it's empty, and now I no longer feel like painting. I am so annoyed about this. I've lost all desire to paint. One cannot rely on anyone.

A Human Relationship

WOLF-MAN: Just imagine, I had stamps in a safe at the bank; they were estimated to have a value of 10,000 schillings at the time. I met Luise, and she runs after me and sees me walk into the bank. I wanted to show her that there's nothing left in the safe. I have nothing left in the safe, I had forgotten that this stamp album was still there. She saw it and said she wanted to have the stamps appraised. You know, one has to know stamps. I don't. They don't have great value. There are also a few Hitler stamps among them. Someone once told me that only one page had any value.

So she said she wants to go with me and have them appraised. And with what result? She went with me to have them appraised. I could have done that myself, and they were appraised at 17,000 schillings. And then she demanded the stamps and said, "When you die, I will be evicted, I cannot pay the rent," and she wanted the stamps. So it went back and forth, you know what I'm like. And she did what she always does, she gets money from me and on the way home, she demands that I go up and bring her money. I said, "Very well, but only on the condition that this will be all except for what E. sends." She promised. It is humiliating for her too, always to act the beggar. So she agreed. So we came to this preliminary understanding. What will come of it, I don't know. I talked to S. and he said, "That could also have been done differently, but now it's too late, and since you have a certain guilt feeling . . ." Constantly new dresses, and now she's already starting in again with her rheumatism. For the stamps, the man would have made a down payment of 5,000 schillings. I don't know how much the auction would have brought. She told me that she knew people who are stamp experts, that she'd certainly sell them at a better price than I could. But now it's done. What do you say?

OBHOLZER: And you believe this is a definitive settlement?

W: No, I don't believe it.

O: Nor do I. Did you take those green happiness pills today?

W: No, I haven't taken any for months.

O: You seem a little keyed up.

O: No. I got here early, so I went into a small restaurant nearby and had a glass of wine.

O: I hope you won't do anything foolish like you did Christmas, with Luise.

W: Sometimes I say to myself, perhaps I should tell her about the book after all. Now she keeps asking, "Were did you get the money?" Because I gave her so much.

O: She wants to know where you got the money?

W: I don't know what to say. I gave her the money I got from the book.

O: Tell her you saved it.

W: I do, but she doesn't believe me.

O: Why not?

W: Why then did I gave her so little before? She thinks I also had the money before.

O: You can say that you hadn't yet saved it at that time.

W: One could say that, I suppose.

O: And now she asks, "Where did you get the money?"

W: She doesn't actually bring it up. Something like, "Mysterious business, your mysterious affairs." Well, the Polish woman said, "For you, every Sunday is an ascent of Mont Blanc." She's Polish, a Slav, there's a certain similarity. And she said, "The way Russians hate, other nations cannot hate; they are capable of a terrible hatred." She said, "I am sometimes afraid of you." That's something she said before. And now she says: "Every Sunday is an ascent of Mont Blanc. It accumulates, it keeps accumulating, and one day, there'll be a terrible explosion." I don't believe that. What would I do? What does that mean, explode? Such relationships often end in a real tragedy. But I think I have that much control over myself that I wouldn't do something completely crazy. One doesn't know, of course.

O: Sometimes you really do feel miserable.

W: The whole thing is impossible. I cannot keep going to restaurants and the theater with Luise until I am two hundred years old. It no longer interests me, and the movies don't either. So it must come to some sort of end. But what sort? That cannot be foreseen at the moment. My God, that Polish woman, she ought to be grateful to me, she married a wealthy man. They just came back from India and Vietnam, and I don't know where else, China. She also fibs a little, you understand. Now she believes in the transmigration of the soul. She told me that I am in a terrible state. When I die, my soul will enter the body of a dog. So prospects are bad. And then there is a Japanese science, flower arrangement. That's what she's doing at the moment.

O: Ikebana.

W: Yes. And then she told me that her mother, who is no longer alive, visited her twice after her death. She believes that's the absolute truth. So you see the kinds of people I am dealing with. But she was no threat. And she was clever. She managed to get all sorts of wealth out of Poland. I don't know how she did it. I got along well with her. Polish women have a particular quality, it's not that they are prettier than other women but they adapt better to men. And she is also an émigrée; her father was a wealthy manufacturer, he was a nouveau riche, I think. And then she has another good quality—she doesn't claim, like other Poles, that she is descended from the king. Because all the rest of them are allegedly descended from the king. In any case, she ruined everything for me. Because I met her Sundays and then some man appeared on the scene who could only come on Sundays, with the result that my Sundays became free.

I couldn't stand them, those Sundays. It's through those Sundays that I ruined everything. . . . I don't believe I am a neurotic; I am schizophrenic, that's my diagnosis. I must have been quite mad at the time. She said, "We'll let three weeks pass, and then we'll see." And this harmless sentence made such an impression on me. Instead of saying, "All right, I agree," and thinking about it, I say to her, "Well, then there's no choice, I'll marry you." It's as if someone else had said that. . . . That's a split, isn't it? It is a split. I hadn't considered marriage at all, and suddenly I say, "Let's get married." And she jumped around, the world is standing still, what great happiness, etc. And then her mother came in, she wasn't that enthusiastic. She said, "We'll see what comes of it." A moment later, I understood that I had committed a terrible stupidity. Well, I think I've already told you all that, haven't I? You know, Russian literature did me a great deal of harm.

O: What do you mean?

W: Well, you see, those women. In *Resurrection,* they always preach that women, that the common people, are human beings just like those who belong to the educated class, that another point of view is prejudice. A woman with no education is also a woman, when all is said and done. This idea is not expressed but it runs through Russian literature like a red thread. One forever raises up downtrodden people. That's not done in other countries. The peasant is glorified. Look at Tolstoi, who bought a peasant blouse for himself. . . . I brought a few letters of hers along which she once wrote me. I must pay such a price for this love. I was going to ask you your opinion of these letters. They sound childish, actually. I don't know, should I read them to you? No, it's pointless.

O: Why? Go ahead and read.

W: "Darling, be sure you don't smoke too much because there are older gentlemen here who have lost a leg through smoking. Darling, a dashing fellow like you, who looks like a lord, surely you don't want to do that. I am already counting the days until Saturday evening . . " Well, in any case, she writes she's impatient, she sits in some corner because her man isn't there, and counts the hours until I come, things like that. What do you say?

O: What can I say? Her way of expressing herself is rather primitive.

W: Primitive, granted. But it is a primitive love because she is a primitive human being. One cannot be offended by that. But she has . . . What she felt, she once expressed like this: "I could not afford you." She had no use for such a love where the man has no money because she has no pension and no medical insurance. She really should not have attached herself to me, that's true. But I cannot help that. Now she holds me responsible; I ruined her whole life, as it were. Who forced her? Or must it be appreciated in some way that the woman loved me? Do I not have an obligation after all? Those are moral questions, you know, and they are confusing. And everybody tells me something else. S. says: "You don't owe her a dime, she just exploited you. You can stop immediately and not give her one more dime if she's that vile." You see the problem.

And E. . . . I got a letter from E., by the way. I'll read it to you. She was so insolent, I don't know if I told you. Of course, when she is so vile and insolent, I also raise my voice, you understand. And she says, "Yes, you are screaming at me," and she has given my name and address to someone and if I scream at her and she has a heart attack and dies, then I am her murderer and that person will know. That's the kind of thing she says to me. Isn't this a crazy individual? She is completely crazy. To get back to E.'s letter. He writes: "Dear Doctor, I am pleased that the check has reached you. I don't quite understand what makes you so nervous every time. In your present financial situation, it cannot matter if the check arrives a week earlier or later. My letter was probably sent a little late. I cannot always stick to the precise date." There you have it. He offered to send money for Luise. It comes to about five thousand schillings.

O: A month?

W: Five thousand per month. But the dollar is falling. I'll send him the exchange rate. It's always a little less. But it is supposed to be five thousand. So you see from the letter that he believes that I still have the money I got from Gardiner for the book. I don't have it. I have given her everything. He will say: "What's this? Am I to send you money so you can give it to that insatiable woman? In that case, I will stop sending it." On the other hand, he is incorrectly informed. He believes I have enough money. . . . I tell S. because S. gives me no money. But that was a mistake E. made. He shouldn't have done that. It would have been better if he had sent nothing because then she would have left me and have looked for someone else. Then I couldn't have given her those 5,000 schillings.

O: How long have you been getting that sum?

W: Ten years, no, longer, fourteen years, something like that, she was still in good health.

O: Every month?

W: Yes. And he ruined everything with that. . . . And now Gardiner has ruined everything for me with that book. I got money, and gave her money. You understand? It should have occurred to her: this man is so old and in the hands of such a woman. This success has only done me harm. This success is ruining me. Don't you see how truly tragic the entire situation is?

I continue: "I should like to make the following comments on your impressive description of the events during the last Sunday afternoon: you know that L. has a somewhat limited intellect, and you should really have known that she would not understand what you wanted to explain to her." I had written about that increment, you know. "Once Luise seizes an idea, nothing can divert her from it." That's the central phrase. When she imagines something, you cannot convince her otherwise. There is no logic that would convince her. "That's an old story and it does not surprise me to hear that she doesn't understand this matter of the increment. I am glad that you finally expressed your feelings of anger; it really was high time." That's also quite false. If I lose control and berate her, things get worse.

O: Really?

W: Of course, then she reproaches me again. And I get nowhere. And then I want to make up for everything so that we don't part as enemies, and I give her money. These people don't understand this situation, you know. At least E. doesn't. You see yourself that he misunderstands everything. "If she declares publicly that she is trying to get witnesses because she will go to court, that gives you the right to break off the relationship." Here's what she did: when I raised my voice a little, she . . . there was a couple, she walked up to them and said, "Look, you can be witnesses, give me your names and addresses, you heard how my husband treats me." She says "my husband," of course. "He isn't Viennese, he's Russian. Testify that he caused an uproar."

O: Incredible. And what did they say?

W: "Carry on your disputes without our help. We don't feel like going to court."

O: That was in a restaurant?

W: No, at a streetcar stop.

O: Recently?

W: Two weeks ago. Dostoevski is a beginner compared to her. What I suffer with this woman! *The Possessed* is nothing, *The Brothers Karamazov* nothing. It's incredible. And in Vienna of all places, in this supposedly jolly city, I have to come upon something like this. "Who would continue a relationship with a woman who tells him to his face that she will take him to court?!" Question mark and exclamation point. "If she continues threatening you with court action, you have an additional reason for pounding the table and telling her that if that is her opinion of you, she will probably no longer be able to count on your visits." That's false too. She claims that it is only on Sundays that she can eat enough to make up for the inadequate diet during the week.

The rest isn't so important. "I notice with great sadness that you are still trying to drag in improbabilities and that you maintain yourself in a state of tension. It is high time to break off relations with this woman. I have said this often and realize perfectly well that you won't do it this time either. I also assume that you have not entered into negotiations with the director of the old people's home. I hope to hear from you soon and remain, yours, E."

Well, what do you say? He thinks it's so easy to end it. It isn't all that easy when one has been with a woman for thirty years. And when that woman is ill besides. The reviewers of my book often compared it to Dostoevski. For example: "The memoirs read like a Russian novel." "It's the atmosphere in which Dostoevski's characters move." There's another passage that says that "in Freud and his most sensitive patient, we have two masters of the language." So the reviews were positive. But what good does that do me? What good? None. Money. There wasn't that much of it. It all went to Luise. There you can see that success doesn't really mean as much as is generally believed. In my personal life, nothing has changed as a result. Wouldn't it be better if the book had never been published? Then I wouldn't have so much trouble with this individual. Or does the success make up for that? What's your judgment?

O: I do think that success is important.

W: At first, I thought it was splendid. It is read in America. And then everything burst like a bubble. Now I no longer get any pleasure from it.

O: I don't quite understand.

W: I arrive at the conclusion that it is really narcissism.

O: What does that matter?

W: An excessively high evaluation of an intellectual, of a belletristic matter. Why is it so important for people to read it? Or that, once dead, I continue to live in the brains of those people who read the book? What is fame? What value is it supposed to have? None.

O: I don't know if one can look at it like that.

W: Well, it's another one of those matters that is difficult to judge.

O: If you had not published the book, you probably wouldn't be satisfied either.

W: Probably not. Then I would ask myself, What did you live for, actually? No one knows anything about you. And no one is any longer interested in you, once you are dead. Tiny, for example. She no longer exists. There's her apartment one floor below mine. She worked and worked, and people don't even know who lived there. My neighbor managed better than I. His wife died, and he took an older woman. She isn't beautiful, but she does a great deal for him. I was too much interested in appearances. I was blinded by appearances. The ambition to write something, that's an appearance. Don't you agree?

O: I has always seemed glorious to me, to write books.

W: It did to me too, I suppose.

O: And aren't you also a little ungrateful, not valuing any of that?

W: That's an idea. Ungrateful because I do not value success. Perhaps it is a lack of modesty.

W: You were brought up to believe that one should engage in intellectual and artistic matters. Your neighbor was presumably brought up quite differently. I'm sure he has no such notions.

W: My father had great esteem for intellectual things, and my sister was talented.

O: In a different environment, ideas like that are dismissed as fantasies.

W: That's how it is with Luise. She has no interest and understanding for these things. Only for practical matters, for money, or how one gets ahead. I wasn't so much interested in that. I painted, wrote a little. . . . Of course, one was brought up that way, but how you stoke a stove wasn't important.

O: And since you had no children . . .

W: That's how I felt. My paintings are my children.

O: And Gardiner was well-intentioned as regards the book. You cannot really blame her.

W: Of course, she thought it would give me pleasure.

O: Didn't it?

W: It did. And that it doesn't last is due to the noxious influence of this woman. She tramples on things intellectual. All she understands is financial success. I have often thought that it would have been better if I had said something about the book. As things are, she always reproaches me for having done nothing. When I was pensioned, I should have accepted a position so that I could have given her more, she says. There's nothing worse, you see, than being with an uneducated woman. That's what I have come to understand. And I thought it was only a prejudice. But it's really true. And my opinion about simple women was a totally false idea. In Russia, they glorified the peasant. That was a reaction against the reactionary czarist regime, and then people simply went too far. But I absorbed all that.

O: But you also have certain grand bourgeois airs. And I think Luise probably adopted some of that. Without your horizon, to be sure.

W: She did adopt things, but somehow misinterpreted them. That's the important question: Am I attached to this woman, or not?

O: I should say so.

W: In spite of all her bad qualities? Is that possible?

O: Yes, it is.

W: Perhaps it is the illusion that one can still change her, the desire. Although one knows that one cannot, that in one's subconscious, one clings to this desire. I ask you as a woman, do you believe that marriage has such importance for a woman like that?

O: For a woman at that age, marriage has immense importance, of course. It's a matter of prestige. In that generation, a woman is only something when she has a husband. No doubt about it.

W: She says the same thing. Sometimes, I have this thought, perhaps it's crazy: all the physicians said I should not marry Therese. But would it not be better if I fulfilled her wish, might not everything turn out well then? S. says that that is an absolutely false idea, that it would change nothing.

O: If everything continues the same in any event, it doesn't matter whether you marry or not.

W: Her narrow-mindedness would remain the same.

O: But it doesn't cost you anything. It takes five minutes.

W: You think it doesn't matter.

O: I do.

W: All right, so you share S.'s opinion that nothing would change.

O: Nothing would.

W: E. believes . . . I don't know, perhaps it's a Jewish trait. . . .

O: Is he a Jew?

W: E.? Yes. Sticking to the letter, you know. Because, when all is said and done, what Freud writes are ideas. And a person's illness is not just a matter of ideas but also of strength. When you are younger, you have a greater volume of strength and energy than at an advanced age. There are a lot of additional things and experiences; it cannot always just be Freud if one wants to make headway. But that's what E. does, he keeps bringing up psychoanalysis. But that is not so fundamental a knowledge that everything can be explained by it.

Well, going to America, that would certainly be radical. I believe that the new impressions would do me good. When I left Odessa on the French ship that transported those officers to Marseille, I had such a happy feeling because I was getting away from that terrible Russia. Life in Odessa, where one did not know what the next day would bring, was very depressing. At one moment it was occupied by the Austrians, then by the Bolsheviks, then the Ukrainians were in power, and so on. I was done with everything I had experienced there. At that moment, everything was as though cut off. It was a marvelous feeling.

O: Did you already know at the time that you would never return?
W: No, I didn't. But I had the feeling, thank God, this phase is over. I am leaving this terrible country where so much unpleasantness has occurred. And now my attitude is similar. Of course, I don't know, perhaps it is my imagination. Now I have the feeling—in this Vienna, I went through my wife's suicide, so many unpleasant things, being arrested by the Russians, that wasn't agreeable either. Although I cannot blame them, of course. When they appeared suddenly, there was quite a clamor. "Traitor! White guardist runaway!" But when they had calmed down and let me go, they were really ten times better than this Luise, who reproaches me for having exploited people as the owner of an estate. The Russians didn't talk about that. On the contrary, the officer addressed me by my first name and my father's name. You know how it is in Russia. "Sergius Konstantinovich, what have you read? What do you know of our literature?" Yet it was unpleasant. I have gone through so much unpleasantness here. I want nothing further to do with this country. I am speaking frankly to you, I want nothing further to do with this city. I would like to do what I did back then when I boarded this ship—go away, and not come back. But of course that

may only be a fantasy. . . . What Gardiner did not take into account. . . . She believes, well, there's a journalist who wanted to find out something about me, and I gave in. But she forgets that I also am only human and that you were really the only person that showed an understanding for everything.

O: I was interested in you.

W: I could not simply say to you, well, I don't want any further dealings with you. She cannot expect that from me.

O: I agree.

W: Isn't that right? She must take into consideration that a human relationship developed here that didn't exist before. She cannot blame me for that. "I told him he should not give interviews." "But he found someone he felt attracted to." But it's pointless to write her that. She would have no understanding; being a woman, she would be jealous. "I have done so much for him," she negotiated, and so on. "He should not have yielded. Now he is too old. . . ." I should not have had the feelings that developed because of you.

O: Why?

W: I really should accept the idea that I did not do what Gardiner recommended. She must know that I have no one and that we understood each other. I could not simply dismiss you: "Leave me alone!"

O: It's not often that one finds people one gets along with. I'm the same.

W: There's no woman with whom I get along as well as with you.

O: She must understand that you are pretty much alone. Never anyone but Luise. And perhaps it also did you good that a younger person took an interest in you.

W: Yes, of course. And one did want this matter to be useful, after all, that it be thoroughly investigated. It's not as simple as Gardiner wrote: "Psychoanalysis helped him and he could deal with all the blows fate dealt him." But one cannot write her that. I can tell you, in any case, that it is difficult to play the role of a showpiece of psychoanalysis.

O: But you did something that a showpiece doesn't do.

W: What's that?

O: You spoke to me, and so you didn't really act like a showpiece.

W: Perhaps that was a mistake.

O: You don't want to be a showpiece.

W: You can see that I don't succeed.

O: The image bothers you in some way.

W: I don't really want to be that. It's a stupid role. One is obliged to constantly repeat what others say. One cannot have an opinion of one's own. That shouldn't be. I have an idea for a novel, a fantasy, really: a man is drawn into a sexually passive role—you know, the sister played the active role—and therefore the woman must be the aggressor. It's only a step from sister Anna to servant Anna. And because the sister didn't want me, she rejected my overtures, and if she hadn't done that, it would have been a relationship between brother and sister, which isn't the right thing either. In any case, I attacked her, and there was a servant girl—it wasn't even a servant girl, it was a very young girl, whom I was giving lessons to.

O: What sort of lessons?

W: And she had the same name. Except that she was from Lithuania, and there she had a different name, she was called Hanne, and I gave her lessons and kissed and held her. . . . No, I am talking about the novel: a person is driven on the wrong sexual path and creates an ideal for himself according to which there must be a component of sadism on the part of the woman. It's not yet a servant girl. . . .

I haven't really had all that much to do with servant girls. Once, in the Caucasus, I had an affair with a servant girl. There was a servant girl there, it was a German girl, who was willing, and I said she should come during the night and she came and we had intercourse. Then I got terribly scared that I might have got gonorrhea, but it turned out all right. Otherwise, I haven't had much to do with servant girls, but then I went to prostitutes. They could be from the upper classes—in Odessa there was a house to which women from the upper classes came and where one paid. In any event, you see that one must give a woman money; she must demand something. I don't know how to describe it further. . . .

O: You are talking about the novel now.

W: Yes, the novel. You know, there are many men . . . A short while back, I read about a woman who complained that she must always deal with sluts because her husband says it is forbidden and therefore exciting for him. And now the novel. Such a man runs into a woman and he suddenly sees that he is on the wrong track, that it is the intellectual woman that is the sexual woman, and not the other one. At this point, when he notices this, he doesn't know what to do. It is too late. He sees that it is not the woman whom he had always taken to be the sexual object that is in fact the sexual object, but that the sexual object is really another woman, the intellectual woman. This is just a fantasy, you understand. . . .

O: But did you always play the passive role vis-à-vis women?

W: No, I never let myself be beaten by women. Some women adopted an imperious tone—I always immediately rejected that. I do not accept women's sadistic role. That is the contradiction, to have women like that, yet to reject them. . . . You know that there are men who have women beat them.

O: Yes. Did you have sadistic sexual tendencies?

W: Not really.

O: You tended to be the aggressor?

W: I felt aggressive. I never really fell into that role of the masochistic male, that's what's strange.

O: Perhaps you would have liked to be more of a masochist and simply didn't want to admit it to yourself?

W: Perhaps I had a block there.

O: Possibly.

W: Who knows?

O: You probably were brought up to play the aggressive male role, and it seems you only had the courage for that when you were dealing with nonintellectual women.

W: That's possible.

O: And with intellectual women, you had difficulties playing the male role.

W: That's an idea.

O: But you are not unique there; that's true of many men.

W: It's a misfortune that this sister seduced me.

O: The incest taboo increased your difficulties.

W: It left me for the first time when you said that you had had gonorrhea.

O: I find it very odd that that should have made such an impression on you.

W: It was an enormous impression. You think I had difficulties with intellectual women in playing the male role.

O: You probably were afraid that they would take the leadership role away from you. Yet that is what men are brought up to do, to behave in a manly, aggressive, and superior manner. It's completely wrong, of course, but that's how they are brought up.

W: Everything is much more complicated than the psychoanalysts believe. You should have appeared earlier, you should be older. You are too young, there's nothing to be done.

O: I can't help that.

W: I have to rely on you—I have no one. I don't believe the psychoanalysts, so I have to rely on you. One must have someone, after all. . . . Gardiner wrote that she is against all interviews, and I did not have the strength to turn you down. You saw we understood each other, and our entire relationship is also a question. . . .

O: How do you mean, a question?

W: One doesn't know what goes on. If I were twenty years younger or around thirty, you see, the relationship would be understandable. . . . I must speak openly with you, there's no point in . . . You understand you entered my life—you'll excuse the expression but another doesn't occur to me—and you did something that you were perhaps not conscious of doing, but you did it.

O: What did I do?

W: You completely changed my attitude toward women.

O: How so? I don't understand.

W: I don't know, should one be that open?

O: But why not?

W: There was the problem with women, you know. You said that I had luck with women. I did have success. I could have started something with any number who would have been more compatible than this Luise. But I clung to an impossible woman and there were reasons for that—the seduction by my sister, that I played a passive role there, or who knows what. All sorts of things could be mentioned, or perhaps a certain masochism, you know, and now I got to know you and have seen that the entire attitude was wrong.

O: Toward women?

W: Toward women. A woman like you would have been right for me. But not like these other women. Now it is too late! At ninety, I can no longer change any of that.

O: Did that never occur to you before?

W: You see that it didn't. You also know where you stand, don't you?

O: What do you mean, where I stand?

W: Your relationship to me.

O: I like you, you know that.

W: Well, but you also understand that the difference in age is colossal. So it could only be platonic.

O: Of course.

W: But actually that isn't quite the way it is.

O: But . . .

W: You understand perfectly well, I don't have to be completely explicit. . . . If I were younger, one could at least try it, make an attempt but . . . You would really be the right woman for me. I get along with you. I don't get along with the other one, and she clings to me. Because you said that you also had gonorrhea, you caused a profound change in me.

O: Didn't you ever in your entire life meet a woman who would have said something like that?

W: I found none, and another one wouldn't have said it. But you said it.

O: You should be glad that you still got to know such a woman. That's not really an occasion for sadness.

W: You believe that one becomes reasonable in old age?

O: That's not my impression.

W: I became reasonable in the sense that I see that I put all my eggs in the wrong basket.

O: The whole thing is astonishing. I suddenly show up a few years ago, and was overwhelmed by you. . . .

W: I really should have reacted with hostility.

O: Why?

W: I did not want people to know me. And you understood me. But I reacted positively.

O: But that's an interesting experience when someone suddenly stands at your door and you find that person likable.

W: I don't know if Gardiner did not also understand the situation and if she does not somehow—you know how jealous women are—if she does not somehow notice that I am attached to you, and that that doesn't suit her.

O: But she doesn't know that we got along so well. She probably thought that I visited you, wrote the article, and that that was it. Does she know at all that you rather liked me?

W: The reason two people get along with each other, that is . . .

O: That is irrational, difficult to explain.

W: It is irrational. You have certain qualities that I like, although you are not really as harmless as you look.

O: Do you think I look that harmless?

W: You look very harmless, but you aren't all that harmless.

O: You have discovered one of the secrets that helps me get quite a few interviews.

W: It's a pity that we are so far apart in age, otherwise we would understand each other better.

O: Doesn't it bother you that I am not so harmless?

W: Oh. One would have to consider that, that hadn't occurred to me that you aren't quite that harmless perhaps. But you are very correct.

O: If we had not liked each other, these conversations would never have taken place. It would have been impossible to talk for such a long time. That was the precondition. . . .

W: Now, all I have is you. . . .

O: There's Luise.

W: Luise.

O: Your acquaintances.

W: The acquaintances.

O: And the analysts.

W: The analysts don't understand. Well, we had many interesting hours, so we can call it a human relationship. And because I have such an unpleasant relation with this Luise, I was all the more attracted to you.

O: That's natural. Everyone seeks contact with others.

W: Yes, and you were the one closest to me. Because I can speak to no one as openly as to you. You showed so much understanding. Perhaps there was also a certain transference from my sister. I don't know.

O: Would that be such a bad thing?

W: No, it wouldn't.

O: All relations are based on some sort of transference. . . .

W: I always dislike leaving here. That's a weakness.

O: Why is that a weakness? I don't think it's a weakness. I am pleased that being here makes you feel good.

W: Yes, I do feel good here. Much better than at Luise's.

·III·
THE WOLF-MAN
AND I

Report on a Death

Old women, a few men, some young people are milling on both sides
of the gate. "No admission until half past one." A sun-tanned man in
a white smock sends back everyone that dares advance a few tenta-
tive steps along the asphalt road on the far side of the gate. In the
Vienna Psychiatric Hospital, the tone is rude, a fact that already
becomes noticeable at the entrance gate, where the young doorman
in his white smock lords it over the visitors.

The August sun beats down between the tall trees of the carefully
tended English park. I make my way up an absolutely straight path,
lined by lamps, at whose end steps seem to lead into nothingness. To
the right and the left of the pebble-strewn path which keeps cutting
across the road with its sweeping curves, I see, at regular intervals,
pink, brownish, and yellow brick pavilions, each with a number on
its door. It is here that the approximately two thousand patients of
the institution are housed. The cultivated atmosphere might make
one believe that this is a resort for the rich. But the pathetic figures
in ill-fitting institutional garb that come toward the visitor, their
gaze lowered in embarrassment, soon undeceive one. Here live the
superfluous and the shelved who could not maintain themselves
outside the confines of this ensemble of Art Nouveau architecture
and English park.

The absolutely straight path ends at the road. The steps that
could be seen from afar lead to Otto Wagner's famous "Kirche am
Steinhof" atop the hill. I turn right and soon see my destination,
Pavilion 22, idyllically set among tress and bushes.

At the entrance one flight up, three good-looking young men sit at a table. But their white smocks do not give them the dignity that may be intended. "Whom do you want to see? What's your name?" the three ask, and laugh. One of them writes something in an open ledger that appears to contain precise data on each visitor. I have to wait for a physician who will take me to the patient I want to visit. "Orders from above," they say in answer to my annoyed objections.

"He's not at all well, don't become alarmed," the physician, a woman in her forties, explains as we walk up to the second floor and I ask why I cannot speak with the patient in private. She takes me down a corridor of green and beige Art Nouveau tiles. In the dormitories to the left, I see patients in striped pajamas, lying in white-enameled iron beds, old men with pallid faces and shining gray stubble. Eyes deep in their sockets stare apathetically in our direction. A few younger men are sitting in the corridor outside the dormitories. They stare at us with a stupid, insolent curiosity and bid us good day. Although these are visiting hours, I see few visitors. At the end of the corridor, the physician stops before a white-painted wooden door into which glass windows have been cut at eye level. She opens the slightly open door further. In a narrow room with high ceilings and whitewashed walls, the Wolf-Man lies in a simple iron bed, his eyes closed, dozing or asleep.

"Dr. Sergius P. . . . born 1886," has been written in black ink in a white piece of paper placed at the foot end of the bed. I have to smile as I remember the many times the Wolf-Man explained to me that he was born on December 24, 1886 of the Julian calendar and therefore on January 6, 1887 of the Gregorian calendar.

The physician stands immobile by the door. I have taken a few steps toward the Wolf-Man, who does not give the slightest sign that he has noticed us. The only window along the rear wall of the room has bars and can only be opened with a special key, which patients do not get their hands on. The door has no handle. In addition to a wheelchair, a wardrobe, a nightstand, and a table with two plastic armchairs, there is a second, empty bed, one of those beds with bars along its two sides in which the patients are kept, defenseless.

"Ah, you are the only one who is not abandoning me," the Wolf-Man murmurs. He has suddenly opened his eyes and recognized me. He pulls me down and embraces me. I push an armchair up to his bed and the Wolf-Man takes my hand. "This is the end, this is the end, they've got me, they've got me locked up," he says despairingly. Now the physician finally consents to leave. "Don't strain him," she admonishes me before she goes, leaving the door half open.

"I made a mistake," the Wolf-Man says. "I got into an ambulance and was driven around Vienna and now you see where I landed, through my own stupidity. . . ." The Wolf-Man seems confused about the circumstances that brought him to this institution. I tell him what happened. Dr. S., his physician of many years standing, the director of this hospital, called me a few days ago: due to the heat, the Wolf-Man had a circulatory collapse and had lost consciousness on the ground floor of his apartment building. He was first taken to a regular hospital. Then S. had had him moved to this institution, in part to protect him from his increasingly hopeless problems.

"You warned me," the Wolf-Man says. 'I should have listened to you." He remembers that I had often urged him to go into an old people's home. "Look at this bed," he complains and points at the bars. "They locked me up in it for a night. It was terrible. S. has no understanding of crazy people, of people that are psychologically ill. How can he run an institution in this way?" And in his ignorance of procedures in psychiatric hospitals, he adds: "Look at this sloppiness, there are no handles on the doors. What sloppiness."

The physician appears in the doorway. "I have to go somewhere for a few minutes," she says. "Don't stay too long. Don't strain him."

"You wouldn't believe what conditions are like," the Wolf-Man says indignantly, displaying the aristocrat he had been in his youth. "No, it doesn't strain me," he adds. And, making sure she hears him, he calls after the physician as she turns to go, "I have no confidence in this hospital!" During our talk, the Wolf-Man recuperates. The sedative he was probably given has lost some of its tranquilizing effect. He speaks with animation, rambles from topic to topic as he always has. His head with its still-full, snow-white hair seems disproportionately large above a frail body that, in the striped hospital shirt, seems even thinner than in the suits he used to wear. His sharp features and the parchment-like skin of his face, his light eyes, which his illness has dulled, his hands, so massive in relation to his body and which show the veins so clearly have always struck me as age-old and ageless at the same time.

"Do you remember Goncharov's *Oblomov?*" he asks. "Then you know that the book is about a man who lies in bed all day long and dreams, dreams, dreams. That's the Russian character. . . .

"The Russian character?"

"Mine, at least, as it presents itself now," he answers with a smile of gentle irony.

"You see me lying here," he starts complaining again. "Without my denture, without a watch. Those things must have been lost in transport. It was a gold watch. I don't even know what time it is." I don't have the heart to tell him that all the patients' personal belongings are collected and kept in storage.

"I would like to have my clothes," he wails. "How can I get up when I have nothing to put on? . . ."

"Why not simply walk around in the shirt you are wearing?" I suggest to him. "It's summer."

"It's summer?" The Wolf-Man seems surprised. "I thought it was fall. . . . I got here through my own fault and stupidity. Now they won't take me at the old people's home. The servants, nurses, attendants—I am telling you, it's a terrible mess. One treats you more politely, another is unfriendly, one should probably tip them. I told one of them that I would get even with him and he immediately became polite. But I have no money. What a mess! Before Dr. S. comes here, they make sure everything is in order, but otherwise no one bothers about me all day long. . . Outside, in the corridor, it's terrible. There's constant shouting and screaming. And then these crazy people here come and stand outside my door and stare at me. They are all crazy. . . . And the food—it's terrible, it's what very poor people eat. Soup with a little bread in it, or odd dumplings, I don't know what they are. . . . And these bare walls, these bare walls all day long. . . .

The physician interrupts this lament and insists that I leave, although visiting hours aren't over yet. "It's too much of a strain for him," she says. And the Wolf-Man, who now really does have difficulty speaking and is panting more and more, fighting for breath, does not contradict her.

"Come back soon," he mumbles as he embraces me. "If I should get back home before then, I'll call."

"Will the servant bring her here?" The Wolf-Man has been startled out of his somnolence. He does not immediately recognize me; his thoughts keep revolving around Luise. She is afraid of visiting him at the hospital and, probably because she does not know about his illness, has sent him the message that she will wait for him at the gate on Sunday, during visiting hours. He has asked an attendent to meet her and to bring her here. Will he do it? Will the servant bring her?

The Wolf-Man takes a postcard from the open drawer of his nightstand and hands it to me. Here's what Luise writes to a deathly ill, ninety-year-old man who, confined to his bed, is constantly fighting for his breath:

"My dear Sergej, I have heard that you are already feeling much better, that your appetite is good and that you can already wash yourself. I am pleased. As you are eating with such a hearty appetite, aren't you thinking of me, that I go hungry, that I am about to be evicted if I cannot pay the rent, that the gas and electricity will be cut off if I can't pay? How can you do that to a person with whom you have spent forty years?

"I would like to see you, talk to you. I was already there a few times, but the attendents always tell me that that young girl is visiting you again, so I didn't want to disturb you. You must be very much in love if you ordered two flannel suits for 4,500 schillings each and pay all that money for her housekeeping expenses as you told me. Unfortunately, I have no money for stamps or letter paper

"So far, I have received nothing of the royalties for August from your book *The Wolf-Man by the Wolf-Man*. They say you gave it to the professor so he would pass it on to me, but he demands that I pick it up at his place, which is absurd, my lawyer says, and I have it from you in writing that I would get the money from Gardiner even after you die. Have it sent to me by one of the male nurses, who are very polite. . . ."

No irruption of reality, no evidence can change anything. After a brief moment of insight during which he mumbles, "The woman is crazy," the Wolf-Man's thoughts return to this fixed point, Luise. At some time in the past, she has managed to break through his generally self-referential train of thought. And since then, and for decades, there has existed this reciprocal effect between those thoughts that revolve endlessly about a fixed point, and a woman who provides ever-fresh nourishment to a neurotic temperament. Will she starve, or not? What is she to live on? Can this be love?

The door opens and two elderly ladies enter. One is the maid who has been cleaning the Wolf-Man's apartment for years, the other a neighbor. The ladies take a seat.

"I finally want to kick the bucket," the Wolf-Man shouts excitedly. He seems beside himself as his three visitors suddenly surround his bed. "But my dear doctor! You mustn's say things like that," the two ladies exclaim as though with one voice.

"He's very poorly, he's very poorly," they whisper to each other. "There isn't much that can be done."

While the old man, suddenly turning inward, wheezes in the background, they tell me in whispers how the circulatory collapse happened. On that day in early July, the Wolf-Man had received his pension for two months, the monthly check and vacation money. Luise supposedly appeared abruptly at his door, he admitted her, and the meeting ended in a loud row. Finally, she simply snatched 10,000 schillings from his hand and ran off. The Wolf-Man had been terribly upset and excited. During the afternoon of this very hot day, as he was coming back from the tobacco shop where he had bought cigarettes, he collapsed.

Month follows month, winter follows autumn, spring follows winter . . . The Wolf-Man lies in his room with its bare white walls, in the depressing atmosphere of the overheated hospital.

His bouts of despair and the rebellion against the hospital stay gradually become muted in the eternal monotony of a regimented existence organized largely to accommodate the personnel. In the meantime, he has recuperated sufficiently to be able to get up. Two female therapists take him up and down the staircase of the building several times a week to bring his circulation back to normal, but the patient has no interest whatever in these exercises and would rather spend the day in bed.

He now wears his own clothes, and his watch, denture, and wallet lie in the drawer of his nightstand. His condition is unstable, a constant ebb and flow. Sometimes, he feels better and thinks more clearly, at other times he fights for air and, during choking fits, gasps out confused phrases. At times, he dozes, his eyes half closed, and seems totally apathetic; at others, there are hints of his former liveliness and irony.

The attendants are not especially taken with him, as far as I can judge. A privileged person—and the Wolf-Man still is that here even if he won't admit it—causes unnecessary work. They have a further reason for being displeased: the term *servant,* appropriate for the personnel in his parent's house, is inappropriate here.

Often, the Wolf-Man has escape fantasies—he wants to get back home, and should that prove impossible because he cannot be alone in his apartment, he wants to go elsewhere. A nurse has recommended a place near Vienna, but who knows whether he would get a single room there, whether he would still have visitors if it is far away, and what the quality of the home may be. Perhaps he'd better stay where he is.

"Luise . . . why doesn't she come? Why doesn't she look after me? I have given her all that money. What should I do? Give me some advice. How do I get away from here? Should I kill myself, should I jump out the window? Couldn't you simply take me with you? S. mentioned something like that, that I might be able to go back home. Why don't you call him and ask what my condition is. And then there's this little Serb, always standing there, staring at me, staring at me."

"What Serb?"

". . . Fairly often, in the mornings, a little Serb comes, stands by the door, and stares and stares. I call out to him to take off but he refuses."

I assume that it must be the child of a Yugoslav cleaning woman. I try to calm him. "It's a child," I say, "and curious." But the neurotic effect this little boy has on the sick man doesn't dissipate so easily.

"Yes, she was here," the Wolf-Man tells me one day. But I cannot get from him any details about this meeting except that it supposedly passed very quietly and harmoniously. I am skeptical and don't really see how such a peaceful meeting could be possible in view of everything I have heard about Luise. But the Wolf-Man sticks to his guns.

"What should I do? Give me some advice! I want to get away from here. . . ." Or: "I want to die, finally. My mother . . . she was so beautiful in death, as I had never seen her. The nurse in the hospital told me that she went through a horrible last agony."

The old man sees nothing but the grayness of November outside his window, and the bare branches of the trees.

The logical sequence of thoughts people cling to and whose dissolution causes fear is becoming increasingly disorderly. It is as if the obsessional neurosis itself were lying on its deathbed. In this ineluctable process of decay, he clutches at some obsessional thought. Everything was for nothing, pointless, false, I would like to start life all over, do everything differently. And only this pathological circling of his thoughts seems to keep him alive.

A nurse is finally hired who will look after the Wolf-man several days a week. There are always fresh flowers on the table now, and the old man's clothing is in excellent condition.

"Anni is nice," the Wolf-Man tells me. He has perked up visibly since the nurse has been taking care of him. "Perhaps I could move in with her. She's not like Luise. I think she's quite harmless."

Sometimes, when I come for a visit, I run into Anni, whom the Wolf-Man occasionally calls Nanja.

"Be a good boy and eat and drink," the well-preserved fifty-year-old, her gray hair always impeccably curled, encourages him.

"Be good and drink," she goes on in a resolute tone and kisses the Wolf-Man on the forehead.

"Yes, yes," he answers as he raises the coffee cup to his lips in a violently trembling hand. The nurse tries to make him eat a piece of cake.

"No, no, little fellow," she says, and pats him on the shoulder. "Don't shake. You'll spill the coffee. He's doing poorly today. Can't expect much any more."

"Good day, miss, very kind." The Wolf-Man, bowing politely, suddenly turns in my direction as if he had just noticed me.

Then he abruptly begins to fantasize about the women he has known, and especially about the many opportunities he has missed. The nurse and I laugh at him—he is really no longer an altogether credible Casanova. The Wolf-Man is surprised that we should be sitting so peacefully at the table and not be jealous of each other. I ask the nurse if Luise was really here. She whispers that she hasn't come once and that it would be best not to mention her name in his presence again. "You and Anni, I can somehow make sense of that," the Wolf-Man explains when the nurse is gone. "But how Luise fits in, I don't know. Everything is so confused." As time goes on, Luise moves more and more into the background. He mentions her less often, and finally he no longer speaks of her at all.

During the last two years of his life, the Wolf-Man developed a strong need for affection, something I had not noticed in him before. He had always made a stiff, almost wooden impression on me and had seemed to feel more secure when he could talk in a somewhat superficial manner about belletristic matters. He expressed his feelings toward me by formally kissing my hand when he arrived and again when he left. Now, when I sit by his bed, he wants to hold my hand for hours, embraces me when I arrive and leave, and sometimes even kisses me.

In the summer of 1978, when the Wolf-Man had been in the institution for almost a year, he passed through a severe crisis. He fell in the corridor outside his room, and his left temple, which was injured, is healing slowly. "What am I to do?" Gasping, the Wolf-Man clutches onto me. He holds on to me as if I could keep him alive. "Give me some advice! Help me!" He keeps gasping the same phrases.

What should I advise him? What can I do? There is nothing more to be done. "Simply let yourself go," I say. "Give up. Let what happens happen, and rid yourself finally of your obsessions."

The Wolf-Man falls back on his bed. But a moment later, his obsessions begin again: "Life was in vain, everything was pointless, we must build something, something new, begin at the beginning once more. . . ." When I have to leave at the end of visiting hours, he won't let me go. "Give me some advice!" he calls after me.

There are times when I find it very difficult to visit him and weeks pass without my being able to make myself drive out to the hospital. This slow dying weighs me down, this gradual extinction of a human being who found it difficult throughout his life to make decisions. And it is really perfectly consistent that even now, he should be unable to make the one decision that is still his to make. Then I force myself to visit him because he is pleased when I come. And I think one should not flinch from being there when a human being is dying.

Nurse Anni has arranged for the Wolf-Man to move next door. Here, he has a washbasin, which he didn't have in the other room. He had often complained that he could not wash himself. A few pictures hang on the walls. A bright red oilcloth has been spread over the table. The nurse is trying to make the last months of his life more pleasant.

The few friends and acquaintances the Wolf-Man has come less and less often. The only ones who still look after him regularly are Dr. S., his physician of many years standing, the nurse who is paid by Dr. E. with funds form America for taking care of this fading monument of psychoanalysis, and Albin Unterweger. The Wolf-Man became acquainted with this friend of Muriel Gardiner many years ago. And Unterweger insists on supplying the almost ninety-two-year-old regularly with periodicals and sweets. "People come and go as they please," the Wolf-Man tells me when I run into the nurse or Mr. Unterweger at his bedside.

Visitors, nurses and physicians enter his thoughts, and fade again. The patient is defenseless against this coming and going. He can keep no one, should he want to, nor can he send anyone away. His desires, which are becoming weaker and weaker in any case, are of no consequence in the schedule of the institution.

In the winter, a radio suddenly finds its way into the Wolf-Man's room. The program of the Austrian pop station Ö3 rings out. I turn off the music and ask the old man what the radio is doing there. He doesn't answer. His eyes are half closed; he lies on the bed and has considerable trouble speaking.

"It's very cold outside," he says suddenly, "look at me." He moves the blanket aside and points at his thin body. "I can't lie down like this outside now." The Wolf-Man has become calmer, his obsessions torment him less. Gradually, he seems to accept the fact that all he has left is a single decision.

Early in 1979, I go on vacation. Returning two months later, I meet Albin Unterweger at the patient's bedside. The Wolf-Man is sitting on the edge of the bed, dressed in a dark blue pinstripe suit.

"I am completely losing my mind," he says and claps his hand together in a slightly theatrical gesture.

We laugh, and this is the last time I see him in one of those harlequin poses he had adopted occasionally and which I had always liked. The Wolf-Man falls back on his bed and stares indifferently into space.

He no longer joins in our conversation. Unterweger goes outside for a moment because he feels that the patient may have something to tell me. The time has come when one must seriously consider that he will die soon. But the Wolf-Man keeps his eyes closed and remains silent.

On a Sunday in early May, I come into the room. The radio has been turned off and the old man lies in bed, motionless, dressed in a white shirt. I pull an armchair toward the edge of the bed and take his hand in mine. The Wolf-Man tries to whisper something, but without success.

"We mustn't talk," I say and stay there quietly for the next hour.

"Give me your hand," he says as I take it away momentarily to light a cigarette. The Wolf-Man, who no longer wanted to eat, has been force-fed for the last two weeks. I find it incomprehensible that one should torment him with this sort of thing. As I sit there, I suddenly have the feeling that he will die soon. Up to now, I had been afraid sometimes that he might die while I was with him. I had thought it would be horrible to witness a person's death. But I really feel no fear on this day. If he had to die now, I would simply go on sitting there. The Wolf-Man makes an incredibly peaceful impression; there is no sign of the horrible death struggle of the last year and a half. He lies there with his eyes closed, very helpless, almost like a child. As I look at him, I suddenly realize that death can be beautiful only when one has overcome the obsessive attachment to life.

When I have to go, I kiss him on the forehead. He pulls my right hand to his lips and kisses it as he used to. While this gesture had struck me as quite formal before, today it expresses deep emotion and gratitude. At the door, I turn, laugh, wave, and call out "All the best!" as I always have in the past. The Wolf-Man looks at me, raises his hand, and waves feebly.

The next day, at about the same time in the afternoon, he dies without further struggle, in the presence of Nurse Anni. No one invited me to the burial, not even S., who had once promised the Wolf-man that he would inform me when he died. On my next trip out there, I am told of his death.